Joseph A. La[...]
New Windsor, Md.

Nov. 1930.

A COLONIAL HOME — THE CORNER STONE OF OUR NATION

Spinning, whittling, and other kinds of work were done by candlelight or by the light of the open fire. The fireside was also the favorite place for reading and story telling. (Page 365.)

OUR NATION'S HERITAGE
WHAT THE OLD WORLD CONTRIBUTED TO THE NEW

BY

REUBEN POST HALLECK, M.A., LL.D.
AUTHOR OF "HISTORY OF OUR COUNTRY FOR HIGHER GRADES,"
"HISTORY OF AMERICAN LITERATURE," AND
"NEW ENGLISH LITERATURE"

AND

JULIETTE FRANTZ, M.A. (Columbia)
DEPARTMENT OF ENGLISH, LOUISVILLE GIRLS' HIGH SCHOOL
FORMERLY TEACHER OF SIXTH GRADE HISTORY IN THE
MARGARET MERKER SCHOOL, LOUISVILLE, KY.

AMERICAN BOOK COMPANY

NEW YORK   CINCINNATI   CHICAGO   BOSTON   ATLANTA

HALLECK'S AMERICAN HISTORY SERIES

FOUNDERS OF OUR NATION
MAKERS OF OUR NATION
OUR NATION'S HERITAGE
HISTORY OF OUR COUNTRY FOR HIGHER GRADES

PREFACE

IN this book the authors have aimed:

I. To tell the fascinating story of our wonderful heritage from the Old World, but to give only so much of the history of the Old World as is necessary for understanding how it could bestow such gifts.

II. To show what use our forefathers made of this heritage in planting colonies, making homes, establishing self-government, winning independence, and framing the Constitution.

III. To tell this doubly interesting story in such a concrete, vivid, simple way that children will take pleasure in projecting the facts on the screen of their imagination.

IV. To increase our patriotism and pride in our country by showing how we have been of service to the Old World, as well as how it has served us.

V. To emphasize the life, work, and progress of the peoples with whom the book deals.

VI. To furnish a text (*a*) to meet the general aim of the Committee of Eight (1909) in teaching the Old World background of American history, and (*b*) to include added features which recent teaching experience has shown to be desirable.

The summaries, usually called *Things to remember*, are merely signposts to call attention to the most important points in the text. Memorizing the words in a summary does not give live knowledge. Pupils should be encouraged to make their own summaries in their own language.

Things to do are suggested after each chapter. The teacher will use her discretion in varying these problems and their assignment to suit the needs of different classes and different pupils.

This book is a constant challenge to pupils to use their imagination. Viewed from this angle, the text of each chapter itself is a series of "things to do" with the imagination. The specific direction given (p. 328) for making "in your imagination" a pageant of the activities of the founders of the Jamestown colony, may be made to apply to all the chapters. Note, for instance, how the use of the imagination called for on pages 33–38 makes it easy to understand the tangled history of the ancient Near East. Again, the pupils can readily imagine themselves playing the rôle of the early colonists in America, building log cabins in the forest (pp. 359–360) and doing the work of colonial boys and girls on the farm and in the home (pp. 361–366).

In conclusion, it is hoped that in this book the readers will find an interpretation of our ancestors' life and progress which will (1) challenge interest by the thrill of the narrative, (2) furnish a substantial background of vital historical facts against which succeeding American history can be effectively projected, and (3) tend to make the readers humble in their appreciation of our great heritage, and at the same time proud to belong to the American nation so solidly established on the accumulated achievements of the past.

CONTENTS

EARLY BOAT MAKING

Our early ancestors learned to make boats from logs, which were hollowed out by means of fire and stone axes.

A MODERN OCEAN STEAMSHIP

This steamship is about 870 feet long and carries nearly 3000 passengers.

OUR NATION'S HERITAGE

CHAPTER I

WHAT OUR EARLY ANCESTORS LEARNED

What we can gain from the study of history. — History tells us what we owe to the people who lived before us. Let us consider the world in which we live to-day. We can fill a dark room with light by simply pressing a button. We can talk to friends at the other end of the city, and we can send messages to relatives three thousand miles away by telegraph or cable or radio. We can travel in trains or in lake and ocean steamships which are like great floating hotels. We can buy food prepared and ready for immediate use. We can purchase every article of clothing, from hat to shoes, without the trouble of taking a stitch. We live in comfortable houses heated by wood, coal, and gas fires. We enjoy moving pictures, plays, and concerts. We are educated and entertained by books, magazines, and newspapers.

Everything mentioned in the paragraph above had to be invented or discovered by somebody. You have heard your fathers and grandfathers tell how, when they were boys, the idea of a horseless carriage seemed foolish. People laughed at inventors who said that they could make ships that would fly in the air or sail under the sea. You know that once these wonderful things did not exist.

There was a time long ago when there were no carriages at all, because nobody had discovered how to make a wheel.

Even bread was unknown, because no one had thought of crushing grain into flour. There were no books, because there was no printing and no writing.

The study of history makes us realize how hard our ancestors worked and how few comforts they enjoyed. It makes us grateful for what they invented and passed on to us. Perhaps we, in turn, can help to improve the world for those who will come after us.

The early inhabitants of North America. — Only a few hundred years ago our country was not the "United States." It had no name. It was the home of many tribes of Indians, or red men, most of whom were savages dwelling in scattered villages of wigwams or rude huts. They often moved from place to place in search of food. Their women did the hard work. The men loved to hunt in the dense forests and over the wild prairie lands which supplied them with plenty of quail, rabbits, deer, bears, buffaloes, and other game. Sometimes the Indian women had gardens or small fields where they raised corn, beans, and squashes.

To-day we see in this country, which we call the United States, great cities with tall skyscrapers, wide fields of wheat and corn, and pasture lands where cows and sheep are grazing. We see few Indians here. Another race from across the Atlantic has taken their place. How did this change come?

Where American history begins. — People from Europe began to settle in our country less than four hundred years ago. These people had learned many wonderful things in the Old World before they crossed the ocean. We may even say that our ancestors had gone to school in the Old World for thousands of years. They had learned many things which the Indian did not know. They knew how to read and write. They had schools. They could use metals and make axes and saws. With these, they built houses that would keep out the wind and rain and

SKYSCRAPERS OF NEW YORK INDIAN VILLAGE

Many buildings in New York and other large cities have ten stories or more. Some have thirty or forty stories. One such skyscraper has room for more people than the largest Indian village in our country four hundred years ago.

cold. They knew how to build ships. They had gunpowder and muskets and many other wonderful inventions. They had learned more about governing themselves than the Indians ever knew.

The United States would not be here to-day if our ancestors had not learned such things before they came to America. This book will show how the history of America really begins in the Old World. It will tell some of the things which our forefathers did in the Old World before they came to America.

The savage life of our earliest ancestors in Europe. — We have seen that there was a time when America was not a civilized land. Thousands of years ago, the Old World, too, was a land of savages. The earliest people in Europe roamed the forests like the wild animals around them. Women followed the men, carrying the babies on their backs. Each person looked for his own food. He ate the berries and nuts that he picked. For dinner he sometimes had a fish or a rabbit or other small animal that he killed with a stone or a heavy stick. He ate the meat raw, for he had not yet discovered fire. At night when the animals prowled through the forest to seek food, this early ancestor of ours found the nearest cave or hollow tree an excellent bedroom.

How fire made the home. — Then one day, we do not know how, this early man discovered how to make a fire. Perhaps a tree near him was struck by lightning, and he kindled another fire with some of the burning splinters. A man boring into a piece of wood with a pointed stick may have noticed that the rubbing caused heat. Early man

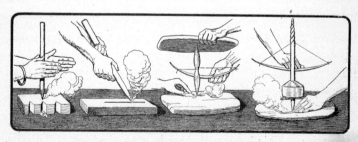

HOW FIRE MAY BE MADE WITHOUT MATCHES

The friction of the pointed stick rapidly rotated (or rubbed) on the larger piece of wood causes enough heat to make fire.

learned how to start a fire by rubbing together two pieces
of wood, or by striking two pieces of rock together until a
spark dropped on a pile of dry moss.

Fire gave man more comfort and better food. It also
changed his ways of living. Fire was the beginning of the
home. A fire once started had to be tended. Watching
the fire became the woman's duty. She had to stay where

CAVE DWELLERS

The man at the left is bringing home a wild goat he has killed. On the ground a small skin
is stretched out to be scraped clean.

the fire was burning. She began to find work to do near
by. Instead of being simply a hunter like her husband,
she became a housewife. In the evening the man came
back to the fire with the food he had found. At night the
glowing embers frightened animals away from the sleeping
family. The fire kept the family together.

Some early homes. — When our early ancestors first
looked about for a shelter for the family and for the fire, they
found a ready-made home in a cave. The door, a great

HOW THE LAKE DWELLINGS PROBABLY LOOKED

In some lakes of Europe, men have found, below the surface of the water, the remains of the piles (posts) on which such dwellings once stood.

stone, kept out the larger beasts.   While most people were still living in caves, others were dwelling in houses built on land or on stilts out in the lakes.

The houses on stilts are called "lake dwellings."   The lake dwellers were safe from enemies, for their village was joined to the land by means of a drawbridge.   When enemies approached, the drawbridge could be taken up.

The earliest houses were small round huts made of boughs interlaced overhead and covered with grass, bark, or twigs daubed with clay.   Tents were made by sticking a few poles upright in the ground and covering them with skins.   In countries where stones were plentiful, stone huts were built. Such were the beginnings of the comfortable and beautiful houses that shelter us to-day.

How early man learned to protect himself. — Living in the forest as he did, early man slowly learned how to make tools and weapons. Nature had not provided him with the great tusks of the rhinoceros, the sharp teeth of the tiger, the swift legs of the deer, or the poison of the snake. Man had only his two hands and his mind to help him. In order to overcome his enemies and gain food, he had to invent weapons and tools. His earliest tools were also his weapons. A stout stick or a heavy stone served either to break the skulls of his enemies or to kill animals for food.

Early weapons.— The "fist hatchet" was a triangular piece of hard stone, chipped until it had a sharp edge. The cave man used it sometimes as a knife, sometimes as a hatchet, sometimes as a weapon. A stick, whittled smaller at one end than at the other, became a club. Pointed at one end and hardened

EARLY STONE HATCHETS
Made of chipped stone.

in the fire, it was a spear. At a much later time man invented the bow and arrow. This weapon gave him an advantage over his enemies. Instead of fighting them face to face with spears and stone axes, he could shoot his arrows at them from a distance and from under cover.

The New Stone Age. — For a long time man's best tools were of rough stone. He made them by chipping one stone with another. This period of time is called the Old Stone Age. After thousands of years he improved his stone tools and polished them until they were smooth. He learned how to sharpen his stone arrows, spear heads, axes, and knives. This later age is called the New Stone Age.

These improved stone tools were much better than we might suppose. A modern carpenter used a sharpened

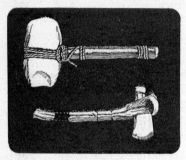

POLISHED STONE AXES

stone ax to learn what the men of the New Stone Age could have done with it. In ten hours he cut down twenty-six pine trees eight inches in diameter. He then used only stone tools to cut up the trees and build a house. He finished it in a little less than three months. He thus proved that it was possible for men in that age to build a comfortable house where pine trees grew.

The men of the European stone ages did not have metal tools or weapons. Probably Europeans did not learn to work with metals before 3000 B.C.

Early woman's duties. — We must not forget that woman did her share in this early world. The man was the hunter and guard of the home, but it was the woman who made the home and who invented many things found in it.

She had few of the duties of a housewife of the present day.   There were no carpets to sweep, no furniture to dust, no dishes to wash, and no stockings to darn. The bones and scraps left from the meals were simply thrown on the ground outside the home. What then did this early housewife have to do? She wandered, with her children, through the woods near her home. She carefully searched trees and plants for nuts, berries, and seeds. With a pointed stick she dug up roots to be roasted in the ashes of her fire. Sometimes honey was found. Then mother and children enjoyed a great feast, usually spoiled a bit by the stings they suffered in getting it.

If the man was unsuccessful in hunting or fishing, he would find a supper of baked roots, berries, nuts, and roasted seeds awaiting him. If he had been lucky, a huge piece of meat or a fish would soon be sizzling over the fire.

Some early inventions. — From the beginning to the present day, woman has been inventing easier and better ways of preparing the family meals. At first a piece of meat or a fish was hung on a stick over the fire or wrapped in leaves and buried in the hot ashes. When boys and girls roast steak over a fire in the woods and bake potatoes in the ashes, they cook in the same way as their early ancestors did. When the early housewife wanted a boiled dinner, she dug a hole in the ground and lined it with bark and hide. Into it she put the meat and water and dropped hot stones in until the water was boiling.

Later, a pot was made by chipping or burning a hollow in a log. Some one discovered that soapstone does not crack in a fire. Pots and griddles were made of it. In some homes to-day soapstone griddles are used for frying pancakes.

It was a lucky day for the world when some one discovered that crushed grains cook more quickly and thoroughly than whole ones. Women learned to make flour by crushing grain with a mortar and pestle. Your druggist to-day uses these tools in mixing drugs. A rock with a groove in the center was the first mortar; a stone, the first pestle. The crushed grain was moistened and baked over the fire on a soapstone griddle or in the ashes. Grinding grain enough for one loaf of bread meant hours of toilsome work. After perhaps hundreds of years, the stone mill was invented, and the task of making flour grew easier.

It was natural that woman should make something in which to carry her seeds. She early learned to weave reeds and grasses into baskets. To make her basket hold water and withstand heat, she covered it on the inside with clay.

POTTERY FOUND IN GRAVES OF THE NEW STONE AGE

Then one day the basket fell away from the clay, and a piece of pottery was left. It was even decorated, for the pattern of the basket was imprinted on it. Baskets were then generally used as molds until some one discovered that clay could be shaped by the hands and that a mold was not necessary.

The early dressmaker. — Making clothes for the family has always been one of woman's principal tasks. Her first materials were the skins of animals, scraped carefully until they were soft. With a sharp bone needle she pierced holes in the skins, which she sewed together with thread made of sinews. The entire family wore the same style of skin garment.   The girls and women decorated themselves with necklaces and bracelets of shells, teeth, and bones. The men also liked decorations.   They painted their bodies with colors prepared from roots and plants.

After the sheep had been domesticated, some one discovered how to manufacture cloth.   Woman rolled fibers of wool between her fingers until she had a thread.   She wove the thread into cloth.   Flax, of which linen is made, was raised after men began to farm the land.   The spindle was an ancient invention.   With it woman spun the fiber more rapidly than with her fingers alone.

Man's first steps in the making of boats and carts. — It is a long step backwards from the comfortable Pullman car and the huge ocean steamship to the first methods of transportation.   The woman's back carried the first passenger, her baby, — and also the first freight car, the basket. Think how woman's strength was spared when her burden was loaded on the back of the dog, the horse, or the ox.

One of the greatest inventions of the early people was the cart with wheels.   The first wheels were solid pieces of wood taken from the trunk of a tree.   Think of all the uses now made of wheels — not only in automobiles and locomotives but also in machinery.

The word for "boat" in many languages first meant "tree trunk."   From this fact we can guess that the earliest boat was a log on which a man sat, using his hands as paddles.   Some one then discovered that a hollow log would float better.   Another man invented the boat with a framework of wooden ribs covered with skin or bark.   Boats were then moved by paddles, oars, and poles, and much later by sails.   Man had many more things to learn before his simple skiff could develop into an ocean liner (p. 1).

How early man learned to speak a language. — There was a time when your early ancestors could not talk at all. They probably just used signs or gestures and made queer noises like animals. Sometimes you use gestures. You beckon to a friend to come across the street. You point to your pocket to tell where your money is hidden. You shake your fist and frown when you are angry. If you are hurt or glad, you cry out, " Oh, oh !" You do just what the early men were forced to do to express their thoughts and feelings.

Little by little the people began to give names to ·the things about them. The men out hunting and fishing built up their own stock of words. The women, working together at home, named many household things. When one tribe was conquered by another, or when several tribes united, the languages were combined. Men and women told the stories of the heroes of the race to their children. History was preserved in this way before writing was invented.

MAMMOTH

Drawing made by cave men who saw this animal. The mammoth has been extinct for thousands of years.

The cave artists. — Some of our early ancestors were artists, too. During their leisure time, as they sat by the fire, they decorated their bone tools with carvings of animals which they knew. On a piece of a mammoth tusk picked up in a cave, is a rough sketch of a mammoth, an enormous elephant that has not existed for thousands of years. Think of a picture of a mammoth drawn by a man who saw it! Some years ago a Spanish nobleman was digging for flint and bone implements in one of the caves on his estate in northern Spain. His little daughter, who was wandering about the cave, suddenly called out, " Bulls! bulls!" The father looked at the ceiling to which she was pointing. The child had seen what no human eye had gazed on for thousands of years. A great procession of bisons or buffaloes had been painted across the ceiling by the men who once lived in the cave. The work was beautifully done.

BISON

One of the procession painted on the ceiling of a cave in Spain.

It is one of the best examples of cave painting. Some of the early paintings tell stories, as of a hunt or a battle. Man's earliest way of writing was by pictures.

How early man became a herdsman. — Our familiar barnyard animals and household pets, such as the cow, the horse, the dog, and the cat, were once wild. They used to roam the forests like the wolves, the tigers, and the bears. How did man tame these animals and make them serve him? Sometimes when the hunter had only wounded an animal, he took it home alive. If there was food on hand, the animal was spared until food was scarce. The women and children cared for the animal and might make it a pet Sometimes hunters brought home the young of dogs, cows, or horses and tamed them. The people discovered that by keeping some animals their work of food-getting was made easier. They could milk a cow or kill a sheep or pig when food was needed. Wool and hides, the materials for the family clothing, were also furnished by these animals.

Gradually man spent less time hunting, and cared for flocks of sheep, goats, and cows instead. Herding was a

more peaceful and more settled occupation than hunting.
When man became a herdsman, he took a long step towards
civilization.

How early man became a farmer. — Our early ancestors
had been in the habit of seeking far and wide for seeds and
berries. Thousands of years may have passed before they
discovered that they could have a crop of seeds near their
homes. They may have noticed that some seeds dropped

EARLY PLOWING, HOEING, AND SOWING

From a relief in an Egyptian tomb. Notice that the Egyptian hoe is shaped very differently
from modern hoes.

in the fall sprouted in the spring. They learned to scatter
seeds near home. By accident they must have discovered
that seeds grow better in loosened soil, and thus found out
something about farming. To stir the soil, they learned to
draw a hooked stick pressed into the earth. This was the
first plow. A long stride toward modern farming was taken
when the domesticated ox was hitched to the stick.

The early garden grew into a field, which with the domesticated cows and sheep furnished the food for the family.
Man thus became a farmer. Our ancestors knew how to
use oxen in plowing and how to raise crops of wheat and
barley long before they came to America.

Progress in civilization. — When our early ancestors began to domesticate animals and to till the soil, they were

no longer savages. Life became more settled. The family, instead of moving constantly, had to remain in one spot until the crop was gathered. Some families might remain in one place year after year until a town was formed.

As the family grew, it became a tribe with the strongest man as the chief. Tribes often quarreled and fought. At first all persons captured in battle were killed. Later, captives were taken as slaves to work on the farms. Agriculture increased as a result.

Some tribes did not become farmers. They were herdsmen and roamed from place to place with their flocks and herds. If they needed clothing or weapons, they bought them from the town people, giving cows and sheep in exchange for their purchases. They were the first traders.

When history begins, we know that some nations were living settled lives on farms and in rude towns; others were wandering about with their herds; and some few others were living the rough lives of cave men.

The following chapters will tell how nations grew up, what they learned, and what they passed on to us.

Things to remember about early man. — 1. History tells us what earlier nations have passed on to us.

2. Our early American ancestors came from Europe.

3. The people of Europe, as well as those of other parts of the Old World, were once savages.

4. They lived in caves, used stone tools and weapons, and hunted their food in the forests.

5. Their most important discovery was fire, because it helped them to improve their way of living.

6. These early men and women slowly developed a language, and made houses, cooking utensils, baskets, pottery, clothing,

AN EARLY CART OF WOOD WITH SOLID WHEELS

Redrawn from the relief on the Antonine Column in Rome. The cart is drawn by two oxen.

wagons, and boats. They also began the arts of painting and carving.

7. After the domestication of animals, some of the people became herdsmen and thus took a step toward becoming civilized.

8. When they learned to plant crops, they led a more settled life.

9. All the early people did not reach the same stage of civilization at the same time. While some were farmers, others were herdsmen, and others were still savages.

Things to do. — Make a list (1) of the conveniences that you use on your way to and from school, (2) of what adds to your comfort in your home, (3) of what keeps you warm out of doors.

Write any facts that you know about America before white settlers came.

Ask some boy scout to show you how to make fire without using a match.

Mention some things that we could not have if there were no fire.

Draw or construct on the sand table a cave, a lake dwelling, and a round hut.

Get a chip of stone and see if you can cut with it.

If you have ever roasted potatoes or broiled meat in the woods, tell the class what you did.

What animals would you have hunted for winter clothing? How would you have caught them and used their skins?

If you have clay or plasticine, model a bowl.

Suppose you had wanted a tame animal, what would you have done? What animal would you have chosen? Which animal was the greatest favorite of Abraham in the Bible?

Write two paragraphs telling how animals help man.

Talk to the class for two minutes on " What Early Woman Accomplished."

Imagine that you wish to film a moving picture with the title: " Man's First Steps in Civilization." Tell in the right order how the savage man who roamed the forest became a partly civilized man who lived in a village.

References for Teachers. — Myres, *Dawn of History*, 7–28 *; Osborn, *Men of the Old Stone Age*, II–VI *; Tylor, *Anthropology*, IV–XIII, XVI; Quennell, *Everyday Life in the Old Stone Age*, II–V; Starr, *Some First Steps in Human Progress;* Wells, H. G., *Outline of History*, 65–91; Tyler, *New Stone Age in Europe*, III, IV, VII, XI; Marvin, *Living Past*, 10–27; Mason, *Woman's Share in Primitive Culture*.

For Pupils. — Wells, M. E., *How the Present Came from the Past*, 1–99; Clodd, *Childhood of the World;* Van Loon, *Story of Mankind*, 9–16; Dopp, *Early Cave-Men;* Dopp, *Later Cave-Men;* Dopp, *Early Sea People;* Holbrook, *Cave, Mound, and Lake Dwellers;* McIntyre, *Cave Boy of the Age of Stone;* Waterloo, *Story of Ab.*

* Note. In the References the Arabic numbers refer to pages; the Roman numerals, unless otherwise designated, refer to chapters.

CHAPTER II

LIFE AND PROGRESS IN EARLY EGYPT

WE left Europe when men were making good stone tools, about 3000 B.C. Europeans had not then invented the

EGYPT AND OTHER LANDS NEAR IT

arts of civilization, such as writing. But the people of some other parts of the world had traveled meanwhile a long way on the road of civilization. Shall we travel along this road with them to learn of their work and life? Let us start with Egypt (ē'jĭpt).

Why we begin with Egypt. — We must study our geographies to see why we begin with Egypt. Let us follow the course of the Nile River from its source in the mountains of central Africa. The Nile flows northward through Egypt into the Mediterranean Sea. The narrow valley and the delta of this river are very fertile, while the rest of the country is a desert. It is the river that makes the soil rich.

Man can do little without the aid of Nature. In some places she helps more than in others. In most parts of the Old World man has had to learn slowly how to provide fertilizer to keep the soil in his fields rich. We may imagine the Nile saying to Egypt, thousands of years before Christ:

"When the snow melts in the mountains, I will bear the flood down to you. I will overflow my banks for many miles. Every year my waters shall bring to your fields a coating of rich black mud. This will make your wheat and barley take joy in their growth. They shall yield more than a hundred fold.

" I will do enough for you, Egypt, so that your sons shall have time to learn the art of building in stone. Five thousand years hence men shall come and stand in silent awe before your temples and your tombs. The work of your sculptors and painters and goldsmiths shall remain to teach the world. I will give to you the lotus flower to remind you that you are to make common things beautiful.

" One of my greatest gifts to you, Egypt, is a simple reed growing in the marshes that fringe my banks. You shall call it the papyrus (pa-pī′rus). From it you shall make material on which to write. Other nations shall long write on heavy clay tablets. Your books shall be of papyrus as light as a butterfly's wing. You shall place some of them in your tombs, where they shall outlast the ages. They shall reveal the beginnings of history to men of future times.

" You shall honor me as a god, but I am only the willing, joyful agent of another, greater Power whom you worship as the Sun."

The Nile might justly have been proud of the land which it made fertile. Not only did it spread a flood of water and rich mud over the fields every summer, but at other seasons it was the source from which the people drew up water to irrigate their crops. The land is warm and can produce two crops each year, one after the other. Egypt is still to-day a land of fertile farms and rich cities, and is often visited by Europeans and Americans. A traveler three thousand years ago wrote this description of one of its towns in the delta of the Nile :

" The place is pleasant to dwell in ; its fields are full of good things. The canals are rich in fish ; the lakes swarm with birds ; the meadows are green with vegetables ; melons with a taste like honey grow in the irrigated gardens. The barns are full of wheat and durra [another kind of grain]. Onions and grapes grow in the inclosures ; and the apple-tree blooms among them. The vine, the almond tree, and the fig tree are found in the orchards. The city canal produces salt. Sea-going ships enter the harbor. Plenty and abundance are perpetual."

What the architecture of old Egypt tells us of its people. — The ancient Egyptians believed that a person lives on after death, and so they cared more about their future lives than about their lives on earth. Most of their architecture shows us how they provided for that future life.

1. *The tombs*. — The Egyptians were the first to build great structures in stone. Their Great Pyramid, the tomb of a king, heads the list of the Seven Wonders of the Ancient World. This pyramid, a few miles west of Cairo, covers thirteen acres and contains 2,300,000 stones, each weighing over 2000 pounds. Egyptian kings did not have palaces so large as this. They said : " Man lives only a

short time in his palace but forever in his tomb." Groups
of pyramids, large and small, extend for more than sixty
miles south of the Great Pyramid. Other tombs were
hollowed out of the rocks.

We have learned more about the life and work of the
ancient Egyptians from their tombs than from anything
else. The tombs of kings and nobles have many rooms,
the walls of which are painted to show scenes from the life
of the dead men. Things which a king or a noble might be
supposed to need after death were placed in his tomb.

GROUP OF MODELS FROM THE TOMB OF MEHENKWETRE

Mehenkwetre, seated on the porch, watches the counting of his cattle. The models from this
tomb are about one eighth life size.

The Metropolitan Museum of Art in the city of New
York exhibits many things that were actually found in the
tomb of Mehenkwet're, a high officer of an Egyptian king.
This officer died nearly 4000 years ago. The models found
in his tomb show how Mehenkwetre lived in this world
and how he wished to live in the next. There are models
of girls bringing him ducks, wine, and meat, of butchers at

STORING GRAIN FOR MEHENKWETRE

Models now in the Metropolitan Museum of Art, New York. Five men are measuring wheat, and five clerks keep the count.

work in his slaughter-house, of his cattle fattening, of his brewers making beer, of men measuring wheat in his granary, with clerks keeping an account on sheets of papyrus. There are women grinding wheat into flour, and a man making it into cakes. There is a pleasure boat in which he is shown traveling on the Nile, waited on by his servants, and listening to a singer and a harper. Two fishing boats, made of papyrus, are dragging a fish net

EGYPTIAN FISHING BOATS MADE OF PAPYRUS

Models found in the tomb of Mehenkwetre.

between them. Other models from the tomb show carpenters hewing timbers and smoothing them with sandstone. Another carpenter is using a ripsaw to make boards, while another is cutting mortise holes in a plank with chisel and mallet. Women are spinning flax and weaving cloth. There were many folds of linen in the tomb — enough, it would seem, to last Mehenk-wetre for an age.

Mehenkwetre thought that the spirits of the little model workmen would supply his soul with food and raiment and boats forevermore.

Mehenkwetre's tomb was not found until 1920. The Metropolitan Museum divided the models with the Museum in Cairo, Egypt, but there are enough for both. Another tomb, that of King Tutankha'men, who had lain in his grave more than 3000 years, was opened in 1923. It contained many rings, bracelets, and necklaces,

ARMCHAIR FROM TOMB OF TUTANKH-AMEN

The back is beautifully overlaid with gold and decorated with colored glass and stone inlay. The scene on the back panel shows the king and queen in the palace.

so beautiful that jewelers in other lands have copied them.

The models found in these tombs not only show how the Egyptians provided for a future life, but teach us a great deal about the work and manner of living in early Egypt. The industries of the Egyptians show how far they were in advance of Stone Age Europe at the same time. Egyptian workmen had tools not only of stone but also of copper. They later mixed tin with copper, making a

SECTION OF THE GREAT HALL OF THE TEMPLE OF KARNAK, AS IT PROBABLY
LOOKED IN 1300 B.C.

Notice the figure of a man at the foot of one of the large columns. In European cathedrals the roof is arched
and is supported by the side walls, and there are no such large columns in the middle of the nave (p. 209).
The clerestory is the upper part of the nave; there are windows in the side wall above the smaller columns.

BRONZE AXES, SWORDS, LANCE HEAD, AND DAGGER

harder metal, called "bronze," of which still better tools were made.

2. *The temples.* — The Egyptians built great temples; greatest of all was the Temple of Kar′nak, one and a half miles in circumference, near the city of Thebes (thēbz). This has been called "the most stupendous religious monument in existence." Sixty men could stand on top of each of its largest columns.

Some of the most famous cathedrals in the world are like the old Egyptian temples in two ways: (1) They have colonnades, or rows of columns, like those first used by the Egyptians to hold up a roof. (2) They have a row of windows on each side of the upper part of the nave. The nave is the main part, or largest room, of the cathedral (p. 209). The upper part of the nave, with the row of windows on each side, is called a "clerestory" (klēr′sto-rĭ) and was invented by the Egyptians.

3. *The obelisks.* — An Egyptian obelisk is a very tall, graceful stone monument, made out of one block of stone. One of the most famous obelisks was brought to America

OBELISK IN CENTRAL PARK, NEW YORK

This was brought from Egypt in 1880.

in the nineteenth century and now stands in New York. Another, still standing by the great Temple of Karnak, is nearly one hundred feet high and weighs three hundred and fifty tons. That obelisk was brought on a boat one hundred and fifty miles down the river from the stone quarry at the First Cataract of the Nile. It was landed at Thebes and then raised into position. The ancient Egyptians had studied mathematics and knew how the wedge and the lever worked, or they could not have raised such great weights. One of the oldest books in the world is an Egyptian manual of measuring.

What we learn of the Egyptians through their art. — The ancient Egyptians rank among the greatest portrait makers in the world. The best of their portraits are statues of stone, and some of them weigh as much as a thousand tons. Egypt's most famous statue is the Sphinx. This is a portrait of an Egyptian king, in the form of a man's head on

the body of a lion. The head, cut out of solid rock,
measures thirty feet from the bottom of the chin to the
top of the forehead. The Sphinx looks wise enough to
answer any question, and he keeps his reputation for wisdom
by saying nothing. To-day we often call a wise-looking
person a Sphinx if he keeps his opinions to himself.

THE SPHINX, NEAR THE PYRAMIDS, IN THE EGYPTIAN DESERT

This huge stone figure is half man and half lion. The nose is 5½ feet long.
There was once a small temple between the front paws.

The Egyptians were good painters, although they could
not draw things so as to show distance in their pictures.
Their cows, sheep, cats, and ducks are usually quite life-
like. Some of their work, on the inside walls of chapels in

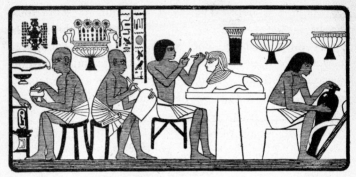

EGYPTIAN ARTISTS

Redrawn from a wall painting in an Egyptian tomb made about 1450 B.C.   One of the artists
is finishing a small statue of a sphinx.   The others are painting vases.

the tombs, is still very beautiful. Egyptian chairs, beds, and chests were carved with rare skill. It pleased the Egyptians to make a drinking glass shaped like a lotus flower, because they wished to make everything beautiful.

Writing, books, and education. — The Egyptians made the first paper, from thin layers unrolled from the papyrus reed. The oldest books in the world are papyrus rolls found in the tombs of Egyptians. The papyrus sheets were pasted end on end, and some of the books were forty feet long. Instead of shutting their books, the Egyptians rolled them. Some of these rolls were story books and told tales of adventure. The earliest *Sindbad* was an Egyptian sailor who was shipwrecked in southern waters. Egyptian children knew *Cinderella* and many of the fairy tales that delight us to-day. The story of *Ali Baba and the Forty Thieves* may have been first told in Egypt.

The first great libraries were those of Egypt. Papyrus rolls in labeled jars stood on the shelves of Egyptian libraries. These libraries were generally used only by priests, nobles, and scribes. The millions of common people could not read.

One of the most important professions in Egypt was that of the scribe, or one who could write. In the early tomb paintings the scribe is seen writing down the number of the cattle as they pass, or making note of the amount of the grain being stored in the granaries. Boys who were to become scribes or priests were put into schools at an early age. They learned how to add, subtract, multiply, and divide, and to work fractions. If the boys showed signs of lagging, the rod was always near at hand.

The oldest Egyptian writing was in the form of a picture for each word. Later the Egyptians used a picture or sign for each syllable, and finally they invented an alphabet.

LINEN GARMENT FOUND IN AN EGYPTIAN TOMB

How the Egyptians measured time. — Did you ever think how the calendar came to be what it is to-day? The cave man told time by the moon. In Egypt, where the sky is cloudless, people studied the heavens. They began the science of astronomy from the study of the stars. Have you noticed that any particular star rises in the east each night a few minutes earlier than it did the night before? The ancient Egyptians watched carefully and found that in 365 days a star will rise at the same hour again. They therefore made their year 365 days long. They noticed also that twelve moon months do not make a year of 365 days. The Egyptians therefore made a calendar of thirty days to a month, and the five days that were left over at the end of the year were set aside as a festival time. The Egyptian calendar was invented in 4241 B.C. A later nation, the Romans, made slight changes that gave the calendar its present form.

Experiments in government. — The cave man ruled his own family and did not have much to do with anybody else. Afterward, a group of related families lived together and formed a tribe. Still later, in connection with manufacture and trade, towns grew up. People had to have rules for living together in tribes or in towns, just as they must to-day have rules for playing football, baseball, or basketball together. There must, for instance, be a rule against stealing. If the town wants paths or roads, there must be a rule for making people work on them or for collecting taxes to pay for them. Such rules are called *laws*.

Sometimes the people of one town or tribe made the laws for themselves. When several tribes or towns were united to form a nation, government became less easy than before. In times of war a man of great ability might get command of the army and make himself king. He would then make and enforce the laws himself.

We know that the Pyramids in Egypt were the tombs of the kings called Pharaohs (fā'rōz). The Pharaoh ruled all Egypt as a nation and was very powerful. The Pharaohs thought that they could have more slaves and more wealth by conquering other nations, so they took another step and made an empire by conquering and ruling other nations. An empire is a group of nations ruled by the strongest nation. For four hundred years (from the early sixteenth to the twelfth century B.C.) the Pharaohs governed an empire that included not only Egypt but also nations in western Asia to the Euphrates (ŭ-frā′tēz) River.

PYRAMIDS, THE TOMBS OF ANCIENT EGYPTIAN KINGS

The passage leading to the burial chamber in each pyramid was skillfully closed with great blocks of stone. All the pyramids, however, were entered and robbed by later conquerors of Egypt.

In these experiments in government we have seen (1) the father governing his family, (2) related families living together and forming a tribe, (3) manufacture and trade bringing people together in towns, (4) a group of tribes or towns joining to form a nation, (5) a group of nations brought under the rule of one conqueror to form an empire.

Things to remember about ancient Egypt. — 1. Egypt became civilized long before Europe.

2. The Nile River made Egypt fertile and prosperous.

3. The early Egyptians had learned the use of copper and bronze. They had advanced from the Stone Age to the Bronze Age.

4. The first paper was made from the papyrus plant in Egypt.

5. The early Egyptians built the pyramids, which rank among the wonders of the world.

6. Articles found in their tombs tell us how they lived.

7. They invented the colonnade and the clerestory.

8. They made great portraits in stone, painted pictures, and made beautiful jewelry, pottery, and furniture.

9. They wrote books and had schools and libraries.

10. They invented a calendar from which our calendar has developed.

11. The kings called Pharaohs, made Egypt a great empire.

Things to do. — Model a map of Egypt on a sand pile.   Show the course of the Nile, the delta, Thebes, First Cataract.

Become the papyrus plant and tell the class how you grew and what you did for people.

Tell the class about an Egyptian city of 3000 years ago.

Talk for two minutes on Mehenkwetre's tomb, and tell what the models show and why they were put in this tomb.

Imagine yourself talking to a person who knows nothing about the Egyptians.   Tell him what progress they made.

Tell what early experiments were made in governing.   Tell why laws are necessary.

References for Teachers. — Breasted, *History of Egypt; from Earliest Times to Persian Conquest*, Vol. I; Seignobos, *History of Ancient Civilization*, III; Hall, H. R., *Ancient History of the Near East*, III, IV; *Cambridge Ancient History*, Vol. I, Chs. XIV–XIX; Myres, *Dawn of History*, III; Maspero, *Dawn of Civilization;* New York Metropolitan Museum of Art, *The Egyptian Expedition, 1918–1920*, Part II.

For Pupils. — Arnold, *Stories of Ancient Peoples*, 7–55; Hodgdon, *The Enchanted Past;* Wells, *How the Present Came from the Past*, Book Two, Ch. I; Church, *Stories of Cræsus, Cyrus, and Babylon, from Herodotus*, IX–XI; Van Loon, *Story of Mankind*, 17–28.

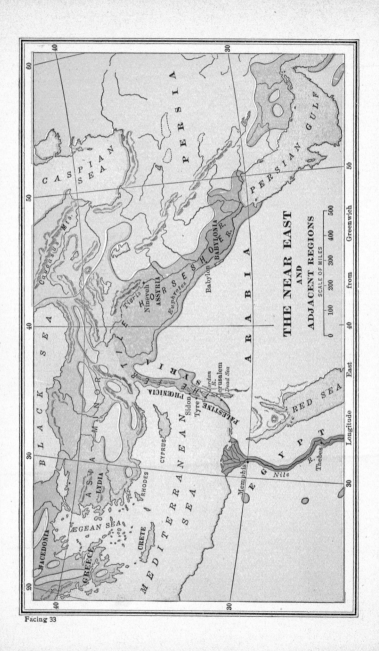

THE NEAR EAST
AND
ADJACENT REGIONS

SCALE OF MILES

0   100   200   300   400   500

CHAPTER III

WHAT WE INHERIT FROM THE NEAR EAST

A map problem. — By the " Near East " we mean that part of Asia which is nearest to southern Europe. It lies south of the Black and Caspian seas and east of the Mediterranean. Let us set ourselves the problem of understanding the important parts of this region by studying the map facing this page. Notice first the Euphrates and Ti'gris rivers flowing into the Persian Gulf. The mouths of these two rivers were " a day's journey " apart in the early period that we are studying. In later times they united and made one river before they reached the Gulf.

The space between the lower part of the Euphrates and the Tigris receives rich black mud when the rivers overflow. This region is fertile like that part of Egypt bordering on the Nile. Irrigation canals were dug through it. In ancient times this land between the two rivers produced two or three crops of wheat a year. One seed yielded from two hundred to three hundred grains of wheat.

To complete the study of the map, find the regions called Pal'estine, Phœnicia (fe-nǐsh'ǐ-a), Syr'ia, Assyr'ia, and Babylo'nia. All together on the map they look like a wide horseshoe. The horseshoe is colored green to show that the country is fertile. Babylonia is shown in a deeper green than the rest to indicate greater fertility. Southern Palestine is drawn in fainter green than northern Palestine to show less fertility.

Arabia, the land south of the horseshoe, is to a great extent desert land. But some of it serves to pasture sheep and cattle if they are driven from place to place. Wandering herdsmen there lived on the meat and the milk of their herds.

Much of the land north of the horseshoe is hilly or mountainous. The valleys between the hills and mountains produce grain, but not so much as the more fertile, irrigated fields between the lower Euphrates and the Tigris. The uplands also furnish good pastures for flocks. A hardy race of people developed in this northern country.

An imaginative problem. — Let us imagine ourselves wandering herdsmen in the desert south of the horseshoe. Our flocks have eaten up the scanty grass west of the lower part of the Euphrates, but we can look across the river and see the green grass, the fields of waving wheat, and the fat cattle there. We should set ourselves the problem of crossing over and then also try to solve the problem of what would happen to us in the new land.

Next, let us become the people to the north of the fertile horseshoe. Travelers would tell us how much more fertile the lands to the south were, how many crops could be raised in a year, how many fine things there were in Bab'ylon, the chief city of Babylonia. What should we wish to do? As people of the north or as the herdsmen of the southern desert, we should have the same wish, — to live in Babylonia. Our problem would be the same, — how to conquer it. The problem of the Babylonians would be how to keep us out. Many wars in the Near East resulted from attempts to solve these problems.

How the problem actually worked out. — For ages the people from the north and from the half-desert grass lands struggled to get possession of the fertile parts of the Near East. One tribe succeeded in seizing these lands and holding them for several hundred years. Then another tribe developed a hardier set of warriors who would take the fertile lands and keep them as long as they could. Then they in turn would be driven out. Some held the river valleys long enough to introduce the arts of civilization, and the newcomers used these arts.

THE LION OF BABYLON

Made of glazed tiles in the time of Nebuchadnezzar II (604–561 B.C.). This is one of a series which line the walls of a sacred street of Babylon.

Those who fought with each other for the possession of these lands were usually different tribes of Semites (sĕm′-īts). The Semites, or Semit′ic race, were so named because they were supposed to be the descendants of Shem, son of Noah. We are not to-day sure of the origin of the race. The Hebrews and the Arabs (ăr′abz) are the best-known peoples of the Semitic race.

Some five thousand years ago the Babylonians, a peaceful Semitic race, were living in Babylonia. They made great progress in civilization.

After a while the Assyrians, a race of Semites to the north, were powerful enough to force their way into the fertile lands. Assyria built up a great empire, with its capital at Nin'eveh. It is often mentioned in the Bible, and its destruction was foretold by the prophets.

PERSIAN SOLDIERS

Tiles from the palace of Darius, a Persian emperor. Notice that the soldiers are armed with bows and arrows as well as with spears.

Next, the Chaldeans (kăl-dē'anz), another race of Semites from the deserts of Arabia and the shores of the Red Sea, grew strong enough to conquer the Assyrians. Students of the Bible find the name of the Chaldean king Nebuchadnez'zar, who destroyed Jerusalem and took many Jews captive. In the fourth chapter of the book of *Daniel* we read of Nebuchadnezzar's dream and the story of how it came true.

The Persian invasion. — The Chaldeans were conquered by men of another race, called the Persians. Under their emperor Cy'rus, the Persians took Babylon (538 B.C.) and swept on to the Mediterranean, conquering all of the fertile horseshoe and surrounding territory.

The Persians were not Semites. They were men of the Indo-European group of nations, like most of the Europeans and most Americans. The earliest Indo-Europeans are sometimes called Ar'yans. It is believed that they came from the grassy plains east of the Caspian Sea. Some went south to Persia. Others made settlements in Europe as far west as the Atlantic Ocean. They were herdsmen. They were rough and uncultured at this time, but from them sprang the Greeks with their poet Homer, the Romans with their Cæsar, the English with their Shakespeare, and the Americans with their Washington and Lincoln.

What the people of Babylonia did for civilization.—Hammurabi (hȧ-mōō-rä'bĕ) was a great Babylonian king. One day at Babylon, more than 4000 years ago, a servant handed him a letter. The letter said that boats could not come up the Euphrates because it was obstructed. The king wished the river to be open for trade; so he dictated a letter ordering men to clear the stream. We know all this because the letters are still in existence. The king's secretary took down the dictation on a clay tablet. He had this tablet baked before sending it. The baked clay tablet, almost as hard as stone, has lasted through the ages, while most letters written on paper have been burned or have crumbled to dust.

Let us see what progress the men of the river region made in civilization. It is not necessary for us to know what part was played by each tribe of invaders. We should remember that most of this progress was due to the Babylonians, and that the Assyrians inherited the larger part of their culture from the Babylonians. The Assyrians were often at war while the Babylonians were cultivating the arts of peace.

The people in the fertile region between the Euphrates and the Tigris showed progress in education, architecture and art, measuring time, the use of domestic animals, trade, and the use of iron.

A STONE TABLET OF CUNEIFORM WRITING

The picture above the writing shows worshipers before the shrine of Shamash, the sun-god, one of the important gods of the Babylonians.

Education. — While Europe was in the Stone Age (p. 7), the inhabitants of the Tigris-Euphrates region could write. Their sign for each word or syllable was made up of wedge-shaped marks, and this kind of writing is called cuneiform (ku-ne'ĭ-form), from a Latin word that means "wedge."

Babylon had schools. Excavations have uncovered a schoolhouse of 4000 years ago and shown the clay tablets on which the pupils worked. One tablet had this for a copy: "He who excels in tablet writing shall shine like the sun." The tablets show what a hard task it was for pupils to learn cuneiform writing. They had to know more than three hundred syllables made of wedge-shaped marks. We can see the thumb print of a boy on the clay where he was trying to rub out a wrong mark.

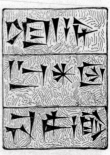

CUNEIFORM CHARAC- TERS

The Babylonians took a step far in advance of most races by educating girls as well as boys.

The people of the river region wrote enough to have a literature and libraries. A library of more than 20,000 baked clay tablets has been found in the upper river region.

Architecture and art. — The Babylonians made much use of the arch in building. The Hanging Gardens of Babylon, one of the Seven Wonders of the Ancient World, rested on a number of arches seventy-five feet high, built to make a square. These gardens were filled with flowers, vines, and trees. Europeans learned of the Babylonian arch and used it. We Americans also use the arch. Our church steeple had its beginning in the temple tower of Babylonia. This was a tower-like building of several stories, each story smaller than the one below.

The Babylonians did not have stone; they had only clay which they dried into brick. Such brick in the temple

HANGING GARDENS OF BABYLON (IMAGINATIVE RECONSTRUCTION)

From a painting used in an old Bible to give an impression of the grandeur of this ancient structure. In the background are shown temple towers.

towers, the Hanging Gardens, and other buildings, did not last so long as stone. The visitor in Babylon to-day does not find any wonderful buildings, statues, or tombs like those in Egypt, which had stone.

The most artistic work in Babylonia was shown in cutting gems and carving pictures on very small stones or seals. A Babylonian, instead of signing his name, pressed his seal against the soft clay of his letter. The Babylonians did good work in copper, and made beautiful rugs.

The Assyrians excelled in sculptures of animals. These were full of life (picture, page 42). The human figures in Assyrian art seem lifeless, showing neither joy nor sorrow.

Measuring time. — The Babylonians invented the week. Each of the seven days was sacred to one of their gods.

On the face of your watch you see twelve hours marked. They represent the Babylonian day of twelve hours. We now divide the day into twenty-four hours, but we number them as two twelves. For measuring time the Babylonians invented the sundial and water clock, the first steps toward our clock. The shadow cast on the sundial points out the hour. In the water clock, water dripped slowly from one vessel to another and measured the time.

The Babylonians, like the Egyptians (p. 29), learned to measure time through the study of astronomy. They learned in this way the true length of the year. They could foretell the time of eclipses.

Beginnings of arithmetic and science. — Do you remember how you used to count on your fingers? You simply repeated the ordinary way of counting used by early people. Counting by fives and tens is the result of using the earliest counting boards, the fingers and toes. The early people of Babylon used a system based on sixty. This number can be divided by many numbers. It comes down to us in the number of minutes in an hour, and in the number of seconds in a minute.

Man also first measured with his own body. Some measures like " foot " prove this fact. The first foot was the length of the king's foot. The " cubit " measure mentioned in the Bible was the length from the tip of the middle finger to the elbow. The Egyptians and Babylonians used weights also. The *mina*, a Babylonian weight, has come down to us under the name of pound. " Dozen " was also a Babylonian measure.

The queer measuring symbols or signs on a doctor's

prescription were invented by the Babylonians. Look at the signs of the zodiac (one for each month) in an almanac. They also come to us from the Babylonians.

Use of domestic animals. — The Babylonians used donkeys to carry things across the desert and to pull small loads. Probably the tamed horse was brought to Babylonia by the Indo-Europeans and reached there about four thousand years ago. A Babylonian tablet (2100 B.C.) describes

ASSYRIAN KING HUNTING LIONS
From wall sculpture in the palace of an Assyrian king (ninth century B.C.). The chariot is drawn by two horses.

the horse as " the donkey from the East." The horse was soon used in both industry and war. The domestication of the horse was then almost as great an event in civilization as was the coming of the railroad in the last century. It caused great changes in Egypt as well as in Asia.

When we next eat eggs or fried chicken, we should remember that the Persians were the first to bring the domestic fowl from India into this river region. From there it was taken to Europe and later to America.

Trade. — The Babylonians were great traders and merchants. They were also farmers and manufacturers. Their fertile soil raised more than they could eat. They traded for other things the food which they did not need.

Their sheep supplied much wool, which they wove into more cloth and rugs than they could use. Trade was necessary for the growth and support of the great city of Babylon.

The accounts on the clay tablets contained such items as these: wheat, dates, figs, oranges, onions, beans, wool, leather, cloth, and rugs. These articles were carried on donkeys over various trade routes. Some of the goods were taken through the Arabian desert to Mediterranean seaports; some went by boat down the Persian Gulf. All these routes led to Europe, which was glad to get products of the East.

How trade was carried on. — Think how awkward it would be to have to drive cows to a store when you wished to buy an automobile. When there was no money, things had to be exchanged for other things. We call such exchange " barter." Only a short time ago a European singer in the South Sea Islands had to barter one of her concerts. The natives gave her three pigs, twenty-three turkeys, forty-four chickens, five thousand coconuts, and more bananas than she could carry. She ate what she could, and then she had to feed the fruit to the pigs and the poultry to keep them alive.

In Babylon and Egypt the first trading was barter. A homemade fan or strip of linen might be exchanged for a fish or for onions. Cattle were for centuries the standard of exchange, a slave, a house, or a ship being worth so many cows. The most valuable things in the ancient world were gold, silver, copper, and iron. Long before money was made, pieces of these metals were used in exchange for things, because they were easy to carry and could be kept any length of time without spoiling. If the singer in the South Sea Islands had been given a half-pound lump of gold, she could easily have carried it away.

Gold, copper, and silver rings finally came into use as money. The oldest known money is this " ring " money. Ancient Egyptian artists painted pictures of men weighing heaps of gold and silver rings. The first real coins used for money appeared about 550 B.C., but long before

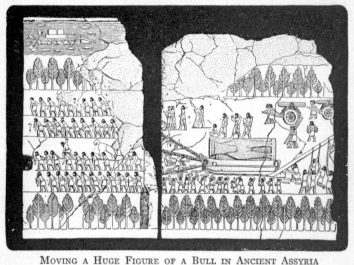

MOVING A HUGE FIGURE OF A BULL IN ANCIENT ASSYRIA

From wall sculptures of an Assyrian palace. The great stone rests on a sledge drawn by four lines of men. Rollers are used to make the hauling easier. They are picked up from behind the sledge, carried forward, and laid down in front of it.

this time the use of precious metals made exchange much easier.

A new age. — Before we leave this river region, we should know that we are in a new age, the Iron Age. The Assyrians lived near iron mines, and they had the first large army that fought with iron weapons. The rise of the Assyrian Empire, the first great world empire, was in part due to the use of iron. The Assyrians had iron-headed battering rams and easily knocked down walls of sun-dried brick.   The Egyptians who used bronze could not withstand those armed with iron.   The Bronze Age had to give way to the Iron Age.   We are to-day living in the age of iron or of steel, a form of iron.

How the western fertile region developed. — Let us glance at the western side of our map of the fertile horse-shoe region (facing p. 33).   This region was invaded by two tribes of Semites, the Phœnicians and the Hebrews, from the Arabian desert.   The Phœnicians took Phœnicia, which is the northern part of the fertile strip along the eastern coast of the Mediterranean.   The Hebrews settled in Palestine to the south of them.   Both Phœnicians and Hebrews were shepherds in Arabia.   Both made contributions to the world, but in very different ways.

What the Phœnicians did. — The Phœnicians became for a time the greatest traders in the world.   They built the harbor towns of Tyre and Si'don and later founded Carthage, another great trading port in the northern part of Africa.   Long Phœnician rowboats, with many oars, swarmed on the Mediterranean Sea.   Their pilots learned to steer by the North Star. They even ventured into the Atlantic to get the tin of the British Isles, which the Egyptians and Babylonians needed for mixing with their copper when they made bronze.   Caravans from India and Central Africa brought gold, pearls, ivory, and jewels to Phœnician traders, who sold them to the countries of the Mediterranean.

PHŒNICIAN SHIP
Redrawn from Assyrian sculpture.

As the Phœnicians went about on their trading voyages, they learned many things from other countries. They found out from the Egyptians how to make beautiful glass and vases, and soon surpassed their teachers. They copied much that they saw in Egypt and Babylonia. After 1100 B.C. the Phœnicians became skilled jewelers and weavers. Their purple dye, made from a shellfish, was so much prized that purple has ever since been called the " royal " color.

How we got our alphabet. — The trade and art work of the Phœnicians were not their only gifts to civilization. Let us see how they helped the world to express its thought.

Suppose that every time we wanted to write a story, we had to draw pictures instead of using words to tell our thoughts. Not many of us could tell a story that would be understood.

The world began with picture writing, which is still used in some cases. The Roman numerals I, II, III stand for pictures of the fingers. V represents a picture of the thumb and forefinger.

The next step from picture writing is sign writing. Suppose that you had been a Babylonian child forced to memorize more than three hundred different signs for writing; also imagine yourself a Chinese pupil of the nineteenth century, memorizing from 10,000 to 40,000 signs standing for as many words. You would be thankful if some one invented an easier way of writing.

The Phœnicians brought to Europe our much simpler modern alphabet. The first true alphabet was made up of twenty-two letters, all consonants. It is probable that the Phœnicians did not invent this entire alphabet. Which nations gave the most or any of the letters we do not know. It is certain that the Phœnicians improved the alphabet. It is also a fact that in their trading expeditions this alphabet was carried to Greece and to all parts of the then known world.

The alphabet made writing so easy that the Phœnicians imported shiploads of papyrus (p. 28) and sold it to other nations, especially to the Greeks. Europe used papyrus for many centuries. The Greek name for papyrus was *biblos*, and this word is the source of our word " Bible."

How the Old Testament came to us. — We now come to a race that gave us the great laws of the Ten Commandments. This was the Hebrew race, much weaker than its mightier neighbors in Egypt and Babylonia. Yet Palestine, the land of the

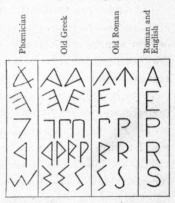

DEVELOPMENT OF THE ALPHABET

Hebrews, is perhaps the only part of the ancient world that most people to-day know anything about. The Hebrews first appear in history as a shepherd race wandering on the Arabian desert with their flocks. From time to time they drifted into Palestine, which is just south of Phœnicia. Later came years of famine, and hosts of the " children of Israel " went to Egypt for wheat. Centuries later we find them still making bricks without straw while held in bondage by the Egyptians. Moses, their prophet, led them from Egypt to Palestine, the " land of milk and honey " which Jehovah had promised them. They lived under " judges " for many centuries. Then they chose a king

Saul, who was succeeded by David. David and his son
Solomon built up a great kingdom whose chief city was
Jerusalem.

A few centuries later the Hebrews were conquered and
carried to Babylon. When Cyrus, the ruler of Persia,
conquered Babylon, he allowed the Hebrews to return to
Palestine.

The Hebrews, unlike the other early nations, worshiped
only one God, Jehovah. These shepherd people thought
of him as a Good Shepherd who watches tenderly over his
flock and guards it from harm. The laws of the Hebrews
are expressed in the Ten Commandments, which have
come to be respected in all the civilized world. Now and
then reformers or " prophets " would urge the Hebrew
people to lead good lives. They pictured Jehovah as one
who hated evil as strongly as he loved good.

That part of the Bible known as the Old Testament gives
the early history and religion of the Hebrew race. It also
tells interesting stories like that of Ruth, and contains
rare poetry, such as the Psalms. The religion of the Old
Testament emphasizes two duties: (1) man's duty to
God, — " Thou shalt love the Lord thy God with all thine
heart, and with all thy soul, and with all thy might" (*Deuter-
onomy*, VI, 5); and (2) man's duty to his fellow men, —
" Thou shalt love thy neighbor as thyself " (*Leviticus*, XIX,
18). We owe to the Hebrews the heritage of the Old
Testament.

**Things to remember about the ancient people of the Near
East.** — 1. The earliest peoples of the Near East belonged to the
Semitic race.

2. Early civilization developed in the fertile valley of the
Tigris and Euphrates rivers.

3. Many peoples — the Babylonians, Assyrians, Chaldeans, Persians (a race of Indo-Europeans), and others, — struggled to live in this fertile region.

4. The Babylonians, like the Egyptians, showed great progress in civilization. They had a system of writing, schools, and libraries.

5. They used the arch in building.

6. They invented the week. They measured the hours by the water clock and the sundial.

7. The horse and the domestic fowl were brought to this fertile region.

8. The people of the Near East were great traders and merchants. Most of their trade was barter, but the precious metals began to be used in exchange. This was the first step toward the use of money.

9. The Phœnicians, the greatest traders of ancient times, brought the alphabet to Europe.

10. Palestine, or the Holy Land, was the home of the Hebrews who gave us the Old Testament.

Things to do. — Make on a sand pile a model map of the Near East. Show the Persian Gulf, the Euphrates, Tigris, Dead Sea, fertile horseshoe, desert of Arabia, Phœnicia, Palestine, Persia, and east shore of the Mediterranean. Locate the chief cities.

Imagine yourself a herdsman of the desert or a dweller among the mountains, and tell the class why you would wish to enter Babylonia.

Imagine yourself a Babylonian, and tell why those outside should be kept out.

Make a two-minute talk on what Babylon did for civilization.

Explain what is meant by barter. What takes the place of barter to-day?

Write one hundred words on the Phœnicians.

Tell the class in three minutes why our alphabet is such a wonderful invention.

How can you tell time by a sundial?

Read in the Old Testament and tell to the class the story of the children of Israel in bondage in Egypt and how Moses led them to the " land of milk and honey."

References for Teachers. — Myres, *Dawn of History*, IV–VII; Hall, H. R., *Ancient History of the Near East*, V–XII; *Cambridge Ancient History*, Vol. I, Chs. XIII–XV, Vol. II, Chs. X, XIV; Seignobos, *History of Ancient Civilization*, IV–VII; Morey, *Ancient Peoples*, II, IV–VI; Jastrow, *Civilization of Babylonia and Assyria;* Rawlinson, *Phœnicia* (Story of the Nations); Kent, *History of the Hebrew People;* Wells, *Outline of History*, XIV, XVI, XIX, XX; Elson, *Modern Times and the Living Past*, III; *Encyclopædia Britannica*, articles "Alphabet," "Babylonia and Assyria," " Phœnicia," " Palestine," " Hebrew Religion," " Bible," " Cyrus," " Persia."

For Pupils. — Wells, *How the Present Came from the Past,* Book Two, Chs. II–VI; Arnold, *Stories of Ancient Peoples,* 81–182; Hodgdon, *Enchanted Past;* Guerber, *Story of the Chosen People* (Hebrews); Luther, *Trading and Exploring*, 9–61 (Phœnicians); Church, *Stories of Crœsus, Cyrus, and Babylon, from Herodotus*, V–VIII, XII–XVI; Van Loon, *Story of Mankind*, 29–48.

SUNDIAL

CHAPTER IV

HOW THE GREEKS BECAME THE FIRST NATION OF EUROPE

CRETAN COOKING UTENSILS OF 2200 B.C.
Found in a tomb at Cnossus.

The scene shifts back to Europe. — We now return to Europe to see what had been happening there while Egypt and the Near East were making such progress.

An island in the Mediterranean Sea was the first home of European civilization. You will notice on your map many islands near Greece. In Crete, the largest of them, there grew up a civilization almost as wonderful as that of Babylon or of Egypt. By 2000 B.C. the Cre′tans had built a beautiful city called Cnossus (nŏs′us). The palace of Minos (mī′nos), the king, contained bathrooms and plumbing — conveniences that we think of as being modern. A Cretan lady in her ruffled skirts, tight-fitting waist, and

51

long gloves would not seem much out of place to us; her four-thousand-year-old costume might easily be mistaken for one only forty years old.   The Cretans had a system of writing.   They knew how to paint, to make pottery, and

to work in metal.   They built ships and traded with Egypt.   On their trading voyages no doubt the Cretans learned many of their industries from the Egyptians.   The Cretans improved upon what they borrowed. We find in Egypt many beautiful Cretan vases which the Egyptians bought because they were more beautiful than the Egyptian vases.   The civilization of Crete spread to all the islands of the Ægean (e-jē'an) Sea and even to the coast of Asia Minor.

CRETAN GODDESS
Style of dress in the sixteenth
century B.C.

European history begins with the Greeks. — Cnossus, like Babylon, was destroyed; how, we do not know. Another race, the Greek, was to build an even more wonderful civilization on the ruins of the Cretan.   The Greeks took for their home the rugged Grecian Peninsula, which juts out into the Mediterranean, and the islands and shores of the Ægean Sea.   The early Greeks were not much better than savages, but they were a bright, wide-awake people and were quick and eager to learn.   They had a love for beautiful things.

The city-states of Greece. — Greece was cut up into many separate districts by mountain ranges and the sea. Each district was ruled by its chief city and was an inde-

pendent city-state. In the district of At'tica, for example,
the principal city was Athens. Every citizen of Attica
was a citizen of Athens and obeyed the Athenian laws.

Though the Greek city-states played an important part
in history, they were not large in comparison with many
cities of to-day. A city-state was about the size of a
county of Iowa or Alabama. Attica may have contained

GREECE IN THE FIFTH CENTURY B.C.

all together only about 250,000 inhabitants. The next
largest city-states, Sparta, Thebes (thēbz), Ar'gos, and
Cor'inth, probably had between 50,000 and 100,000 people
each. The history of Greece is chiefly the history of her
two most important city-states, Athens and Sparta.

Every city-state had its own government and its own
god or gods. In Greece there was no central government

like ours at Washington to hold all the states together. To-day in America a citizen of California or Pennsylvania is first an American and then a Californian or a Pennsylvanian. An Athenian was first an Athenian and then a Greek. Our country has become one of the great powers of the world because the first thirteen states very early discovered that they had to work together as one nation, the *United* States, or perish. The Greek states did not learn this lesson; they were jealous of each other and even fought many wars against each other.

Who lived in a city-state. — There were three classes of people in a city-state: (1) the citizens, or those whose ancestors for many years back had been born in the state; (2) the foreigners, or those who came from other places; (3) the slaves, or those who belonged to masters and had no rights of their own. Only the citizens could vote. If a citizen of Thebes, for instance, moved to Athens, he lost his vote. In Athens he was considered a foreigner, and though he lived there fifty years, neither he nor his sons could vote. There was one exception to this rule: if a foreigner performed a valuable service for the city, the assembly of citizens might permit him to become one of them. Most of the slaves were captives taken in war, or were the children of slaves; but some persons — men, women, and children — were sold into slavery to pay debts.

There were hundreds of thousands of slaves in Greece. A rich man might have as many as a thousand to work on his estate. Slaves raised the food, made the clothes, built the homes, and even taught the children. In Athens slaves were generally considered members of the household. Wise men of Athens said that a slave worked better if he was well treated and believed that some day he would be free.

Sometimes, however, the masters were so cruel that the slaves ran away to the altar of the god, where they would be protected. The slave could then ask to be given to another master. We find in later Greek history that many people were beginning to consider slavery wrong.

How the Greeks carried on business. — The earliest Greeks were farmers, like the earliest people of other great ancient nations. They raised wheat, barley, olives, grapes, figs, and peas, beans, and other vegetables. Grapes were made into wine or dried into raisins. As the cities grew, manufactures developed, and certain cities became noted for certain articles. Miletus (mī-lē′tus), Chios (kī′ŏs), and Sa′mos were noted for their wool-

A SHOEMAKER'S SHOP IN ANCIENT GREECE

From a vase painting. The girl is being measured for a pair of shoes. She is standing on the leather on which the shoemaker is marking the outline of her feet. Notice his curved knife. The man at the right is directing the work. On the wall hang the shoemaker's tools.

ens, purple dyes, and carpets; Corinth and Argos, for metal work; and Athens, for olive oil.

In a city like Athens, persons engaged in the same trade lived in the same street, which was named for them, as "the street of the sculptors" or "the street of the bakers." The manufacturers' wares and the farmers' produce were generally sold in the Ag′ora, or market place. There the merchants were grouped together in sections known by such names as "the books," "the wine," "the slaves." If you wished to buy a salmon, you would have been directed to "the fish." Proprietors stood behind their counters and called: " Buy my wine ! " " Buy my beans ! " " Buy my roses ! " Huge loaves of bread were sold by old women. Even in ancient Greece, as in our American cities to-day, the market was not complete without its street vendors, some of whom told how their medicines would cure any illness under the sun.

Sometimes the honesty of the merchant was questioned. He was accused of mixing wine with water, of stuffing the birds and chickens to make them seem fatter, or of mixing artificial dressing with the cloth to make it seem thicker.

How the Spartans lived. — Since the cities of Sparta and Athens were so different, we shall study each one separately. We sometimes hear expressions like these : " He has Spartan courage," " That school gives regular Spartan training." Let us see what these terms mean. The Spartans were the citizens of Sparta in southern Greece. They loved war and believed that the soldier was the most important person in the state. It was the purpose of Sparta to make soldiers of its citizens.

Sparta said that a child belonged to the state and not to its parents. When a baby was born, it was brought before the elders of the city ; if it was sickly or badly formed, it was left on a lonely mountain side to die. In other Greek city-states it was usually the father who decided whether or not the baby was to live. This custom seems cruel to us, who give even more than ordinary care to a weak child, but to the Greeks it did not seem cruel.

When a boy was seven years old, he was taken from his home to live in a camp under the care of a captain. He practiced running, jumping, and wrestling to strengthen his body. His captain taught him how to fight. Every Spartan boy had to be courageous. When wounded he was expected to give no sign of his pain. He would die under the whip rather than utter a cry. When a boy was eighteen, he entered the men's camp. The men ate at a common table and slept in buildings like soldiers' barracks. You see that the citizens of Sparta had little freedom to do as they pleased. An Athenian said: "A Spartan's life is so unendurable that it is no wonder he throws it away lightly."

Sparta aided in the wars of Greece, but she had no hand in developing the artistic life for which the Greeks are famous. Sparta has, however, given to us many examples of courage and honor. She has also shown us how to make strong, sturdy bodies through hard training and simple living.

How the Athenians lived. — The most famous of the Greek cities and the one which has had most influence on the history of mankind was Athens. Life in Athens was in some ways like that in Sparta, but there were also some differences. In the first place many of the Athenians disliked war and loved peace. They could, however, fight if it was necessary. Their love for their city and for independence made them win many battles. It was the work of the Athenians in times of peace, rather than the warlike deeds of the Spartans, that made Greece famous.

A SCHOOL IN ANCIENT GREECE

Redrawn from a Grecian vase. One pupil is taking a lesson in music (lyre playing); another is reciting to a teacher who has a manuscript "book" or roll.

In Athens the boys' minds were trained as well as their bodies. Writing, reading, music, grammar, and oratory

GREEK CHILDREN PLAYING WITH A SWING
From a Grecian vase.

as well as physical training, swimming, and dancing were taught them. Since Athenian citizens took part in the government, the boys learned how to make speeches. Boys were taught manners: " Rise from your seat before your elders when they approach, and do not behave ill towards your parents. Be ashamed at what is disgraceful."

The following is the oath sworn by Athenian youths on entering army service: " I will never disgrace these sacred arms, nor desert my companions in the ranks. I will fight for gods and home, both alone and with many. . . . I will observe both the existing laws and those which the people may hereafter make; and if any person seek to annul or to disobey the laws, I will do my best to prevent him."

GREEK CHILD PLAYING WITH A TOY CART AND A PET DOG
From a Grecian vase.

Athenian women and girls stayed at home. In Greek history we read of no women lawyers, of no women voters, and of hardly any women teachers, writers, or artists. Sappho (săf'o), a Greek woman of 600 B.C., is considered the greatest poetess that ever lived. Hypatia (hī-pā'shĭ-a), also a Greek woman, was a famous teacher of mathematics at Alexan'dria (in Egypt) about nine hundred years later. The Greeks, however, thought that women should not be trained to do anything but care for the home.

Greek experiments in self-government. — The Greeks, particularly the Athenians, loved freedom. They experimented with different kinds of government until they found one that allowed citizens the most freedom. The same state at different times would be a kingdom, an ol'igarchy ruled by a few nobles, and a democracy. In the fifth century B.C. Pericles (pĕr'ĭ-klēz), a great man of Athens, said: " It is true that we are called a democracy, for the administration is in the hands of the many and not of the few." We get the word *democracy* from the Greeks. It comes from two words: *demos*, which means " people," and *kratos*, which means " power."

The assembly of the city-state. — Each city-state was so small that the citizens did not live very far away from the assembly place. Each citizen went to the assembly himself and voted. He lost his vote if he was not present. Greeks considered it a disgrace not to take part in the government.

Let us see how the Athenian assembly was conducted. It met four times a month. The council, a body of five hundred citizens chosen each year, prepared the business of the assembly. At the meeting the citizens discussed, and accepted or rejected, the laws put before them by the council. Those who took part in the debate had to be well-trained public speakers. If they mispronounced words or were uninteresting, the crowd would hoot and bawl at them to finish.

The Athenians believed that in a true democracy all citizens were equal. They thought that all citizens should take part in making the laws, and also that they should have the right and the opportunity of serving as officers to carry out the laws and as judges to decide lawsuits. We must remember that the Greeks had the first free governments in which the common man had a voice.

What the Greeks learned through trading. — In early times Phœnician traders had landed on the coasts of Greece. They pulled up their boats on the shore and displayed their wares to the Greeks who crowded around them. Greek women were eager to buy the ivory combs, beautiful purple cloth, gayly decorated vases, and golden chains from the East, and the men were glad to obtain bronze and iron knives to replace their stone ones.

Gradually the Greeks learned how to make these things themselves. They began to build the kind of ships the Phœnicians used. As their trade increased they constructed ships too large to be dragged up on the shore. It was then that the anchor for holding ships at sea was invented.

Greek traders touched at every point in the Mediterranean. They learned all that the Egyptians, Babylonians, and other nations could teach them about art, architecture, sculpture, dyeing, weaving, and metal work. The ideas which the Greeks borrowed from other nations were very valuable. The important thing to remember about the Greeks is that they usually improved what they took from other nations.

The Greeks received the alphabet from the Phœnicians. At first a merchant now and then learned to write Greek words with Phœnician letters. Gradually the alphabet was employed by all the Greeks. They added to it the vowels a, e, i, o, u, which the Phœnician alphabet did

not have. It was the Greeks who first used the alphabet
in writing plays, poetry, and history which have come
down to us.

During their travels the Greeks noticed that the Lyd'ians
in Asia Minor paid for their purchases with small silver
coins stamped with the king's seal. One of the Lydian
kings, Crœ'sus, was so wealthy that we
still use the expression " as rich as
Crœsus." Since a sackful of coins on
a trading voyage is much more convenient to carry than a herd of cattle,
the Greeks adopted this invention of
their neighbors.

A LYDIAN GOLD COIN

The colonies of the Greeks. — Many Greeks left the
homeland altogether and started colonies on the coast of
Asia Minor, Africa, Italy, Sicily, Sardinia, on the shores of
the Black Sea, and in the delta of the Nile. There are
two main reasons why they emigrated. (1) Greece was

GREEK COINS

The middle coin represents the Acropolis at Athens (p. 75).

growing too crowded. In other lands there was more room
and more chance to make money. (2) As traders, the
Greeks were becoming important. For years the Phœnicians had jealously guarded the secrets of the trade routes.
Greek ships followed them until they learned these secrets.

Little by little the Phœnicians were driven out. Some
of their trading centers were taken by the Greeks, who established colonies at those places. Greece gradually became the chief trading nation in the Mediterranean, and
she grew very wealthy.

Most of the Phœnician colonies had been simply trading
posts. The Greek colonies were not so. When the Greek
colonists went to their new home, they carried some of the
fire that was kept burning on the sacred hearth of the
" mother city." The fires of the new " daughter city "
were kindled with it. The tie between the " mother city "
and the " daughter city " was very strong and accounts for
the great patriotism in the scattered Greek colonies. In
its government, however, the new city was an independent
city-state. The Greeks carried with them to the colonies
not only some of the sacred fire of the mother city; they
took also the knowledge of art, science, and literature that
the Greeks at home had developed. They built beautiful
temples like those of the homeland. Statues of the gods
were carved and set up. In the Greek colonies some of the
greatest poets and thinkers lived. Thus Greek civilization
was spread over Mediterranean lands that were hundreds
of miles from Greece.

How the freedom of the Greeks was threatened. — An
enemy nation from the east threatened the freedom of
Greece. The Persians were growing in power and in numbers. Under Dari'us, their emperor, they were sweeping
over the world, conquering everything in their path. We
have seen how Babylonia and other lands of the near East
fell before them (p. 36). Next the Persians took Egypt
and Asia Minor, and in 490 B.C. they landed an army in
Attica.

The battle of Marathon. — On the plains of Mar'athon, near the seacoast, the Athenians met the Persians, who were drawn up ready for battle. Miltiades (mil-tī'a-dēz), the Athenian general, knew that the Persians would send a terrible hail of arrows before his men could get near enough to fight.   He ordered the troops to run toward the Persians. This act so took the Persians by surprise that the Athenians were upon them before they could prepare for a hand-to-hand fight.   Thousands of Persians were killed, and the others were sent rushing madly toward their boats drawn up on the shore. The Athenians hotly chased after them and even ran out into the water. Some caught hold of the orna-

GREEK SOLDIER
The chief weapon of the Greek soldier was his spear.

ments at the head of the boats, captured the vessels, and then set fire to them. Seven Persian ships were destroyed, and those that escaped sailed away.

Why this battle was important. — The battle of Marathon is called the first very important battle in the history of the world. Let us see why. Suppose the Persians had been victorious. Attica and finally all of Greece would have belonged to the Persian emperor. The Greeks would have been little better than his slaves, and could not have made the beautiful buildings and done many of the other things that we shall read about in Chapter V.

The Persians return to Greece. — Themistocles (thĕ-mĭs'to-klēz), an Athenian general, knew the Persians would return. He persuaded his countrymen to prepare for them by building a fleet of two hundred ships.

Ten years later the Persians did return. Their emperor Xerxes (zurk'sēz), the son of Darius, assembled a vast and strange army. In it were soldiers from the entire Persian Empire: Persians in gay robes, savages in leopard skins, shepherd people whose only weapon was a lasso, Arabs on swift horses, Greeks from Asia Minor in bronze armor, and soldiers from India in white robes. A long train of horses, mules, and camels followed, carrying the provisions. Xerxes had a bridge of boats built across the Hel'lespont so that his army might cross easily.

The battle of Thermopylæ. — It is no wonder that some of the Greek city-states surrendered to Xerxes. Athens and Sparta, however, decided to fight him. The Spartans resolved to meet the Persians at Thermop'ylæ, which was a narrow pass between the mountains and the sea, on the road into Greece. Three hundred Spartans and several hundred other Greeks under Leon'idas, king of Sparta, bravely held back the Persian host for several days. The struggle was a terrible one. From time to time Persian troops attacked the Spartans, who sometimes appeared to run away. Then when the Persians were upon them, the Spartans turned and killed great numbers. Herod'otus says: "It is said that Xerxes, who was watching the battle, thrice leaped from the throne on which he sat, in terror for his army." A Greek traitor offered to lead the Persians over the mountains to a path on the other side of Thermopylæ. His offer was accepted. The next day the Spartans were awakened by cries of their scouts.

The Persians were coming from the other direction! Now the army was trapped, but Leonidas and his Spartans determined to fight to the last man. When the mighty Persian armies swept toward them on both sides, the little band fought with great courage. All the Spartans were killed, but the story of their bravery helped to stir other Greeks to fight against the Persians. An inscription was set up over the graves of the heroes. It reads:

> " Go, stranger, and to Sparta tell
>   That here, obeying her commands, we fell."

The final defeat of the Persians. — When the Persian army advanced from Thermopylæ, the Athenians were terrified and fled from their city to an island.

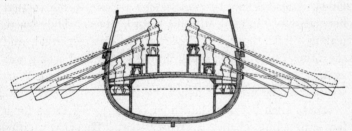

HOW A GRECIAN TRIREME WAS ROWED

This is a cross section of a trireme, the most usual kind of warship in ancient times. A side view of such a ship is shown on page 120.

The Persians destroyed Athens, and then their fleet sailed to the bay of Sal'amis to fight the Athenian fleet. The Persians, however, were poor sailors, and in spite of their much greater fleet they were overcome by the Greeks in the naval battle of Salamis. Those ships that were left hurriedly sailed away to Asia. Most of the Persian army also went home, and the part that remained was defeated.

Athens becomes the leader of the Greek cities. — When the other Greek cities saw that Athens would save them from the Persians, many of them united with her and formed a league. In return for her protection, they sent her money, which the Athenians used in rebuilding their city.

The homes of the Athenians were luxurious and filled with treasures from Egypt and Persia. Theaters supplied the people with entertainment. Painters and poets produced great works. Beautiful temples of marble, decorated with wonderfully carved figures, arose on the Acrop'olis. For fifty years the Athenians were the leaders of their nation. This time is called the "Age of Pericles," because Pericles was then the great leader of the Athenians.

Athens grew more and more eager for gold. The other Greek cities became tired of paying tribute to her so that her citizens might lead idle, selfish lives. They were jealous of her strength. Sparta, her greatest rival, and the other cities of the south united and waged a long war against Athens. This, known as the Peloponne'sian War, resulted in the defeat of Athens.

Sparta then became the leader of the Greek cities for a few years, but Thebes overthrew her. The Greek cities fought much among themselves. This wasted their strength and money. When a conqueror from another nation came along, they were unable to resist him.

Macedonia conquers Greece. — A king in a country just north of Greece watched his fighting neighbors for many years. In the meantime he drilled and equipped a great army. He massed his soldiers and their long spears so that they formed a solid wall of spears. This man was Philip of Macedonia (măs-e-dō'nĭ-a). He had studied in Thebes and had learned how the Greeks fought. His plan was to make Greece a part of his kingdom so that he would have her help in overthrowing the Persian Empire.

He marched south and conquered the cities of northern Greece. Athens did not seem to realize her danger. Demosthenes (de-mŏs'the-nēz), one of the world's greatest orators, warned the Athenians in a series of speeches to prepare for Philip. In thundering tones he cried out to them: "Here you are, Athenians, sitting still and doing nothing. What I wonder at is that you Athenians, who in former days fought for freedom against Sparta, now shrink from personal service and payment of money for the defense of your possessions."

But the Athenians were unwilling to return to the hard life of the army after living so comfortably in fine houses. They disliked to give money for weapons when they might spend it on beautiful statues, theaters, and rich clothing. They laughed at Demosthenes, who lived to see his advice taken, but too late to save Greece. When Philip approached Athens, the Athenians and Thebans united to fight against him, but the Macedonian conqueror overcame them. Greece became a possession of Macedonia.

How Alexander the Great conquered the East. — Philip had a son, Alexander, who was a fearless, headstrong youth and a born fighter. When Alexander was a boy, he complained to his playmates that his father would leave nothing for him to conquer. Even in his boyhood he showed the courage that was to make him one of the great leaders in history. His father had bought a fine horse which was so wild that no one dared to go near it. Philip was about to send it away when Alexander asked to be allowed to ride it. He had noticed that the horse was afraid of its own shadow. Alexander turned the animal's

ALEXANDER THE GREAT, HUNTING THE LION. From the so-called sarcophagus of Alexander.

head toward the sun. Then he patted the horse's neck, leaped upon its back, and soon tamed it. From that time on, the horse Buceph'alus was his property.

At his father's death in 336 B.C., Alexander, who was then twenty years old, became king. He was determined to finish the work of conquering the Persian Empire. He first took the cities along the coast of Asia Minor and Phœnicia. Then he added Egypt to his possessions. At the western end of the Nile delta he built a city which he named Alexandria, for himself. From Egypt he marched across to the Tigris-Euphrates valley, the home of the ancient kingdoms of Babylonia and Assyria, but now a part of the Persian Empire. The mighty Persian army could not stop the Macedonian warriors and their dauntless leader. The Persian Empire came to an end, and its vast treasures fell into Alexander's hands.

Alexander, not content with this conquest, pushed on to India. In the scorching desert the lack of water destroyed a great part of the army. Some of his soldiers discovered a small spring in the desert. They collected the water and brought it to Alexander as if they were bringing him a great gift. Alexander thanked his men and then poured the water on the ground in the sight of his army. When the men saw that their leader would not take what every man could not have, they marched on, strengthened as if each man had been refreshed by the water Alexander had thrown away. Alexander was finally forced to return to Babylon. In 323 B.C. he was stricken with fever and died before he had reached the age of thirty-three.

At his death he left his empire " To the most worthy," — meaning one of his generals named Perdic'cas. No one but Alexander could have held the empire together. It broke into three parts: the kingdoms of Asia, Egypt, and Macedonia.

Alexander's conquest of the East is one of the turning points in history because he carried Greek civilization into all parts of his empire. The countries that bordered the Mediterranean formed a kind of Greek world where Greek was the language of the educated and where Greek books were studied. For several centuries Alexandria, in northern Egypt, was the center of learning of the whole world. A great library and a museum were built there, and many men from Greece and from other countries went there to study.

Things to remember about the ancient Greeks. — 1. The island of Crete was the home of the earliest civilization in Europe.

2. The Greeks were the first great nation of Europe.

3. From the nations of the Near East and from Egypt, the Greeks learned the alphabet and many other things.

4. Greece was made up of many city-states; the most important were Sparta and Athens.

5. Sparta trained her citizens to be fighters.

6. The Athenians trained the minds as well as the bodies of their boys.

7. Some of the Greek city-states were the first democracies, with free governments in which the common citizens had a voice. The Greeks, however, had slaves who did not vote.

8. The Greeks founded colonies on the shores of the Mediterranean. Greek civilization was thus spread.

9. The Persians threatened the freedom of Greece.

10. The battles of Marathon and Salamis, in which the Greeks defeated the Persians, are for us the first very important battles in history.

11. Athens became the leader of the Greek cities for a period known as the Age of Pericles.

12. The Macedonians conquered Greece. Alexander the Great, king of the Macedonians, conquered most of the known world, and spread the Greek civilization over his empire.

Things to do. — Find on the map Crete, the islands of the Ægean Sea, and Greece. Notice how near they are to Egypt and Asia.

Give an example of Spartan courage from life to-day.

Read in Haaren and Poland, *Famous Men of Greece*, 133–138, *Leonidas at Thermopylæ*.

Imagine yourself to be Xerxes on the golden throne and describe the battle of Thermopylæ as you see it.

Tell to the class the story of Alexander and the taming of Bucephalus. (See *Famous Men of Greece*, 215, 216; Harding, *Stories of Greek Gods, Heroes, and Men*, 184, 185; or any Greek history.)

References for Teachers. — Hall, *Ancient History of the Near East*, II; Baikie, *Sea-kings of Crete;* Myres, *Dawn of History*, VIII–IX; Zimmern, *Greek Commonwealth;* Seignobos, *Ancient Civilization*, IX, XI–XIII, XV, XVI; Wells, *Outline of History*, XXI, XXIII; Bury, *History of Greece* (second edition); Morey, *Ancient Peoples*, 81–186, 241–296; Whibley, *Companion to Greek Studies*, 428–588, 633–663; Abbott, *Pericles* (Heroes of the Nations), I–XVII; Fowler, *City State of the Greeks and Romans;* Webster, *Readings in Ancient History*, 6–153; Davis, *Victor of Salamis* (fiction).

For Pupils. — Haaren and Poland, *Famous Men of Greece*, 128–146 (Miltiades, Leonidas, Themistocles), 163–172 (Pericles), 210–226 (Philip, Alexander); Guerber, *Story of the Greeks;* Macgregor, *Story of Greece;* Church, *Story of the Persian War from Herodotus;* Harding, *Stories of Greek Gods, Heroes, and Men*, 137–165; Van Loon, *Story of Mankind*, 48–65, 74–87; Tappan, *Story of the Greek People*, 24–135, 151–239; Church, *Three Greek Children* (fiction); Snedeker, *Perilous Seat* (fiction).

CHAPTER V

WHAT WE OWE TO THE GREEKS

The religion of the Greeks. — The Greeks believed that the earth was ruled by powerful beings called gods, who

ATHENA, OR PALLAS
From the antique marble statue in the Vatican Museum at Rome.

dwelt in the clouds on the summit of Mount Olym′pus, the highest peak in the land. Zeus (zūs) was ruler of heaven and earth and hurled the thunderbolts across the sky. Like other Greek gods, he is now most often mentioned by his Roman name, which was Jupiter or Jove. He′ra (Juno), his wife, was goddess of the home. Posei′don (Neptune), to whom sailors prayed before their voyages, was the god of the sea. Pluto was king of the underworld, the dark region where the dead lived. Aphrodi′te (Venus), the most beautiful of all the goddesses, was queen of love and beauty. On valentines you have probably seen her son E′ros (Cupid), the god of love, with his bow and arrows. Athe′na (Minerva) was the goddess of wisdom and needlework. Her poetic name was often Pallas.

In books and magazines we shall often find references to these and to other gods, goddesses, and heroes of Greece. In one of Shakespeare's plays we find the line: "She'll not be hit by Cupid's arrows." Those who read *The Raven*, by the American poet Edgar Allan Poe, can see the croaking raven " perched upon a bust of Pallas."

Greek myths. — What the Greeks could not understand in nature they explained by means of stories or *myths*. They picked out certain stars and groups of stars, and invented stories about them. The Greeks imagined that a certain group of seven stars represented seven sisters called the Pleiades (plē'ya-dēz). Zeus had changed them into stars, and we can see them to-day in the autumn sky. They are followed by the hunter Ori'on and his dog; the dog star Sir'ius is the brightest of all the fixed stars.

This is how the Greeks explained the rising and the setting of the sun : Every morning I'ris, the goddess of the dawn, lifts the purple curtains of night in the east. Phœbus Apollo, the sun god, in his fiery chariot, makes his daily journey across the sky. One day Apollo allowed his son Pha'ethon to drive the chariot. The boy lost control of the horses. They ran so near the earth that some of the people were burned black. They have remained so till this day. The earth in one place was so badly scorched that it is still the Great Desert, the Sahara.

The Greeks believed that now and then the gods, disguised as mortals, visited the earth. One day Athena, in the form of an old woman, was passing the home of Arachne (a-răk'ne), the finest weaver in Greece. She heard Arachne boast, " I can weave better than Athena herself." Athena entered and challenged Arachne to a contest. Of course, the goddess of needlework won. She changed Arachne into a spider so that she could go on weaving forever.

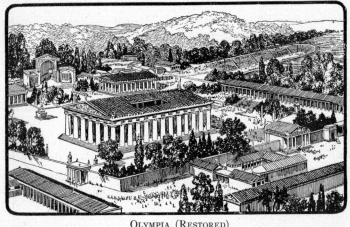

OLYMPIA (RESTORED)

The stadium for the games can be seen in the background at the right.

Religious festivals. — Sometimes men from all over Greece met in great religious festivals which lasted for days. The most famous was celebrated every four years at Olym′pia in honor of Zeus. Every youth in Greece was eager to enter the Olympian games. To receive the olive wreath, the sign of victory, at Olympia was the highest honor a Greek could know. Even wars between Greek states were sometimes stopped during the Olympian games.

The modern Olympian games are held every four years in some city of Europe or America. Nearly all nations take part. In 1908, when the Olympian games were held in London, an American named Johnny Hayes won the long-distance race known as the "Marathon." The Mara-

thon is so named for the following reason: After the battle
of Marathon (p. 63) a soldier ran to Athens, a distance of
about twenty-five miles, with the news. He shouted:
" Ours the victory," and fell dead.

Greek architecture. — The first great buildings of all races
have usually been temples to their gods. Man has never
built a more beautiful structure than the Par'thenon. This
temple was built at Athens in honor of the goddess Athena.
The great ideal of the Athenians was wisdom, and so they
chose Athena as their special goddess. The Parthenon
was built after the Persian wars (finished 434 B.C.). It
stands on the Acropolis, as the fortified center of any
Greek city was called. The Acropolis of Athens is a high
hill. The Parthenon can be seen from far away.

The Greeks used three different kinds of columns: Dor'ic,
Ion'ic, and Corin'thian. The Parthenon has the Doric
columns, which are plain. The Ionic column has at the
top an ornament that looks like a scroll. The top of the
Corinthian is adorned with leaves.

CAPITALS OF GREEK COLUMNS
Showing the three types: Doric, Ionic, and Corinthian.

The Greeks could not endure things out of proportion.
Every part of a Greek building was in harmony with
every other part and with the whole building. The columns,
for example, were neither too large nor too small.

The Parthenon is only one of a large number of beautiful Grecian temples, some of which are still preserved, in Greece and Italy.

THE PARTHENON AS IT APPEARS TO-DAY
It was ruined by an explosion of gunpowder stored there in 1687.

All the civilized world shows the influence of the architecture of the Greeks. There are few cities or towns in the United States that have not copied Grecian architecture in some of their buildings. If we see handsome columns in front of a public building, a bank, or a home, we may nearly always find that they were copied from Greek models.

SCULPTURES OF PART OF THE PARTHENON (RESTORED)

Sculpture. — The Grecians excelled in sculpture as much as in architecture. They gave grace, beauty, and strength to the modeled human form. They had such skill that they could make the folds of marble drapery on their statues seem like soft muslin.

The sculptor joined with the architect to make the Parthenon beautiful. Phid′ias, the world's greatest sculptor, and his pupils worked on it for years. Part of their sculptured relief figures are shown in the picture on page 76.

It is easy to get prints of famous pieces of Greek sculpture and to notice its beauties for ourselves. Two of these are the Venus de Milo, the most beautiful statue in the world, and the Winged Victory (p. 79), which combines energy, grace, and beauty.

One reason why the Greeks made beautiful statues was that they had fine models. They put their love of beauty into practice every day by making their own bodies as nearly perfect as possible. Men and boys spent hours

GREEKS RACING IN ARMOR
Redrawn from a vase given as a prize.

running, jumping, and playing outdoor games. They trained their bodies to be strong and healthy and therefore beautiful. A weak or sickly body was considered ugly. The

Greeks demanded grace in their athletes. They even hissed a winning athlete in their games if he was awkward.

Suppose that you could have three wishes. What would you choose? Plato quotes these three wishes from a Greek proverb: to have (1) health, (2) personal beauty, (3) wealth honestly gained. The playgrounds of our schools show that we also want health for our boys and girls. Doctors say that beauty and wealth will more easily take care of themselves if we are healthy.

Greek vases and painting. — The Greeks loved to have the common things of life beautiful. They would not drink from ugly cups or sleep on ugly beds. Even the earthen jars and pots used in the kitchen were of graceful shape.

Greek vases, jars, and urns are so beautiful that the world has never ceased to admire them. The vases were of

GREEK VASE

different shapes and had varied uses, as we use china to-day. Sometimes they were given as prizes to athletes. They were often buried in tombs, so that the spirit of the dead might have something beautiful for use in the next world.

It is from Greek vases that we learn most about the art of painting in Greece. The paintings on the vases are graceful and natural (pictures on pages 55, 57, 58, 77). They tell stories of the gods and of the everyday life of the people. The paintings of the Egyptians show only a flat surface. The Greeks learned how to give an idea of depth and distance. One Greek painter is said to have painted a bunch of grapes so naturally that the birds pecked at them.

WINGED VICTORY OF SAMOTHRACE

This statue was set up in 306 B.C. to celebrate a naval victory. It is very beautiful, even in
its present mutilated condition.

The Greek drama. — The Greeks had another great art worthy to rank beside their architecture, sculpture, and painting. They were the first people to pay as much attention to the acting and writing of plays as to their other arts. The Greek plays, or dramas, still rank beside the greatest in the world. They have served as models for later dramatic writers.

How the Greek drama began. — The Greek drama began as a festival or an act of worship of the god Diony'sus. This god, the Greeks believed, was the power that called the trees, flowers, and vines to life in the spring and that ripened the grain and loaded the vineyards with grapes in the autumn.

We know that as early as five hundred years before Christ, the Greeks acted tragedies in honor of Dionysus. A tragedy is a serious play, often connected with death; but at first the word meant merely a " goat song." The early tragedies were called " goat songs," probably because a goat was sacrificed when the song was sung. The first actors were a " chorus " of men dressed like sat'yrs, the fabled attendants of Dionysus. Satyrs had long pointed ears, snub noses, and goats' tails. The chorus sang songs in honor of Dionysus, which perhaps told tales of his adventures. Important parts of every Greek tragedy were sung by a chorus of men.

The Grecian comedies or humorous plays probably developed in connection with songs at rustic festivals and banquets at the time of harvesting grain and gathering grapes. Comedy was given to mirthmaking. The Greeks did not make as great an art of comedy as of tragedy, although they had one great comic dramatist, Aristophanes (ăr-is-tŏf'a-nēz).

The flower of Grecian tragedy. — Three Athenian poets wrote the best Greek plays. All of these were tragedies. These dramatists were all born within forty-five years of each other: Æschylus (ĕs'kĭ-lus, 525 B.C.), Sophocles (sŏf'o-klēz, about 495 B.C.), Euripides (ū-rĭp'ĭ-dēz, 480 B.C.). Their plays dealt with the religion, history, and heroes of Greece.

The government of the city-state of Athens thought that attendance at these plays would make the citizens more religious, more patriotic, and more proud of the deeds of the Athenians. The government, therefore, bought tickets to the plays for those who could not pay for them.

Once in a while some of these great Greek plays, such as the *Antigone* (ăn-tĭg'o-nē) of Sophocles, are acted to-day. For the chorus of this play Sophocles wrote a song that shows the pride of the Greeks in the work of man. The *Antigone* chorus sings: " Of all strong things, none is more wonderfully strong than Man. He can cross the wintry sea, and year by year compels with his plow the unwearied strength of Earth. He seizes for his prey the airy birds and teeming fishes, and with his wit has tamed the mountain-ranging beasts, the long-maned horses, and the tireless bull. Language is his, and wind-swift thought and city-founding mind; and he has learned to shelter himself from cold and piercing rain; and has devices to meet every ill but death alone. With his boundless skill he moves on, sometimes to evil, but then again to good."

The theater at Athens. — The first theater was a simple hillside; the first stage, the level spot at the foot of the hill. The Theater of Dionysus was on the south side of the Acropolis at Athens. The seats of the theater were partly cut out of the Acropolis rock so that one tier rose

RUINS OF THE THEATER OF DIONYSUS AT ATHENS

Notice a small part of the stage at the left; the orchestra, or level space in front of the stage; and the seats for spectators.

above another in semicircular form. Between the stage and the seats was a circular place called the orchestra, where the chorus sang or danced during the play.

The actors who took the parts of gods and heroes dressed so as to appear larger than ordinary men. They wore high, thick-soled buskins, half boot and half stilt, padded clothes, and masks to cover their faces (picture, p. 83). The masks were often beautifully painted. To-day the mask is the sign of the theater. The heroic size of the chief actors enabled them to be more easily seen when an audience of 20,000 or more was present.

Socrates, the wise man of Greece. — In the Greek temples there were no preachers to tell the people the difference between right and wrong or to give them rules of behavior. Instead, teachers known as *philosophers* gathered groups of men about them and taught the best way of living. One of the greatest of philosophers was Socrates (sŏk′ra-tēz), an awkward-looking man with a flat nose and large forehead. He was a great trial to his wife, Xantippe (zăn-tĭp′ĕ), who scolded him for talking in the market place instead of sticking to his trade of stone cutting.

Pla′to, one of his pupils, says of him: "He used to dispute with all who would converse with him; not with the purpose of taking away their opinions from them so much as of learning the truth himself." Socrates said: "I go on my way and question the

MASKS OF GREEK ACTORS (p. 82)
The upper two were used in acting tragedies and the lower two in comedies.

wisdom of any one who appears wise; if he is not wise, I show him that he is not wise." His habit of questioning people and proving to them how little they knew angered many. Sometimes he was treated with great rudeness and was pulled about and beaten.

One of the teachings of Socrates was that there is one God who rules the world. Socrates taught people to think out the truth for themselves and not to depend on having it given them by others. His influence is felt in our education to-day.

Finally the enemies he had made caused him to be imprisoned and put to death (399 B.C.). They said he did not worship the old gods of Greece and was ruining the minds of young men.   Before he drank the cup of poison hemlock, he said: " Be of good cheer about death, and know this of a truth, — that no evil can happen to a good man either in this life or after death."

Plato, his pupil, was also a famous philosopher.   One of his beliefs was that girls should have the same education as boys, and that women should vote as well as men ; but this plan was not adopted in any Greek state.

The Iliad and the Odyssey. — The Greeks wrote beautiful poems which many later poets used as their models. Two of the best poems that the world owns and reads to-day are the *Il'iad* and the *Od'yssey*.   A blind Greek poet named Homer is called the author of them.   They are epics, or narrative poems of heroes and great deeds.   The *Iliad* is the story of the Trojan War.   It tells how thousands of Greek warriors sailed over to Troy in Asia Minor to bring back Helen, a beautiful queen who had been stolen by the Trojan prince Paris.   For ten years the Greeks camped near the walls of Troy, fighting the Trojans and waiting for a chance to destroy the city.   Ulysses or Odysseus (o-dĭs'ūs), a crafty leader of the Greeks, had built a wooden horse big enough to hold many soldiers.   It was placed before the gates of Troy.   The Trojans, thinking it a sign from the gods, dragged it into the city.   That night the Greeks crept out of the horse and opened the city gate, and the army entered.   Troy awoke to find herself in flames.

The *Odyssey* is the story of the wanderings of Ulysses on his way home from the Trojan War.   He had all sorts of adventures and met many strange creatures such as the one-eyed giant Cy'clops, the six-headed monster Scylla (sĭl'a), who grabbed six men at once off the ship, and the enchantress Cir'ce, who changed the sailors to pigs.

Note how simply Homer has Ulysses tell the story of the way in which his men were changed back into human form :

" So I spake, and Circe passed out through the hall with the wand in her hand, and opened the doors of the sty, and drove them forth in the shape of swine of nine seasons old. There they stood before her, and she went through their midst, and anointed each one of them with another charm. And lo, from their limbs the bristles dropped away. And they became men again, younger than they were before, and goodlier far, and taller to behold."

The *Iliad* and the *Odyssey* were composed before the Greeks knew how to write. Men learned these poems by heart and passed them on until writing was introduced.

Two Greek historians. — The desire to learn all about other lands and other people made the Greeks great travelers. Herod'otus, a famous Greek traveler, visited Egypt and all the rest of the known world. He made a map and published a history of the Persian Wars. The Athenians gave him a large sum of money as a reward for his work. His is the first long history that has come down to us, and therefore he is called the "Father of History."

Another great Greek historian was Thucydides (thŭ-sĭd'ĭ-dēz), who wrote an account of the Peloponnesian War (p. 66). His book is full of life. It is not a dry record of happenings. Thucydides told in clear, forceful language what he saw and heard. Later historians have imitated his style of writing history. Herodotus said that the gods caused wars and the downfall of nations. Thucydides, like modern writers of history, showed that historical events were caused by men on earth.

Æsop's fables. — Six hundred years before Christ there lived in Greece a slave boy named Æsop. His master, seeing the boy's unusual cleverness, set him free. Æsop became the most famous writer of fables in the world. Most fables written since are copies of his.

You know, or should know, the story of the crow and the cheese, of the dog and his shadow, and of the frog that tried to make itself as big as an ox. From Æsop's fables come many of our common expressions, such as "sour

THE FOX AND THE GRAPES

Redrawn from an illustration in Caxton's *Æsop's Fables*, one of the earliest books printed in England.

grapes" and "a wolf in sheep's clothing." Find out and tell the class the fables in which these expressions occur.

Greek books. — The free discussion in the market place led to a desire for reading books. Much of the wisdom of the great thinkers was written down by their pupils. Plato put into writing the sayings of his teacher, Socrates. Books were widely read in Athens in the fifth century B.C. A Greek historian, in describing shipwrecks on the coast of Asia Minor, mentions books being washed up on the shore along with chests and beds. The books of ancient Athens were not the printed and cloth-bound books of the twentieth century. They were hand-written rolls of papyrus much like the Egyptian books (p. 28). Some of the rolls were 150 feet long.

What the Greeks did for science. — The Greeks desired to know things, not for the purpose of making money, but just for the sake of knowing the truth. They tried to discover the distance of the earth from the sun, and to find out whether the earth moves around the sun or the sun around the earth. The Egyptians and the Babylonians had taught that the earth is a flat disk. Pythag'oras, a Greek teacher, said : " The world is a sphere, a sphere whirling in a circular orbit around a central fire." Many Greeks believed that the earth is round, but only a few that the earth revolves about the sun. Most of them believed that the sun moved around the earth.

The Greeks made great advances in mathematics, particularly in geometry. Euclid's geometry is so complete that many schools of England still use it. It is the oldest school book in use to-day.

The Greeks stopped believing that diseases are caused by demons and angry gods. Doctors looked for the natural causes in the human body. They studied the organs of the body and learned all they could about them. Greek physicians were so famous that the Persian king called one to his court. Hippocrates (hǐ-pǒk'ra-tēz), the first great man in the science of medicine, used to put broken arms and legs in slings. In several cases that he describes, he used exactly the same treatment that the doctors prescribe to-day. He says that " the love of the art of healing is the same as the love of man."

The secret of the Greeks. — How did Athens in less than fifty years of the fifth century before Christ produce such art and literature that they remain models for the

THE DISK THROWER

This statue, of which many copies have been made, is one of the famous examples of Greek sculpture.

world? What Athens did then is called the " miracle of history." Let us try to explain this seeming miracle.

I. Every free Athenian had an equal voice in government and took pride in making his city great.

II. The Greeks were simple and direct in their art and literature. They did not overload their columns or buildings with ornament. Homer (page 84) and Thucydides tell their stories simply and in few words.

III. Pericles gave one reason for the work of the Atnenians when he said: " We are lovers of the beautiful." This means the love of truth, because art cannot be beautiful unless it is true to nature. It also means the triumph of the higher nature of man over the lower. It is the higher nature that loves art and poetry, while the lower nature is satisfied with food, drink, dress, and the other common things of life. The Athenians began their education by trying to make common things beautiful.

IV. The Athenians tried to do their work as well as they

could.   The men who laid the marble blocks in the walls of the Parthenon fitted them so exactly that the edge of a thin knife blade could not be inserted between them two thousand years later.

V. In addition to these reasons, the Greeks had genius or the natural ability to do their great work.   They also had power of will to match their genius.

Things to remember about our debt to the Greeks. — 1. The Greeks believed that the world was directed by Zeus, Poseidon, Pluto, Hera, Aphrodite, Athena, and other gods and goddesses.

2. The Greeks made up myths to explain natural happenings, such as the rising and setting of the sun.

3. The Parthenon and other buildings of the Greeks showed grace, beauty, and proportion.   The world still imitates the Grecian columns and Grecian sculpture.

4. The drama was one of the great arts of the Greeks.

5. The *Iliad* and the *Odyssey* were the first great epics.

6. Herodotus and Thucydides showed men how to write history.

7. The Greeks had books written on papyrus rolls.

8. Socrates taught people to find out truth for themselves.

9. The Greeks made progress in science, mathematics, and medicine.

10. The Athenians were able to do so much because they were (1) free men in a democracy, (2) simple and direct in art and literature, (3) lovers of beautiful things, (4) eager to do their work well, (5) possessed of great natural ability.

Things to do. — Read the myths in Kingsley's *Greek Heroes*, Hawthorne's *Wonder Book*, or some other book of mythology, and be able to tell some myth that you like.

What were the first three wishes according to a Greek proverb?   What would be your best three wishes?

Tell why the Greeks paid so much attention to athletics.

Explain why we copy Greek architecture and sculpture.

Write " An Interview with Socrates " for a paper.

From Æsop tell in one hundred words each the fable of " The Wind and the Sun " and " The Lark and her Young Ones."

Draw or model in plasticine the three kinds of Greek columns. See if you can find any examples of these columns in your city.

Bring to the class pictures of temples, churches, and public buildings which have Greek columns.

Imagine that you are talking to some one who does not know why the Greeks are great. Explain to him the secret of their greatness.

References for Teachers. — Livingstone, *Legacy of Greece;* Marvin, *Living Past*, 48–90 ; Tucker, *Life in Ancient Athens;* Mahaffy, *What Have the Greeks Done for Modern Civilization?* Seignobos, *Ancient Civilization*, X, XIV ; Whibley, *Companion to Greek Studies*, 117–428, 606–610, 663, 670 ; Wells, *Outline of History*, XXII, XXIV ; Abbott, *Pericles*, XVII, XVIII ; Morey, *Ancient Peoples*, 186–240 ; Butcher and Lang, *The Odyssey of Homer, Done into English Prose; Cambridge Ancient History*, Vol. II, Chs. XVII, XVIII, XXII ; Walters, *Art of the Greeks;* Tarbell, *History of Greek Art;* Gardner, Percy, *Principles of Greek Art;* Gardner, Percy, *Grammar of Greek Art;* Gardner, E. A., *Handbook of Greek Sculpture; Encyclopædia Britannica*, articles on " Homer," " Pericles," " Socrates," " Greek Art," " Greek Literature," " Drama."

For Pupils. — Tappan, *Story of the Greek People*, 136–151, 190–195 ; Creighton, *Heroes of European History*, 14–22 (Greek art) ; Haaren and Poland, *Famous Men of Greece*, 186–195 (Socrates), 227–236 (Demosthenes) ; Church, *Story of the Iliad; Story of the Odyssey;* Kingsley, *Greek Heroes;* Colum, *Children's Homer;* Hodgdon, *Enchanted Past*, VII ; Van Loon, *Story of Mankind*, 66–73 ; Guerber, *Myths of Greece and Rome;* Harding, *Stories of Greek Gods, Heroes and Men*, 3–124, 166–188 ; Baldwin, *Old Greek Stories;* Hall, Jennie, *Men of Old Greece.*

CHAPTER VI

HOW THE ANCIENT WORLD BECAME ROMAN

How ancient nations grew. — Each one of the ancient empires had much the same kind of history. A nation began as a small settlement in a favorable spot, the people being farmers or shepherds. They began to take the land nearest them. Not satisfied with that, they spread out and continued to conquer until all the known world was theirs or until another nation overcame them.

Of all the ancient nations Rome was the most powerful. No other nation has left so many monuments in so many different places. From Chester in northern England to the cities of northern Africa, and from Tole'do in Spain to Constantinople, are scattered crumbling Roman walls, archways, and columns, ruined temples, baths, and monuments. It is hard for us to realize that Britain and all the lands bordering the Mediterranean once obeyed the same law. We shall see how Rome gained her empire and how she held it, what she learned from those she conquered, and what she passed on to us. (See map following page 110.)

What happened in early Rome. — While Greece was reaching the height of her glory, Rome was still a village of little round huts clustered on a hill overlooking the Tiber River in central Italy. She had no handsome temples, no theaters, no books. Six hills, inhabited by various tribes, surrounded the hill on which Rome was built. The Romans, after much fighting, conquered their neighbors. By 500 B.C. Rome was a city of seven hills.

The Etruscans were a more highly civilized race who lived north of Rome. From time to time they threatened to overcome the young city. The Romans loved to repeat the stories of their early heroes who held back these enemies. One of these stories tells how Lars Por'sena, an Etruscan king, had gathered a mighty army and was marching to Rome. Between the terrified Romans and the advancing army stood a wooden bridge by which the enemy would cross the Tiber and enter Rome. To save the town the consul asked for volunteers to hold the bridge at one end while he and the rest of the army chopped it down at the other. As the poet Macaulay tells the story,

So-called "Hut of Romulus"
This shows the form of the earliest houses in Rome.

Then out spake brave Horatius,
  The Captain of the Gate:
"To every man upon this earth
  Death cometh soon or late.
And how can man die better
  Than facing fearful odds,
For the ashes of his fathers
  And the temples of his gods?

Hew down the bridge, Sir Consul,
  With all the speed ye may;
I, with two more to help me,
  Will hold the foe in play;
In yòn strait path a thousand
  May well be stopped by three."

So the three standing at one end struck down many of the Etruscan leaders. The bridge creaked, and the crowd shouted to Horatius and his companions to return. Two fled across the bridge, which plunged into the river just as they stepped from it. They looked back to see Horatius still on the other side. He knew that he was at the mercy of the Etruscans. There was only one thing to do. He plunged into the rag-

HORATIUS AT THE BRIDGE

ing river and swam across to safety. The Romans never tired of telling

How well Horatius kept the bridge
In the brave days of old. [1]

The republic of Rome. — Just as the Greeks had a talent for making beautiful things, so the Romans had a talent for governing. According to Roman legends, the first rulers of Rome had been seven kings, the last three of whom were Etruscans; but the kings grew so cruel that the people drove the last one away. The Romans then set up a republic. Every year they elected *two* consuls or rulers so

[1] Macaulay's *Lays of Ancient Rome*.

that no one man could become powerful enough to make himself king. A council called the senate (from *senex*, meaning " old man ") was composed of the oldest and wisest men of Rome. The Senate made some of the laws, while others were voted by the citizens.

Rome showed her wisdom in government by the way in which she treated the people whom she conquered. You will recall that the Greeks did not allow foreigners to become citizens (p. 54). Naturally the foreigners in a city-state felt no interest in the government. Rome, however, grew to be much wiser. Some of the people whom she conquered were told that they might become Roman citizens instead of slaves. Rome expected them, as her citizens, to help her in building up their country, to assist her in war, and to consider Rome as their mother city. In return they had the right to come to Rome and vote.

By 275 B.C. the Romans had subdued not only several tribes of Italians much like themselves, but also the Etruscans in the north and the Greek cities in the south. The city of seven hills now owned all Italy. Rome allowed the Italian cities which she conquered to govern themselves. They became her allies and were very loyal to her.

Patricians and Plebeians. — The people of Rome were of two important classes. The *patricians* (pa-trĭsh'anz), or nobles, were the smaller but more powerful class. They were generally wealthy and very proud of their noble birth. Between the patricians and the slaves was the large class of *plebeians* (ple-bē'yanz), or common people.

Though Rome was a republic, the plebeians at first were no better off than they had been under the kings. Only the patricians could hold office. Moreover, in order to vote, every citizen had to go to Rome. Plebeian farmers living a few miles outside of the city found the journey too long and costly. A small body of patricians, therefore, ruled to suit themselves.

How the plebeians won their rights. — During the early wars the plebeian farmers had to leave their farms and fight. Many came home poor and in debt. The patricians divided among themselves the lands, gold, fine statues and other spoils taken from the conquered people. Though the plebeians complained bitterly of this injustice, the patricians paid no attention to them.

One day "a certain aged man" thrust himself into the Forum or market place. His clothes were ragged, his body shockingly thin, and his face pale and sunken. He was recognized as a brave soldier who had fought for Rome. Those who crowded around him told how

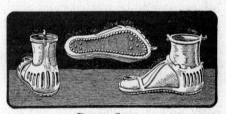

ROMAN SHOES

courageously he had fought for the state. The old man displayed the scars of many battles in which he had been engaged. He told the people how his house had been burned, his cattle stolen, and how finally, when he could not pay his debts, he was thrown into prison. His back was covered with scars where he had been beaten.

When he had told his story, there was a great uproar in the Forum. The noise spread throughout the city. When it was at its height, messengers came running with news of a fresh attack from one of the rebellious tribes outside the city. The plebeians were ordered into the army.

Instead of obeying the command, they left Rome and

quietly remained on the Sacred Mount three miles away. This strike of the plebeians lasted for some days until the patricians gave them the right to elect two " tribunes." These were representatives of the plebeians and had the right to " veto " or forbid any official act that they considered unfair.

The laws of Rome were not written down. Now and then the plebeians had cause to believe that the patricians changed laws to suit themselves. Finally, twelve bronze tablets of written law, called the Twelve Tables of law, were put up in the Forum for all to read. When the laws were known to every one, patricians and plebeians came to be treated more nearly alike. Later, many plebeians through trade and work became wealthier and married patricians. One office after another was thrown open to plebeians as well as to patricians, and the struggle between these two classes gradually came to an end.

How the Romans of the republic lived. — Most of the early Roman families, patricians and plebeians alike, lived on small farms outside the city walls of Rome. They raised grain, vegetables, and olives. Their simple clothes and farming implements were made at home. Even great heroes lived this simple sort of life.

The Romans of later times loved to tell the following story: During a war with a neighboring city-state, the Romans felt the need of a dictator, or general who for a short time had unlimited power to rule. Cincinna'tus, whom the Romans selected, cultivated a little farm of four jugera (two and a half acres) across the Tiber. There he was, busy plowing, when the messengers of the Senate came. After saluting him they bade him put on his toga and listen to the commands of the Senate. He called to his wife to bring his toga from the hut. When he had wiped off some of the sweat and dust, and had put on his toga, he presented himself; and the envoys at once congratulated him and saluted him as dictator.

THE ROMAN TOGA
Statue of Augustus in National Museum at Rome.

Cincinnatus led the Roman army to victory. Instead of remaining in the city and continuing to rule as dictator, he returned at once to his farm and took up his work where he had left it sixteen days before.

Carpenters, potters, coppersmiths, dyers, and other workmen lived in the city. They were united in guilds or unions to help each other in times of sickness or unemployment.

The Forum, or market, was an open meeting place in the center of the city. On one side of the Forum was the basil'ica, where trials were held. Along the other side were shops of all kinds. Near by were several temples. The Forum took the place of newspapers and magazines. Every important event or bit of news was discussed there.

Some results of Rome's earliest conquests. — The wealth of Rome increased as her territory was enlarged. The Romans began to build ships and to make trading

THE ROMAN FORUM AND SURROUNDING BUILDINGS (RESTORATION)
As they must have looked in the time of Augustus.

voyages to other lands. Instead of giving oxen and grain
in return for foreign wares, they sometimes used bars of
iron and other metals stamped with the figure of an ox.
The Latin word for money, *pecunia*, comes from *pecus*,
which means "ox." A metal bar of a certain size represented the value of so many oxen.

From the Greek merchants, the Romans learned the alphabet. They changed the Greek letters into the forms
which we know as the capital letters of the English alphabet.
Most nations of the white race to-day use the Roman alphabet, which first came from the Phœnicians (pp. 46–47).
We sometimes also use Roman numerals, but we should
find it awkward always to write 1925 as MDCCCCXXV
or as MCMXXV.

How woman influenced the Roman republic. — In some
Greek cities and in the eastern nations, women were treated

almost like slaves. The Roman matron, or married woman, was mistress of her house and her slaves, and her husband asked her advice on business questions. She met his guests in her home. At public games and religious ceremonies a place was reserved for her.

HAIRPINS WORN BY ROMAN WOMEN

Roman women had a great influence in public life. At a later time, when some leaders of the government were preparing for a civil war, they asked fourteen hundred of the richest women to contribute money for the necessary expenses. The women refused, saying that they would give money to fight an outside enemy but would not aid Romans to fight each other.

How Roman children were trained. — The family was the foundation of Rome. The father was the head of the household. The old Roman law (afterwards changed) gave him the power to put his wife and children to death or to sell them into slavery.

The children of a household were carefully reared. They were taught to obey their parents and the state, to respect the gods, to tell the truth, and to rely upon themselves. These habits in which the people were trained at home helped to make Rome one of the greatest nations that ever lived. For instance, the obedience which the son gave his father was transferred to his general in time of war.

The father undertook the education of his sons; the mother, that of her daughters. All the children were

taught to read and write. The language of the Romans is
called Latin. Memorizing the Twelve Tables of law was an

A BABY CARRIAGE IN ANCIENT ROME

important part of every
Roman child's education.
At the age of seven the
boy was sent to school
under regular teachers.
His most important sub-
ject was oratory, because
when he became a man
he would need to make
speeches. After school
hours he was the com-
panion of his father, or
perhaps of a tutor, who
taught him to ride, to handle a spear, to swim, and to
wrestle. The boy also studied politics in the Forum, so
that he could take his place later as an intelligent citizen.

The girl, on the other hand, stayed at home and was
taught by her mother how to cook, weave, sew, and care

for a house. She
was being fitted for
her duty in life, the
management of her
own household.

When a boy be-
came a man, he was
given a toga, a kind
of cloak which was

A CHILD'S NECKLACE

Small toys were strung together and hung around the child's
neck to ward off evil spirits and to keep him amused.

the badge of a Roman citizen (p. 97). A solemn ceremony
was held in the Forum to celebrate his coming of age.
Henceforth he was a citizen and soldier of Rome.

Every family had a precious collection of wax busts of its ancestors. Now and then these images were shown to the children. Each child was told to behave so that he would not disgrace the fair names of his ancestors.

How Rome conquered Carthage, her rival. — Rome watched with jealous eyes her dangerous rival, Carthage, a city in northern Africa. The Phœnicians, you remember (p. 45), had built Carthage, which had become the most powerful city in the western Mediterranean world. Until Rome could conquer Carthage, she could not continue to add to her possessions.

The struggle between them, known as the Pu'nic Wars (from the Latin word for "Phœnician"), began in Sicily, the island just beyond the "toe" of Italy (264 B.C.). At once the Romans realized that they needed a fleet. Without one, they were no match for the seafaring Carthagin'ians. The Romans succeeded in building a navy that defeated its enemy. They also conquered Sicily.

The Carthaginians were fortunate in the possession of a family of great generals, the first of whom was Hamil'car Bar'ca. After Rome took Sicily, Hamilcar led his son Han'nibal, then a boy of nine, to the altar at Carthage. He said to his son: "Swear that you will never make friends with Rome so long as you shall live." The boy took the oath. When Hamilcar went over to conquer Spain for Carthage, he took Hannibal along. In Spain the boy learned from his father how to become a leader of men.

After his father's death Hannibal was made leader of the Carthaginian forces. Remembering the oath to his father, he determined to conquer Rome. He knew that he would be defeated if he sailed directly to Italy. Instead, he decided to march overland to Rome. Besides his army of about forty thousand men, he had hundreds of mules and horses and thirty-seven war elephants. He passed through Spain and Gaul. His crossing of the Alps was one of the most marvelous feats ever performed by a general. We must remember that his army and his elephants came from a warm land where snow was unknown. There were no well-made roads over the Alps. Every step over the moun-

HANNIBAL CROSSING THE ALPS

tains was filled with danger. At times a misstep or a slip meant death. To add to the terror of the march, the tribes in the mountains hurled great stones at the army. By the time Hannibal had reached the Po River, half of his army and elephants had perished.

Hannibal fought his way through Italy, winning battle after battle. At the battle of Cannæ forty thousand Romans perished; it is said that the Carthaginians gathered there a whole bushel of gold rings from the dead. Rome was in great sorrow, but it did not occur to her to surrender. Hannibal thought that the Italian provinces would be glad to join his dwindling army in order to be freed from Roman rule. But Rome's sensible government of her allies was rewarded at this time. The Italian states refused to join with Hannibal. The Romans raised new armies. Hannibal at length left Italy and returned to Africa.

In 202 B.C. the Carthaginians were defeated at Zama. Hannibal fled to Macedonia and Asia Minor for help. The Romans followed him and conquered Macedonia. In 183 B.C. Hannibal killed himself to escape capture.

The city of Carthage was finally wiped off the face of the earth, and fifty thousand Carthaginians were carried to Rome as slaves. A Roman general named Scipio (sĭp'i-o), in charge of the burning of the city, is said to have burst into tears at the sight of the flaming ruins.

Rome was now free to continue her conquests. Spain, northern Africa, Greece, Macedonia, and Asia Minor fell into Roman hands. The city on the Tiber had become mistress of the Mediterranean world.

What Greece taught Rome. — Rome's conquests brought her in touch with civilizations higher than her own. She became greater because she learned from them. She was wise enough to make the Greeks her model. One writer says: "Rome conquered Greece, and then Greece conquered Rome."

Rome had little art until she conquered Greece. By copying Greek treasures, the Romans developed their own art. They never succeeded, however, in equaling the Greeks; the Romans had not the love of beauty that inspired the Greeks. The important thing is that Rome preserved Greek civilization, spread it, and passed it on.

In Greece, the Romans saw houses more comfortable than their own, and temples handsomer and more richly decorated than theirs. The wealthy Romans were no longer

A WEALTHY ROMAN'S HOUSE (INTERIOR)
Such a house was built around a small courtyard (seen at the right) which was not roofed over

satisfied with their small houses of only one or two rooms. They copied the more spacious houses of the Greeks. Besides the kitchen, dining room, bedrooms, and reception room, the Roman house came to have a courtyard beautified by flowers and by marble fountains and statues brought from Greece and other conquered lands. There were bathrooms with hot and cold baths. The whole house was heated by a sort of hot-air furnace.

Greek slave artists painted beautiful frescoes on the walls of the rooms. Many of the floors were fine mosaics brought from other countries. Thick Oriental rugs, soft couches, and rich silken draperies found their way into the new Roman houses. In the early days of Rome, an ex-consul had been fined for having more than ten pounds of silverware in his house. About thirty years later, a rich Roman was using ten thousand pounds of silverware and nobody thought it wrong. Gold rings, jewels, and silks, once the property of Egyptians, Greeks, and Gauls, now adorned the bodies of the Romans.

Roman cities began to build temples in the Greek styles of architecture. Theaters, too, were built like those of the Greeks. The Romans improved their theaters by stretching an awning over the seats as a protection against the hot sun. They also added the curtain, which had not been used in the Greek theaters. Greek plays were presented, but were not much appreciated by the common people of Rome. They preferred shows in which men called *gladiators* fought with each other or with wild animals (p. 106). Such

ROMAN THEATER TICKET

For Cavea II (Second Division), Cuneus III (Section 3), Gradus VIII (Row 8) for the play *Casina* by Plautus. Roman theater tickets were of metal or bone.

shows would have been disagreeable to the more refined Greeks. Once when a program of Greek music was given at a public entertainment in Rome, the audience told the musicians to put down their instruments and start a boxing match.

Educated Greek slaves became the teachers of Roman children. It was considered necessary for every educated

Roman to learn Greek so as to be able to read Greek books, because Rome had few books of her own. Later her people translated Greek books into Latin.

The Roman gods. — The Romans were not so imaginative as the Greeks. They had invented no beautiful myths about their gods. Their most important gods were those that could help them most. To receive aid in time of battle,

GLADIATORS FIGHTING WILD BEASTS (p. 105)
From a relief in the Theater of Marcellus at Rome.

they offered sacrifices to Mars, their god of war. To reap bountiful harvests, they worshiped Ceres (sē'rēz), goddess of the fields. Our word *cereal* comes from her name. To protect the boundaries of their land, they worshiped Ter'minus, the god of boundaries.

One of the most important of the Roman gods was Ja'nus, who had two faces. One face looked backward into the past; the other, forward into the future. On the first day of January festivals were held in honor of Janus. Friends and relatives exchanged calls and good wishes, a custom which we still observe on that day.

After Rome conquered Greece, she discovered that many of her gods were like those of the Greeks. The Roman god Jupiter held the same rank as the Greek god Zeus. Roman names were given to other Greek gods (p. 72). The Romans took over the Greek myths and learned from the Greeks how to make statues of their gods and how to build temples to them. The Roman names of the gods are more familiar to us than the Greek names because, as we shall see later, the Latin language was so widely spread.

Why the Roman republic came to an end. — Many causes led to the downfall of the republic. In the first place, the victorious generals of the Punic Wars and later wars brought to Rome several million captives who were sold as slaves. Among them were well-educated teachers from Greece and Alexandria, actors, artists, weavers, farmers, and shepherds. The Roman farmer no longer did his own plowing like Cincinnatus, because he had from ten to several hundred slaves to work for him. The Romans began to feel that it was degrading for a man to work with his hands. Consequently they became lazy.

The Punic Wars marked the beginning of another evil in Rome. At the outbreak of the war, many farmers in Italy left their homes and joined the army. Some of those who returned after the war found their homes destroyed, their farms ruined, and their wives and children gone. The women and children had fled to Rome when Hannibal swept down through Italy. Some of the bravest of the men who again took up their farming discovered that they received too little for their grain in the city of Rome to pay them for their work. Grain was cheap because millions of bushels were pouring into the city from Sicily and Africa.

Many Italian farmers sold their land to powerful nobles who built up great estates worked by thousands of slaves. The ex-farmers went to Rome and became part of the mob of idle people. To keep these people from causing trouble, the state sold grain to them at half price and entertained them with shows. Later the grain was distributed free. By the year 63 B.C., 320,000 citizens were receiving free grain. Any dishonest politician who wished to be elected to a government office needed only to promise the mob free food and free shows.

A Roman of the time says: " The majority of the heads of these Italian families have slipped within our walls, leaving the scythe and plow; they prefer clapping their hands at the circus to working in their fields and their vineyards." Most of the Roman citizens no longer took an interest in the republic. They did not care who ruled them. The Senate was governing to suit its own ends. When the citizens in a republic take no part in the government, the republic fails.

Certain rich and powerful men collected armies about them and began to fight for control of the Roman world. In 78 B.C. there were four such armies paid and commanded by private citizens. What Rome now needed, to save her from ruin, was a single strong ruler.

Julius Cæsar. — Help came in the person of Julius Cæsar. He had gone to subdue the fierce natives of northern Gaul and bring them under Roman rule. The Gauls were commanded by Vercingetorix (vur-sin-jĕt′o-riks), their fearless chief. He led them in many battles against the Romans. Seeing defeat ahead, Vercingetorix gave himself up to the

Romans to save his people from being wiped out. He was finally put to death in Rome. Cæsar made Gaul a province of Rome.

MOUNTED GAULS

Cæsar even crossed over to Britain, but the Britons resisted him so stubbornly that he left them unconquered. It was nearly a hundred years later that Britain became a Roman province. Germany, the land of the barbarians beyond the Rhine, was never conquered by Rome, though Cæsar attempted to subdue it.

The news of Cæsar's victories had traveled to Rome. Some of the leaders of the government, who were jealous of him, persuaded the Senate to command him to give up his army or be considered an enemy of the state. Cæsar quickly decided. He fearlessly crossed the Ru'bicon River, the northern Italian border, exclaiming: " The die is cast." With his army he marched to Rome and took possession of the city. He then conquered his enemies who had fled to Egypt and to the East.

Now all of the Roman world was under his rule. Members of the Senate, jealous of him, and thinking he planned to make himself king, killed him with their daggers in the Senate hall.

Roman Emperors. — Cæsar's grandnephew Octa′vian, afterwards called Augustus, succeeded him. Augustus took for himself the title *imperator*, meaning "head of the army," from which the word "emperor" comes. When Augustus became emperor, in 31 B.C., the Roman republic came

ROMANS BESIEGING A CITY

Relief from the column of Trajan in Rome. When Roman soldiers attacked a town, they protected themselves by fitting their shields together over their heads to form a screen.

to an end. From that time on, for about five hundred years, Rome had one emperor after another. He was usually a general. The soldiers stood behind him ready to support or overthrow him according as his rule pleased or displeased them.

The following map shows the Roman Empire as it was in the fourth century. The government and life of the empire are described in the next chapter.

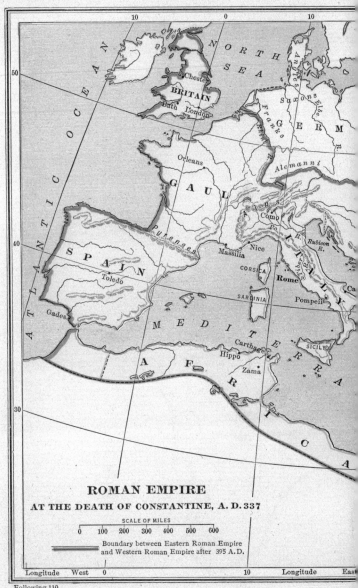

ROMAN EMPIRE

AT THE DEATH OF CONSTANTINE, A.D. 337

SCALE OF MILES

0   100   200   300   400   500   600

—— Boundary between Eastern Roman Empire
and Western Roman Empire after 395 A.D.

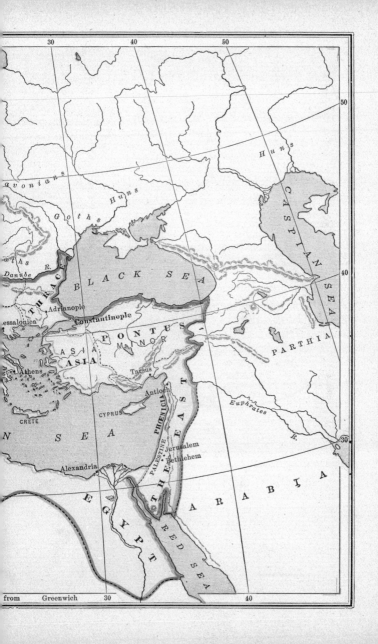

Things to remember about the ancient Romans. — 1. Rome, the most powerful of the ancient nations, began as a little town and gradually subdued all Italy.

2. The Romans set up a republic. They showed their talent for governing by making the conquered Italians first allies, and finally Roman citizens, instead of slaves.

3. The Romans of the early republic led simple lives; they honored their women and carefully trained their children to be useful citizens.

4. Rome waged a long war against Carthage, her rival, and defeated her in 202 B.C.

5. Rome then conquered most of the lands bordering on the Mediterranean Sea.

6. Rome preserved Greek civilization, copied it, spread it, and passed it on.

7. The Roman republic failed when the Roman people lost interest in their government.

8. Julius Cæsar, a Roman general, made himself ruler of Rome. His grandnephew Augustus became the first emperor of the Roman Empire, in 31 B.C.

Things to do. — Find on the map Italy, Rome, and Sicily.

The Romans told an interesting story to explain how their city came to be built. Read the story of Romulus in *Famous Men of Rome* by Haaren and Poland, or in any other Roman history.

Read or ask your teacher to read to you the whole poem of Horatius from Macaulay's *Lays of Ancient Rome*. Learn by heart the three stanzas you like best.

What does the story of Cincinnatus tell you about the Romans?

Write two paragraphs comparing the life of a Roman boy with that of a Spartan boy (pp. 56–57, 99–100).

Read the description of Hannibal's march in Davis, *Readings in Ancient History*, Vol. II, 62–67.

Imagine yourself to be one of Hannibal's soldiers. Write a letter to a friend describing the march across the Alps to Italy.

Read the story of *Vercingetorix, the Bravest of the Gauls*, in Dutton, *Little Stories of France*, 12–14. What do you think of Cæsar's treatment of Vercingetorix?

Read the description of Julius Cæsar in Webster, *Readings in Ancient History*, 218–221, or in Davis, Vol. II, 159–161.

Ask your teacher to read to you the account of Cæsar's crossing of the Rubicon (Davis, *Readings in Ancient History*, Vol. II, 149–150).

References for Teachers. — Seignobos, *Ancient Civilization*, 199–288; Marvin, *Living Past*, 92–117; Fowler, *Rome*, 7–186; Abbott, F. F., *Common People of Ancient Rome;* Wells, *Outline of History*, 380–450; Morey, *Ancient Peoples*, 297–453; Webster, *Readings in Ancient History*, 154–226; Fowler, *Julius Cæsar* (Heroes of the Nations); Morris, *Hannibal* (Heroes of the Nations); Church, *Roman Life in the Days of Cicero;* Davis, *Friend of Cæsar* (fiction); White, *Unwilling Vestal* (fiction).

For Pupils. — Haaren and Poland, *Famous Men of Rome*, 9–218; Clarke, *Story of Cæsar;* Harding, *City of the Seven Hills*, I–XXV; Hodgdon, *Enchanted Past*, 187–197 (Rome); Guerber, *Story of the Romans*, 11–203; Van Loon, *Story of Mankind*, 88–118; Gould, *Children's Plutarch;* Johonnot, *Stories of the Olden Time*, 117–168 (Romans); Tappan, *Story of the Roman People*, 1–167.

CHAPTER VII

WHAT THE ROMANS TAUGHT THE WORLD

How the Roman Empire was governed. — All the land washed by the Mediterranean Sea, as well as most of the island of Great Britain, belonged to the Roman Empire. The northern European boundary of Rome was along the Danube and Rhine rivers. Beyond these rivers lived the Germans, a barbarous race so fierce that the Romans could not conquer them. A Roman army was always stationed along these frontiers to hold back the Germans.

The emperor ruled this vast empire, and he was worshiped as a god. Behind him stood the army that could be rushed to any rebellious province or region belonging to the empire. A good emperor was one who traveled about to see if his people were satisfied. He saw that they were not overcharged by those who had goods to sell. He kept a watchful eye on all parts of his possessions. Thousands of governors and other officers carried out his orders in all the provinces and saw that his laws were obeyed.

The emperors seem to have interested themselves in all matters concerning the provinces. Some letters from one of these governors to the emperor Tra'jan show that the emperor was consulted about repairing a public bath, building an aqueduct, and completing a theater in a city in Asia Minor. The emperor, in reply, commanded the governor " to act mildly in collecting taxes." Some of the emperors, such as Nero, were noted for their cruelty

towards their subjects.   Such an emperor rarely ruled long.
The army or his enemies rose against him and killed him.

Life in the Roman Empire. — The progress which was
made in the Roman Empire was very remarkable.   A

ARCH OF TITUS AT ROME

Erected in honor of the victories of the emperor Titus (reigned 79–81 A.D.).
The Latin inscription begins: "The Roman Senate and People, to the god
(late emperor) Titus, son of the god (late emperor) Vespasian."

writer in 200 A.D. said: " The world is every day better
known, better cultivated, and more wealthy.   The roads
are open to commerce.   The deserts have been changed
into fruitful lands; agriculture is pursued where once rose
forests; sowing where once could be seen only barren rocks.
Drained are the marshes.   No more do the flocks fear the
wild beast.   Everywhere there are houses, people, cities.
Everywhere there is life ! "

Remember that this description was written by a man
who saw what he described.   It shows that Rome taught
her provinces how to improve their methods of raising

fruit, vegetables, and farm animals. She showed the Britons, for instance, how to cultivate apples and pears.

Many buildings in the Roman Empire were erected by wealthy citizens. One record states that a man spent $440,000 on his native town, Como, in northern Italy. "He founded there a library, a school, and a charity institute for poor children; also a temple to Ceres." A monument to a certain Vale′rius reads: "He cleaned out and restored the watercourses for a distance of three miles, and restored the two baths for men and the bath for women, all at his own expense."

A traveler along one of the roads of the empire would pass through numbers of busy cities with their forums, temples, and shops. As he left a city he might stop to read the inscriptions on the tombs that lined the road. Here and there on a tombstone he might see scribbled in chalk an election notice, such as: "Vote for Fabius. He is a good man."

The traveler would notice many small shops in the towns through which he passed, but he would see no large factories. They were unknown in Rome because the Romans had little machinery. The Romans did not need machinery, for the thousands of slaves, working by hand, made cloth,

ROMAN COINS

The engravings on various Roman coins showed not only gods and emperors but, as in the first and third examples above, other Roman officers. The fourth coin shows the mother of an emperor.

furniture, flour, and the hundreds of things that our factories manufacture for us. Trade between the different parts of the empire was made easier by Roman coinage (picture, p. 115). If a traveler bought a vase in Greece, ivory ornaments in Africa, or a bronze knife in Britain, he paid for them in Roman money.

What the Romans taught the world about building. — The Romans were great builders and engineers. They built what was useful and lasting. Even the tomb of the emperor Ha'drian, erected in Rome in 130 A.D., was so solidly constructed that it was used as a fortress thirteen hundred years later. It is still standing to-day, as are many other Roman buildings. The Romans copied the beautiful features of the Greek temples, the columns and decorations, and used them in their own buildings. From

RUINS OF THE CLAUDIAN AQUEDUCT
Some of the arches of this aqueduct were over 100 feet high.

the older nations of the Near East (p. 39) the Romans borrowed the arch, and they in turn have taught the builders of the world its importance in constructing bridges, aqueducts, and buildings.

BRIDGE ON A ROMAN ROAD, NEAR ROME
The round arches were probably built by the Romans about 2000 years ago.

One of the most prominent structures in Rome was the forty-mile Claudian *aqueduct* (water carrier) which carried water into the city of Rome. Roman aqueducts carried the water almost on a level, as a gently flowing stream. Engineers have since learned how to make strong pipes in which water can be forced uphill, and so aqueducts can be built running down and up hill. People in large cities to-day, thanks to aqueducts, do not have to rely on wells and cisterns which may go dry in summer. The Romans were the first great builders of aqueducts.

Since the Romans loved shows, they made a specialty of building great amphitheaters; the most famous is the Colosse'um (picture, p. 124). It could seat 50,000 spectators. Though four great palaces have already been built with stone taken from it, one third of it is still standing.

Among the remarkable things in the Roman Empire were the roads on which armies, traders, and travelers could move quickly from one place to another. Rome taught the importance of good roads in the development of a country. From Rome as a center, perfect roads, hard, wide, and smooth as city streets, radiated to all parts of the empire. The Roman roads have given us one of our proverbs: "All roads lead to Rome." Important roads went directly in straight lines from place to place. In planning them, the Romans were not blocked by mountains, rivers, or swamps in the way. Mountains were tunneled, and rivers and marshes were spanned by bridges. We say to-day: "Run a Roman road through it," an expression which means "go right ahead and allow nothing to block the way." When we ride to-day over parts of the old Roman roads in Italy, France, and England, we cannot deny that the Romans were the great road builders of the world.

What Rome has taught us about government. — You will recall (p. 94) that when Rome conquered Italy she showed her wisdom by making the Italians loyal allies. Later (after a civil war), she allowed them to become Roman citizens. Gradually she gave the rights of Roman citizenship to all the provinces of her empire. Egyptians, Jews, Greeks, Gauls, Arabs, and Britons were included among the citizens. Rome permitted these widely different races to practice their own religions, but all citizens had to worship the emperor as a god. This meant that they said the same words before the statue or shrine of the emperor as before that of Jupiter or Neptune, acknowledging his power and praying for his favor and protection. In all parts of the empire the citizens were called on to go through this form, as we in this country now make our pledge of allegiance to the flag.

Rome realized that she would have untold work if she tried to settle all the problems of each city in her empire. She very wisely did not attempt the task, but allowed each city to carry on its own government. She has proved a valuable example to other nations in this respect.

In all the countries in the empire the Roman law was established and cases were tried in Roman courts. The law was the same everywhere, and it helped to hold the empire together. Roman law had improved much since the days of the Twelve Tables. Laws were much more just and much less harsh. A man, for example, no longer had the power of life and death over his wife and children.

The master who killed a slave was to be punished as a murderer. A guilty slave could be condemned to death or prison only by judges. Slaves could no longer be sold as gladiators. One Roman writer, Sen'eca, says to cruel masters: " Is not a slave of the same stuff as you, my lord? Does he not enjoy the same sun, breathe the same air, die, even as you do? Let then your slave worship rather than dread you. For love casts out fear."

The Roman law gave this definition of justice: " The steady purpose to give to every man that which is his own." If freedom naturally belongs to men, then it should be given to slaves. Many just masters gradually set their slaves free.

As Roman citizenship was extended to all the freemen of the empire, the improved Roman law was spread throughout the western world. It became the foundation of the systems of law in Italy, Spain, France, and Germany, in the Spanish-American countries later, and in our state of

Louisiana, which once belonged to France. The law of
Rome is one of her most valuable gifts to the world.

How the people of the ancient world became Romans. —
Rome passed on to the countries she conquered many things
that it had taken her and the other ancient nations

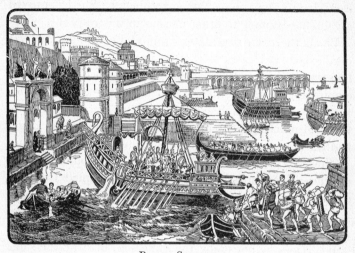

ROMAN SHIPPING

From a wall painting at Pompeii. Commerce in the Roman Empire was very active by sea
as well as by land.   It was protected by war ships like the one in the front of this picture — a
trireme, so called because it was propelled by three "banks" of rowers on each side. (For
position of the rowers, see page 65.)

hundreds of years to learn.   Rome improved all her conquered lands by building handsome temples, excellent
roads, baths, and aqueducts.   Throughout the empire she
spread the civilization called Græco-Roman, made up of
Greek and Roman ideas and ways of life.

After a generation or two most of the people of the
provinces actually became Roman. They gave up the
dress, the customs, the literature, and the language of their
own nations. The grandsons of the Gauls, Greeks, and

Britons who had fought against their Roman conquerors, considered themselves Romans.

Rome Romanized not only the people she conquered but also those who at last conquered her. Germans who had come into the empire some years before had become so Roman that they fought against their own countrymen. When the Germans overran the empire later, they could not entirely destroy the Roman civilization; instead they copied and preserved it for us.

How Latin became the foundation of many modern languages. — Wherever Roman law and coinage were found, Latin, the language of Rome, could be heard. This was a great convenience, because Spaniards, Gauls, and Italians could talk to each other and to people of other nations with whom they traded. Latin is the parent of five important modern languages: French, Italian, Spanish, Portuguese, and Rumanian. For instance, the Latin word for " good " is *bon-* with various endings, as *bonus* and *bona;* the French is *bon;* the Italian is *buôno;* the Spanish is *bueno;* the Portuguese is *bom;* and the Rumanian is *bun*. The alphabet of these languages, as well as of English, is the Latin alphabet.

How the Latin literature was begun. — The Romans, as we have seen, were very practical. Unlike the Greeks, the Romans did not class art, science, and literature as occupations at all, but called them *schola*, meaning " being at leisure." From this word comes our " school." A Roman painted or wrote or studied science in his leisure time. When Cæsar was fighting in Gaul, he wrote an account of his campaigns during his spare moments between battles. His *Commentaries* are read by the students who study Latin to-day.

What the Romans knew of art and literature was learned from the Greeks.   Men like Cæsar had studied in Athens or in Alexandria.   They spoke Greek and were familiar with Greek writings.   Androni′cus, a Greek slave, translated the *Odyssey* (p. 84) into Latin.   It gradually took the place of the Twelve Tables of law as the chief school textbook of Rome.   Roman poets and prose writers copied the work of the Greeks.   Vergil, a Roman poet, wrote a new work, the *Æne′id*, which tells of the wanderings of Æne′as, as the *Odyssey* relates those of Odysseus.

Latin plays, modeled on Greek plays, were produced in the new theaters.   But coarse and rough comedy, rather than the beautiful tragedies of the Greeks, appealed to most of the Romans.

Though the Roman writers studied Greek books, they wrote their own in Latin.   After Latin was succeeded

WRITING MATERIALS USED BY ROMANS

At the left is an ink bottle and a reed pen.   The tablet, commonly used for writing letters, was covered with wax on which the writing was scratched with the sharp-pointed style.   At the right is a papyrus or parchment roll.

by other spoken languages, it remained the chief written language for hundreds of years, — the language in which nearly all books were written.   Even to-day your doctor uses Latin in writing prescriptions for medicine.   The scientific names of animals and plants also are in Latin; for example, French, German, English, and all other scientists call the two species of elephants, respectively, *Elephas indicus* (Indian elephant) and *Elephas africanus* (African elephant).

How we owe our calendar to Julius Cæsar. — You will remember that certain peoples whom Rome conquered were more highly civilized in some ways than she. For instance, when Julius Cæsar was in Egypt he saw that the old Egyptian calendar was more sensible than the Roman moon calendar, which was altered in various ways from time to time to make up for the difference between twelve months and one year. Julius Cæsar introduced the Egyptian calendar into Rome after he had made a few changes in it. He ordered that the odd-numbered months, that is, January, March, May, July, September, and November, should have thirty-one days. Each of the other months except February was to have thirty days. February was to have twenty-nine days every year except leap year, when it was given thirty. Julius Cæsar's calendar would have been an easy one to remember.

Later, Augustus wanted the month bearing his name to have as many days as July, which was named for Julius Cæsar. So that Augustus should not be slighted, a day was taken from February and added to August. February since then has had only twenty-eight days except in leap year. Three months of thirty-one days each, July, August, September, then came in succession. Therefore, September was made a month of thirty days, and the last three months were changed as we now have them. Because of the vanity of one man, many of us have to learn the rime which begins, " Thirty days has September," in order to remember the number of days in each month. Pope Greg'ory XIII (1582) made one further slight change (calling for 97 leap years instead of 100 in each 400 years).   As thus altered the old Roman calendar is still in use to-day in Europe and in America.

How the emperor grew too powerful and patriotism died out in Rome. — After several hundred years the Romans of the empire became simply the subjects of a monarch,

RUINS OF THE COLOSSEUM AT ROME (INTERIOR)

This was the most famous of the amusement places in ancient Rome. It was not roofed over. The open arena in the center was the scene of gladiatorial combats (p. 105). Here, too, many Christians were put to death.

like the ancient Egyptians or Babylonians. We have seen that the once powerful Egyptian and Babylonian kingdoms came to an end. History was to repeat itself in the case of Rome. Little by little the emperor had taken more control over the free city governments of the empire. He sent officials to the cities to carry out his orders. In time these men became the real rulers of the cities. The Roman people had no interest in a government in which they had no voice. One emperor after another was placed on the throne by the army. The people seemed to care little whether one man or another was their ruler.

That patriotism was dying out among the old Romans was shown by the fact that after 100 A.D. Italy no longer furnished all the emperors. Africans, Gauls, and even Germans occupied the throne. In the fourth century the capital of the empire was moved to Constantinople. A little later the empire was divided into two parts — the Eastern Empire with its capital at Constantinople, and the Western with its capital at Rome.

Heavy taxation. — Huge sums of money were needed to provide grain and amusement for the great mob of idle people in Rome. Huge sums were paid to the emperor and his many officials. This money came from taxation. As expenses became greater, the taxes were increased. Each tax collector was obliged to turn over a certain sum from his province or section. He kept for himself whatever he could collect in addition. Naturally he used every means, including torture, to force the proprietors to pay their taxes. The burden fell heaviest on the poor, who, as time went on, paid to the government nearly every cent they made above a bare living.

How these poor men lived is a mystery. In 301 A.D. the wages of a carpenter, a bricklayer, a stone mason, or a blacksmith amounted to a little less than twenty-two cents a day. Butter cost nearly ten cents a pound, fish seven cents, beef nearly five cents, and milk six cents a quart. You can see that the Roman laborer could not afford these foods. He probably lived on a small quantity of coarse bread and vegetables. Then out of the miserable wages the tax collector took his share. A writer who lived at that time says: "The stock of the cattle (of a certain town) was much diminished, and many men died; yet the taxes continued still to be levied even for those who were dead; to such misery men were reduced that even death did not put an end to it."

As the years went on, the tax collector was often unable to collect the sum demanded by the government, and had to complete it out of his own pocket. The position of tax collector at last became one that meant ruin.

How the free laboring class disappeared. — In some nations, the greatest number of people are neither very rich nor very poor. They form what is called the "middle class." In the early days of the Roman Empire the middle class was made up of small farmers, workers at various trades, and shopkeepers.

It was not long before the farmers began to disappear in various parts of the empire for the same reasons that had led the Italian farmers to desert their farms after the Punic Wars (p. 108). A small farmer would often sell his land to a wealthy noble, and would himself sometimes remain as a tenant on the land. More often he went to Rome or to some other large city and became one of the mob fed by the government.

The competition of slave labor was another reason for the disappearance of the middle class. A freeman with a trade had no chance to get a fair price for the shoes, cloth, or furniture that he made, when slaves worked at the same trade for masters who paid them no wages. Like the farmer, many a free workman gave up his occupation.

Slave labor by the wholesale could not last forever. Slaves died off rapidly, many from bad treatment and from the plague, a disease which swept over the empire several times. New slaves did not take their places, because the Romans conquered no more new lands. Before long the emperors grew frightened when they saw that there were not farmers or workers enough to supply the people with food, clothing, and utensils. The state required every one to stick to his trade. Moreover, every son was to follow the trade of his father. Officers in every city watched to see that no laborer disobeyed.

A boy was now deprived of any chance to better himself. A carpenter's son had to be a carpenter even though he might want to be a goldsmith or a lawyer. Every person in the Roman Empire, from a senator to a guard on the frontier, was bound to his occupation.

When enemies came, it is no wonder that the majority of Roman citizens did not band together to drive them out. The average laborer felt no interest in fighting for a government that taxed him too heavily and forbade him to make any change in his occupation.

How the Romans failed to protect their boundaries. — Meanwhile, another danger was besetting Rome. Hordes of barbarians who lived north of the Roman Empire were being driven by other barbarians toward Rome. The Romans either could not see, or they did not want to see, these millions of Germans straining to pass the Rhine and Danube frontier. The protective army on this frontier became smaller as the years passed. Roman citizens felt less and less interest in fighting to protect their land. Consequently, the army was largely made up of the Germans who had been conquered in frontier battles. Sometimes Germans were even invited to help protect Rome against other Germans. It is no wonder that when the Germans began to cross the boundary of their own accord, they could not be stopped.   So in the fifth century Rome and the Western Roman Empire "fell."   The German conquerors set up many independent kingdoms, some of which grew gradually into the countries of modern Europe.

ROMAN SOLDIERS ON THE MARCH

First come the officers, then the standard-bearers, and after them the great mass of soldiers armed with spears and shields.

What Rome did for the world. — Rome set later nations an example in government.   She showed them how to hold an empire together by making its inhabitants one people ruled by one law.   Roman history has taught us that a country can remain great only so long as its citizens support it.

Another important thing Rome did was to promote civilization.   To the Greek civilization Rome added her own.   Throughout all the countries of the Roman Empire she spread this *Græco-Roman* civilization.   By means of her powerful government Rome united the Mediterranean world and held it together until her civilization had taken such firm root everywhere that it remained even after the German conquest. Rome herself remained the most important city in Europe for many centuries, largely because of the Christian Church, which we shall study in the next chapter.

Things to remember about our debt to Rome. — 1. The Roman Empire included western Europe, Britain, and the lands bordering on the Mediterranean Sea.

2. The world made remarkable progress in civilization at the time of the Roman Empire.

3. The Romans taught the world how to build bridges, arches, roads, and aqueducts that would last hundreds of years.

4. One law, the Roman, helped to hold the empire together and to give justice to all Romans. It became the foundation of the laws of many modern European countries.

5. The Latin language was used throughout the empire, and it became the foundation of several modern European languages. Even when Latin was no longer spoken, it continued as almost the only written language used in Europe for hundreds of years.

6. The Roman people became mere subjects of the emperor, without responsibility in their government or interest in protecting their country against the barbarian Germans. Then the Western Empire came to an end.

7. We are grateful to Rome because (1) she set later nations an example in governing large territories, (2) she saved Greek civilization from destruction, and (3) she spread her own civilization so well that it was never entirely destroyed, but became the seed from which European and American civilization grew.

Things to do. — Imagine yourself to have been a traveler in the Roman Empire. Tell the class what you saw.

Can you name any ways in which some wealthy citizens have used their money for the good of our country?

Find pictures of Roman buildings, statues, and ruins.

Look for examples of arches in your city or in pictures.

Ask your father or some older member of your family about the source of the water supply in your house. Compare with the water supply of a Roman city.

What problems of government does your city have to settle?

Read and learn so as to tell to the class the story of the wanderings of Æneas in Church's *Æneid for Boys and Girls* or in Guerber's *Myths of Greece and Rome.*

Compare the way in which taxes were collected in the Roman Empire with the way in which they are collected to-day.

Make a chart showing what we owe to each of the ancient nations, beginning with Egypt and Babylonia and ending with Rome.

References for Teachers. — Seignobos, *Ancient Civilization,* 289–328, 343–359; Fowler, *Rome,* 187–251; Abbott, F. F., *Common People of Ancient Rome;* Wells, *Outline of History,* 451–492; Tucker, *Life in the Roman World of Nero and St. Paul;* Firth, *Augustus Cæsar;* Firth, *Constantine the Great;* Thorndike, *Medieval Europe,* 17–71; Webster, *Readings in Ancient History,* 227–260; Morey, *Ancient Peoples,* 454–537; Marvin, *Living Past,* 92–117; Bulwer-Lytton, *Last Days of Pompeii* (fiction).

For Pupils. — Haaren and Poland, *Famous Men of Rome,* 219–269; Hodgdon, *Enchanted Past,* 197–224; Guerber, *Story of the Romans,* 203–278; Harding, *City of the Seven Hills,* XXVI, XXVII, XIX (Empire); Church, *Helmet and Spear,* 154–337; Tappan, *Story of the Roman People,* 168–237; Benezet, *World War and What Was Behind It,* 25–36 (Rome).

CHAPTER VIII

THE BEGINNINGS OF CHRISTIANITY

How religion helped to civilize the early world. — Anything which makes the world a better place to live in is a forward step in civilization. Religion has been an important force in civilizing many peoples, by giving them a reason for improving their surroundings. Man has offered to his gods the finest things he possesses. Among the early peoples, the largest sheep or ox or even a beloved son was sacrificed on the altar of the gods. This desire in man to give of his best and most beautiful to his gods led to the development of " fine arts ": sculpture, painting, architecture, music, poetry, and drama.

Early man made images or statues of his gods in clay, wood, and stone (pictures, pp. 52, 72, 79). In the ancient world the first handsome buildings were not the palaces of the kings but the temples of the gods (pictures, pp. 24, 40, 76). While building their temples, early men invented forms of architecture such as the arch, the column, the tower, and the clerestory.

Early poetry and music were in praise of the gods. The first dramas or plays were the celebrations in honor of the Greek god Dionysus (p. 80).

What was lacking in most of the early religions. — The religions of the ancient empires failed in one important way. In the beautiful temples the people offered sacrifices to please the gods, but they were not carefully taught to lead a good life for that purpose. The preaching and teaching that help people to be good and to do what is right were not the chief duty of the priests in the early religions. The people usually feared and admired their gods but did not love them. When disease, earthquake, or defeat visited a nation, it was thought that the gods were angry. Sacrifices were hurriedly offered to stop the trouble. The myths or stories of the ancient gods show us that they were believed to have the faults as well as the virtues of men. One myth, for example, tells how Dian'a, the goddess of the moon, and her brother Apollo killed Nio'be's fourteen children because of anger and jealousy at the mother's pride in them.

How Christianity came into the world. — One ancient nation built up no powerful empire but is remembered because of its noble religion. This was the Hebrew nation. The Hebrews, you will recall (p. 48), worshiped only one God. Their Ten Commandments laid down certain rules for good living, such as " Thou shalt not steal." It is not surprising that many great religious teachers came from this race.

One of these teachers, Jesus, called the Christ, became the founder of the Christian religion. He was born in the village of Bethlehem, in Palestine, the land of the Jews, during the reign of Augustus. We count the years now from the birth of Christ. The year 1900 means the 1900th year after the birth of Christ. " A.D." stands for *Anno Domini*, or " in the year of [our] Lord." Dates earlier than 1 A.D. are counted backwards. For example, the first Olympic games were held in 776 B.C., or 776 years " before Christ"; the second, four years later, were in 772 B.C.

Jesus was loved by the common people and by those in

trouble, for, we are told, he "went about doing good." He healed the sick; he comforted the sorrowing; he fed the hungry.

He spoke in simple language and taught great lessons by means of parables or stories, so that even the dullest

© Keystone

THE OLD WALL OF JERUSALEM

Jerusalem was the scene of some of the chief events in the life of Jesus and in the founding of the Christian Church.

person could understand them. For instance, "Love thy neighbor as thyself" Jesus taught by the parable of the Good Samaritan:

A certain man went down from Jerusalem to Jericho, and fell among thieves, which stripped him of his raiment, and wounded him, and departed, leaving him half dead.

And by chance there came down a certain priest that way; and when he saw him, he passed by on the other side.

And likewise a Levite, when he was at the place, came and looked on him, and passed by on the other side.

But a certain Samaritan, as he journeyed, came where he was; and when he saw him, he had compassion on him,

And went to him, and bound up his wounds, pouring in oil and wine, and set him on his own beast, and brought him to an inn, and took care of him.

And on the morrow when he departed, he took out two pence, and gave them to the host, and said unto him, Take care of him: and whatsoever thou spendest more, when I come again, I will repay thee.

Which now of these three, thinkest thou, was neighbor unto him that fell among thieves?

Jesus said : " Whatsoever ye would that men should do unto you, do ye even so unto them." This is called the Golden Rule.

How Christianity spread in the Roman Empire. — The fine roads, the common language, and the peace that Rome had given the world, enabled missionaries of the new religion to spread their beliefs even to distant places.

One of the missionaries was Paul, a Jew of Tarsus and a Roman citizen. The account of his travels in Asia Minor and Europe shows plainly the advantages of being a Roman citizen at a time when this citizenship had not yet been granted to all freemen. Once when Paul had been taken prisoner, and the officers wanted to torture him to make him confess, some one said : " Take heed what thou doest, for this man is a Roman." They all knew that it was against the law to torture a Roman citizen and that if they did so, they themselves would be punished.

In the Roman Empire there were millions of poor unhappy freedmen and even more wretched slaves. They had nothing to live for on earth. All that many slaves could look forward to was to be sent out on the streets to die in their old age. Many of them eagerly turned for comfort and hope to the new religion that promised peace and happiness to Christians after death.

A slave's soul, according to the new religion, was as important as that of the master who owned him. A slave who might be bought for a hundred dollars could become a bishop of the church. It is no wonder that these unhappy people were converted by hundreds to the new religion. People other than slaves and poor workmen also began to join the disciples or followers of Jesus.

Christianity steadily spread throughout the empire. Paul founded Christian churches in Asia Minor, Greece, and Italy. He kept in touch with them by sending letters, or epistles, in which he explained the teachings of Jesus. From Jerusalem westward to Rome, Christian centers were formed in all the large cities. By 300 A.D. almost one tenth of the population of the empire was Christian.

Persecution of the Christians. — The path of the new religion was not an easy one. The Christians were often annoyed, beaten, and sometimes killed by the people among whom they traveled. The Roman government considered the Christians dangerous for several reasons. First, the Christians refused to worship the emperor as a god and to bow down to his statue (p. 118) ; they said they worshiped only the one true God. Second, the Christians would not attend the inhuman gladiatorial shows, and tried to have them stopped because the cruelty practiced in these shows was against Christian teaching. Third, since Jesus preached peace, many of his followers refused to join the Roman army. Fourth, the Christians held secret meetings, a practice forbidden by Roman law because of the fear of plots against the government.

During the reign of Nero, one of the most cruel rulers in history, the city of Rome was almost destroyed (A.D. 64) by a fire which raged for several days. It was whispered about that Nero had set fire to the city. To put an end to this report, he laid the guilt upon the Christians and inflicted the most cruel punishments upon them.

From time to time other emperors ordered terrible persecutions, in which hundreds of Christians were killed.

A ROMAN of that time writes: "If the Tiber overflows its banks, or the Nile does not; if there be drought or earthquakes, famine or plague, the cry is raised, 'The Christians to the lions!'"

Sometimes Christians were hunted down so mercilessly that they were forced to seek safety underground. To-day you can visit the catacombs at Rome, which were the cemeteries of the early Christians. The catacombs are underground rooms and narrow tunnels which branch out in all directions like the boughs of a tree. The walls of the catacombs are lined with slabs about one foot deep and six feet long. Each slab marks the grave of a Christian. Dolls, rattles, and children's money boxes have been found in some of the graves. The larger rooms in the catacombs

A PASSAGEWAY IN THE CATACOMBS OF ROME

The openings in the walls were used for graves. They were at one time sealed with slabs of marble or tiles of terra cotta.

were used as chapels where funeral services were held.   The catacombs were five and six stories deep, and small iron gratings in the roof of rock allowed a little air and light

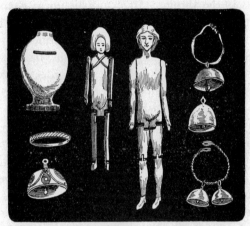

CHILDREN'S TOYS FOUND IN THE CATACOMBS

The dolls found in the graves are of ivory.   Some of them have wires by which the joints may be worked.   The vase in the upper left-hand corner has a slit through which money could be put; it probably served as a savings bank.   Beneath the bank is an ivory ring.   The bronze bells were part of a child's rattle.

to enter.   A person who was being searched for by the Roman soldiers was sometimes obliged to stay in the dark and almost airless catacombs for days.   A writer of the third century tells of a wealthy Roman lady hidden in the catacombs, " trembling, fearful of the capture of her maid on whom she depended for daily food."

How Christianity became the religion of the Roman Empire. — The patience and cheerfulness of the *martyrs*, or those who died for Christianity, led others to believe that there was something good in it.   Opposition to a movement may sometimes really help the movement to grow stronger; and so it proved with Christianity.   In spite of continuous and terrible persecutions, the converts to the new religion increased.

When Con'stantine became emperor, he had to fight rival claimants to the throne. In a campaign near Rome he saw a flaming cross in the sky and under it the words which mean " In this sign conquer." Constantine, so the story goes, became a Christian and won the battle. In 313 A.D. he sent out over the empire this order: " We grant to Christians and to all others free choice to follow the mode of worship they wish."

A few years later, Christianity was made the state religion of the empire. The worship of the old Roman gods was forbidden on pain of death. Temples to Jupiter, Venus, and the other pagan gods were torn down or changed into Christian churches.

The organization of the church. — Even in the early days of the new religion, the life and teachings of its founder had been written in four books called *Gospels*. These, along with the Epistles or letters of some of the Christian leaders, form the greater part of the New Testament, which served as the guidebook for the Christian church.

The first Christian churches were small gatherings of believers who met in various parts of the large cities to worship together. In each of the groups there was a leader who taught the members of his congregation. In time the leaders were called *priests* or *elders*. Those who looked after the poor of the community were known as *deacons*. The head of the church in each city was called a *bishop*, a name meaning " overseer." The bishop of Rome was regarded as the head of the church and was called the *Pope*.

The Pope, bishops, priests, and deacons formed the *clergy*, who were very important in the history of the Middle

Ages, as you will see in a later chapter. After the fall of the Western Roman Empire the Pope took the place of the emperor as the most powerful person in Europe. Even kings bowed before him. Most of the missionaries to the still heathen parts of Europe were sent out from Rome, which as the home of the Pope continued to be the leading city in Europe.

Monasteries. — Monks (from a word meaning " alone ") were men who believed that they could be good Christians

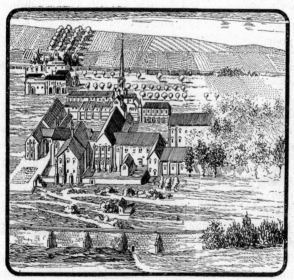

A MONASTERY IN FRANCE
Redrawn from a manuscript of the twelfth century.

only by leaving the world and its wickedness. They lived together in buildings called monasteries. There were homes of the same kind, called convents, for women called sisters or nuns. Both monks and nuns promised to give up all their wealth, to obey the rules of the home, and not to marry.

Most of the early monasteries followed the rules laid down by Saint Benedict, a monk who was head of a monastery in Italy in the sixth century. In these rules he said: " Idleness is an enemy to the soul. To labor is to pray." The Benedictine monks were expected to raise their own food, to make their own clothing, to care for the sick, and to teach the boys who lived in the monasteries. One of the great teachings of Christianity was that work is not a disgrace. Another Christian teaching, " Bear ye one another's burdens," led to the founding of asylums for orphans and old people, and of hospitals for the sick who were poor.

Things we should remember about the beginnings of Christianity. — 1. Religion has been an important influence in civilizing man.

2. The religion of most of the ancient nations consisted in the worship of many gods; and these gods were supposed to care more for sacrifices than for the good conduct of people.

3. The religion of the Hebrews was an exception among the early religions. (1) It taught that there is but one God. (2) It laid down certain rules of conduct, known as the Ten Commandments.

4. Jesus, a member of the Hebrew race, was the founder of the religion known as Christianity.

5. The perfect roads, the common language, and the peaceful condition of the Roman Empire made it possible for missionaries to spread the new religion rapidly.

6. The Roman government considered the Christians dangerous and sometimes persecuted them. Some were forced to hide at times in the catacombs.

7. Christianity was tolerated by decree of Constantine in 313 A.D.; soon afterwards it became the state religion of the empire.

8. The Christian church was gradually organized into a working body with the Pope at Rome as leader.

Things to do. — Reread chapters II, III, V, and VI. Prove by examples from these chapters that "religion helped to civilize the ancient world."

Recall some of the Greek myths. Were the gods kind or unkind?

Tell to the class any parables that you know.

Why was it fortunate for the Christian religion that it appeared at the time of the Roman Empire?

How do you explain the rapid growth of Christianity?

Read in Webster, *Readings in Ancient History*, 232–235, the account of the burning of Rome.

References for Teachers. — Adams, G. B., *Civilization during the Middle Ages*, III, VI; Seignobos, *Ancient Civilization*, 329–342, 352–359; Wells, *Outline of History*, 493–534; Emerton, *Introduction to the Middle Ages*, IX; Robinson, *History of Western Europe*, II; Fisher, *Beginnings of Christianity*; Robinson, *Readings in European History*, Vol. I, 14–27, 62–82; Sienkiewicz, *Quo Vadis* (fiction).

For Pupils. — Van Loon, *Story of Mankind*, 119–123, 131–137; Hodges, *When the King Came*; Haaren and Poland, *Famous Men of Rome*, 254–261 (Constantine); Guerber, *Story of the Romans*, 221–227; Harding, *City of the Seven Hills*, XXVIII (Christianity in Rome); Tappan, *Story of the Roman People*, 215–224 (Constantine); Tappan, *Christ Story*.

CHAPTER IX

THE TEUTONS: HOW THEY CONQUERED THE WESTERN ROMAN EMPIRE

A problem in remaking the western European map. — Why is the map of modern Europe so different from that of the fourth century, when Constantine was emperor? The Roman Empire then included all western Europe as far as the Rhine and the Danube. Look at the map following page 110. We see that the purple line marking the boundary of the Roman Empire encircles all the land touching the Mediterranean in both Europe and Asia and includes what is now England. Most of Germany then had no settled government and was outside the Roman Empire.

We may note on this map the dividing line between the Western and the Eastern Roman Empire (p. 125). The Eastern Empire, with its capital at Constantinople, lasted a thousand years longer than the Western. The result of the breaking up of the Western Roman Empire was the formation of the countries of modern western Europe. It was from them that the first colonists came to America.

If we now look at a map of modern western Europe, we shall see the names of countries that we know. Whence came these countries?

The race that counted most in this change. — One answer that we can give is very simple. This change was due chiefly to the activities of one race, the Teutonic, which included many tribes of Germans, Northmen, and other peoples. They were part of the Indo-European or Aryan race (p. 37). The Teutonic peoples, overflowing from beyond the Rhine and the Danube, conquered the Western Roman Empire. Roman civilization and the Christian religion helped prepare the Teutons for their great work in altering western Europe. We are specially interested in the Teutons because some of them — Angles and Saxons — settled in England and founded the English nation. Their descendants afterward came to the New World and planted the English colonies in what is now the United States.

To the small, dark Romans, the tall, fair Germans and other Teutons seemed like giants. Their bodies were powerful and well developed. Their eyes were blue or gray, and their long hair, golden or red. This light hair was a source of wonder to the Romans, who made wigs of the hair taken from German prisoners. Many a Roman lady proudly wore the hair of one of her barbarian neighbors.

The home of the Germans, east of the Rhine and north to the Baltic Sea, was a land of dark forests, swamps, and small patches of cleared land. Long winters of fog, rain, snow, and ice killed off all but the strongest. The struggle for food in this land of short summers helped to make the Germans a race of warriors. They fought to get food wherever they could find it. We shall see how they tried to conquer people toward the south.

The Teutons, men and women alike, were a brave race and despised cowards. It was considered a disgrace for a man to desert his chief or to leave his shield on the battle-field. The women followed closely behind the army, shouting encouragement to their husbands and sons, carrying food to them, and dressing their wounds. Once when a small tribe of Teutons was overcome in a battle

with the Romans, the victors found the bodies of women
in armor among the slain.

The Teutons, unlike some of the early peoples, had great
respect for their women. Warriors fought against cap-
tivity with five-fold vigor to save their women. To-day

GERMAN VILLAGE ATTACKED BY ROMANS
Relief from the Column of Marcus Aurelius (emperor 161–180 A.D.) at Rome.

Americans and the people of western Europe are like their
ancestors in showing great respect for women.

How the Teutons lived. — Like most uncivilized peoples,
the early Teutons were herdsmen, wandering about with
their flocks. Gradually they settled down into villages —
not villages of neat frame and brick houses, shops, and well-
paved sidewalks, but small collections of round huts rudely
constructed of twigs and branches woven together and
plastered with mud, and roofed with layers of grass. According to a story of the time, a bear once broke loose, made
a rush at a hut, and turned it over. The woman inside
was rescued from death only by the quick action of her
daughter.

The " mead hall " was an important building in each

village. There the warriors gathered around their chief at night, drank mead (a kind of beer), and listened to the harpers who sang of the deeds of Teutonic heroes. The Teutons did not read or write during their leisure time, because they did not know how. Neither could they paint or draw or carve fine statues. When there was no fighting or hunting to be done, the men often drank and gambled. The women and slaves took care of the house, tilled the small garden, and made the clothing.

The occupations of the Teutons. — After the Teutons became farmers and village people, a few trades gradually developed among them. The women made fine linen cloth. Some men began to manufacture metal and wooden things, such as spears, shields, and carts.

From two occupations of the early Germans we get two of our common surnames, "Smith" and "Wright." A worker with metals was called a *smith ;* a worker with wood was called a *wright*. There was the goldsmith, for instance, who made gold rings and ornaments, and the cartwright and wheelwright who made carts and wheels. We have added "smith" to many words and thus formed the name of trades, as "locksmith," "silversmith."

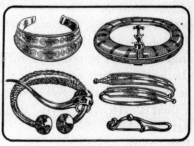

GERMAN ORNAMENTS OF GOLD AND BRONZE
Neckband, crown, bracelet, and brooches.

At one time a man was known by his trade, as John the smith, or William the wright. Later, the names became simply John Smith and William Wright. So many workmen were called "smiths" that we have many families named Smith.

The Teutons highly respected people engaged in certain occupations. The goldsmith was counted a noble workman. Special punishment was given to any one who injured the hand of the harper, of the goldsmith, or of the woman who could embroider.

The Teutons were not great traders, but they had a little commerce with the Romans. Many Roman couches and pillows were stuffed with the down from German geese. The Romans were glad also to exchange their weapons and ornaments for the linen and amber of their German neighbors.

The religion of the Teutons. — The Teutons lived in a country where the forces of nature seemed to be in bitter warfare. The frost giants of the winter killed the children of the summer — the leaves, blossoms, and fruit. They bound the happy, gurgling brook with fetters of ice. The Teutons thought that life must be a battle. It is no wonder that they were a nation of warriors. Their religion shows the warlike spirit of the race. Their leading deity, Odin, or Woden, was their god of war and victory. He dwelt in Valhal'la (Heaven). His daughters, the Valkyr'ies or battle maidens, flew over the battlefields and carried to Valhalla those who fell. Only the warriors slain in battle might sit at the table as Woden's guests and drink from the river of ale. Thor, the god of thunder, was another important god of the Teutons. He sent the thunderbolt against his enemies.

Like the Greeks, the Teutons invented stories to explain what happened in nature. Here is an example: Baldur, the god of light, was beloved of gods and men. Under the direction of the mischief maker Loki, Baldur was slain by the blind Hoder. This story shows how the light of spring and summer is overthrown by the darkness of winter and death. After the long winter from October to April, the people of the northern land welcomed back the glory of the sun on May Day, the first of May. Maypoles, deco-rated with flowers, were erected in honor of Nanna, Baldur's wife, who was the queen of flowers. A queen of the May was chosen, and children danced around the May-

TEUTONIC WAR GOD, ODIN (WODEN)

pole, singing: "We have brought the summer home." To-day, in England and in America, the season of light and warmth is sometimes ushered in with dancing about the Maypole.

Though you may never before have heard of the German gods, do you know that you mention the names of several almost every day? Each time that you say "Wednes-day," you are really saying "Woden's day." Thursday is "Thor's day." Friday is "Freya's day"; Freya was the goddess of love, like the Roman Venus. Tuesday is "Tiw's day," from the name of the ancient German god of war. Sunday is the "Sun's day"; Monday, the "Moon's day"; and Saturday, "Saturn's day."

How the Teutons governed themselves. — The Teutons were noted for their love of liberty. They were not willing to have their laws made by a king. In the first place, the king was elected by the people at the " assembly," or meeting of freemen. In the second place, the king did not have the power to make laws. Laws were drawn up by a council of the older and wiser men and put before the assembly. A clashing of spears from the assembly meant that the laws were pleasing. A murmur of discontent caused the laws to be cast aside or changed.

The assembly was a very important part of Teutonic life. When a boy became of age, he was brought before it and presented with a spear and a shield. He thus became a member of the assembly and a fighter for his tribe.

The early Germans, like most barbarian peoples, believed in taking the law into their own hands. The family of a murdered man was expected to kill the murderer by way of revenge. We can see how a quarrel between two families might continue for years. When the Germans began to mingle with the Romans, they discovered that it was more sensible to turn the murderer over to the government for punishment. Generally the law forced the guilty man to pay a fixed sum of money called *wergeld*, or " man-gold," to the murdered man's family.

The poetry of the Teutons. — The Teutonic peoples, like the Greeks and the Romans, have left us many entertaining stories of their heroes. Siegfried (sēg'frēt) is the great German hero. He won a great heap of treasure by slaying the fearful dragon that guarded it. His deeds and those of other heroes were kept alive by the harpers, who accompanied their singing by playing on a harp. The harpers traveled about from one village to another. They were welcome visitors, for their songs helped to cheer the dreary evenings. The stories about Siegfried are a part of the

Nibelungenlied (nē'bē-lōōng-en-lēt) which has been called "the German *Iliad*" (p. 84). The stories of Siegfried and the German gods were used by Richard Wagner as the basis for his great operas. To-day they are sung in Europe and in America.

Beowulf (bā'o-wōōlf), one of the great Teutonic poems, was probably begun by the harpers. It was taken to England by the Angles and Saxons. It is a story of a hero's battles to free men from evil powers which took the shape of monsters and dragons.

How the Roman Empire was invaded by the Teutonic peoples. — Even as early as the first century after Christ, Germans had crossed the Rhine to become soldiers in the Roman army. From that time on, Germans had entered the empire in great numbers and settled there. By the fourth century the Rhine boundary was guarded by an army made up mostly of Germans. In 376 A.D. a Teutonic nation, the Goths, asked to be allowed to enter the empire. The Huns, a terrible yellow-skinned, black-haired race, were driving them from their land north of the Danube. Rome allowed these people to settle just within the borders of the empire. Trouble with the Roman officers soon followed and led to war. In 378 A.D. the Goths fought a battle against the Romans at Adriano'ple and killed the Roman emperor. At the beginning of the fifth century the Goths and other Teutons broke through the boundaries and swarmed into the Western Roman Empire.

We can imagine what would happen to the empire when a half-civilized race such as the Teutons became the masters of it. The Romans had sunk so low that they made no great effort to keep out the Teutons. We have seen (p. 127) that to the average Roman, the empire was not worth fighting for. Saint Jerome, a Christian leader of Rome, said : "It is through our sins that the barbarians are strong and that the Roman armies are conquered." He wept as he thought of the destruction of the great city " which had taken captive all the world." In a letter to a lady of Gaul he describes the invasion of the barbarians. He speaks with horror of

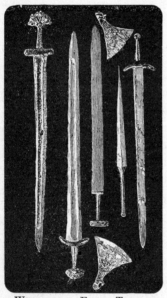

the countless hordes who swept from the Rhine to the Pyrenees. "Great cities have been wiped out. Thousands have been butchered, even in churches ; horses are stabled at the altars ; and famine has completed the work of the sword."

The raids of the Goths.— For the first time in eight hundred years enemies stormed at the gates of Rome (409–410). Messengers from the city asked Al'aric, the leader of the Goths, what terms he would make. "Give me all your gold, all your silver, all your movable property, and all your barbarian slaves, or

WEAPONS OF EARLY TEUTONS
Swords, battle-axes, and spear head used by the Angles and Saxons. Now in the British Museum.

the siege goes on," said Alaric. "What, then, will you leave us ?" asked the Romans. "Your lives," was the answer.

Though the Romans bought off Alaric at this time, he and his barbarians later invaded the city. Alaric commanded his men to spare the churches and temples. All statues were stripped of their gold and silver, which were easily carried away. The Goths did not hesitate to rob palaces of their costly furniture and ornaments. The wagons which followed the train of soldiers were piled high with heavy sideboards filled with silver dishes, wardrobes packed with silk and purple robes, and beautiful vases. Such people could not be expected to understand the beauty of many things which they saw. They melted down wonderfully carved golden, silver, and bronze statues. It is said that a Teutonic soldier, puzzled by a handsome mosaic floor representing white swans floating on a blue lake, shattered it with his battle-ax to discover whether the swans were real.

By the Goths, as well as by the other Teutonic tribes, books were considered to be magic and to possess evil powers. When the Goths were plundering Athens, they piled all the books from the libraries in a heap to be burned. One Gothic chief said: " Let the Greeks have their books, for so long as they spend their days with these idle toys, we need never fear that they will give us trouble in war."

An Athenian scholar, Dexip′pus, remembering the ancient greatness of his people, collected some brave men and burned the Gothic ships in the harbor. Most of the other leading Greeks, however, were not like Dexippus. Wrapped up in the study of their books, they made very little struggle against the invaders.

End of the Western Roman Empire. — Many German tribes followed the Goths, ransacked the empire, and then settled down. One tribe, the Vandals, settled in Africa. They set up a kingdom and built their capital on the site of Carthage (p. 103). Their pirate ships destroyed the towns on the Mediterranean coast. In 455 A.D. the Vandals sacked the city of Rome so ruthlessly that ever since we have used the term "vandalism" to describe willful destruction.

The lofty Roman cities were in ruins. Rude villages took their place. The proud people who once had dozens of slaves at their command themselves became slaves to barbarian masters. Centuries before, the Romans had forced the more talented Greeks to build temples for them, carve statues, and teach the Roman children. Now, Roman artists, teachers, tailors, and other trained workers were forced to toil for Teutonic masters who were wise enough to see that their slaves were more skillful than they. Others who were not trained workers were forced to become herdsmen or farmers. A Roman nobleman might have been found digging in the soil beside one of his former servants, both slaves of the same German master.

GERMAN WARRIOR

Armed with sword, spear, shield, and battle-ax. Redrawn from old representations of a Frankish chief.

What the Teutons gave to the world. — The Teutons added fresh blood that gave new life to the western world. Rome was like an old man, broken and worn out, ready to pass the burdens of the world to stronger and healthier shoulders. The Teutonic race was like a youth, full of life and ready to advance. Like all youthful peoples, the Teutons had much to learn from the older nation. The Teutons, however, were willing and able to learn. This gift was one of their strong points.

During her centuries of power, Rome had discovered many things. She could save her conquerors, the Teutons, the time and trouble of finding out things for themselves. She passed on to them her alphabet, her books, the art of constructing stone buildings and bridges, and her ways of controlling her empire. The Teutons had conquered one of the most highly civilized races that ever lived. It took a long time, though, for them to learn all that the Romans could give. In their ignorance they destroyed much. It was many centuries before Europe became again as highly civilized as it had been in Roman times. To the old civilization the Teutons added some of their own ways of thinking and of doing things.

Love of freedom. — Every Teuton loved freedom and independence. This feeling was especially strong among the Angles and Saxons — the tribes of Teutons who conquered Britain and became the ancestors of the English and of most Americans. No one dared cross the boundary of a Saxon's estate without first calling out to the owner. If he entered without permission, the owner had the right to kill him. To this day the English-speaking people have a saying: "A man's house is his castle." This love of freedom is expressed in our Declaration of Independence, in which the Americans said that all men have the rights of "life, liberty, and the pursuit of happiness." Then they added that whenever any government trespasses on these rights, the people can alter or do away with that government. It was this love of freedom that helped to make us the " United States of America " and not the American colonies of the English government.

Things to remember about the Teutons. — 1. The map of the Roman Empire was changed as a result of the activities of the Teutonic race.

2. The home of the Germans and other Teutons was the land east of the Rhine River and north of the Danube.

3. The Teutons were brave and warlike; they had great respect for women.

4. The Teutons were divided into tribes. They lived in small, rude villages and had few trades.

5. The Teutons, like the Greeks and Romans, worshiped many gods.

6. The Teutons loved liberty, and a village or tribe carried on the business of its government in an assembly of freemen.

7. The Teutons have given us some famous hero stories, such as *Beowulf* and the *Nibelungenlied*.

8. The Teutons conquered and laid waste the Western Roman Empire, including the city of Rome. In the centuries that followed, the Teutons learned many things from the conquered Romans.

9. Tribes of Teutons settled in England and became the ancestors of the English and of most Americans.

Things to do. — Read or ask your teacher to read to you the description of the Teutons by Tacitus (a Roman historian of the first century after Christ). See Davis, *Readings in Ancient History*, Vol. II, 313–316, or Webster, *Readings in Ancient History*, 261–268.

Make a list of occupations ending in *smith* and another ending in *wright*. Are there any members in your class whose names are those of occupations, such as Fisher or Baker?

Let each section in the class read and tell to the rest of the class one of the following stories: *Iduna's Apples*, *The Death of Baldur*, *Sif's Golden Hair*, *Thor's Hammer*. (See Mabie, *Norse Stories;* Guerber, *Myths of Northern Lands.*)

Read and tell to the class the stories of Beowulf (Leonard, *Beowulf, a New Verse Translation for Fireside and Classroom*), the Nibelungs and Siegfried (Haaren and Poland, *Famous Men of the Middle Ages*).

Imagine yourself to be a boy or girl living in Rome when Alaric raided it. Write a letter to a friend living in another part of the empire and describe what happened.

References for Teachers. — Adams, G. B., *Civilization during the Middle Ages*, 64–105; Thorndike, *Medieval Europe*, IV, V, VII, IX; Tacitus, *Germania;* Gummere, *Germanic Origins;* Robinson, *Readings in European History*, Vol. I, 39–49; Emerton, *Introduction to the Middle Ages*, 11–91.

For Pupils. — Haaren and Poland, *Famous Men of the Middle Ages*, 7–35 (Teutonic invasions); Holbrook, *Northland Heroes* (Beowulf); Guerber, *Myths of Northern Lands;* Van Loon, *Story of Mankind*, 124–130 (fall of Rome); Brown, A. F., *In the Days of Giants;* Mabie, *Norse Stories;* Webster, *Readings in Ancient History*, 261–268; Benezet, *World War and What Was Behind It*, III (Teutons); Tappan, *European Hero Stories*, I–V (Teutons, their gods, fall of Rome); Church, *Helmet and Spear*, 343–376; Harding, *Story of the Middle Ages*, II–VI (Teutons, fall of Rome).

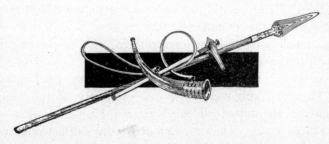

CHAPTER X

HOW NEW NATIONS AROSE IN EUROPE

The end of the Roman Empire in the west. — By 476
A.D. the Western Roman Empire had come to an end. The
last of the western emperors had been overthrown. Where
there had once been one powerful empire ruled by one man,
there were many new kingdoms each ruled by a Teutonic
chief or king. The Goths held Italy, southern Gaul, and
Spain; the Franks owned northern Gaul. Some Angles
and Saxons had sailed over to Britain and settled there.
Other Teutonic tribes were dwelling in other parts of the
empire.

Although little progress in civilization seemed to be made
during the next thousand years, many important things
were begun. When the Teutonic tribes took possession of
the Western Roman Empire, ancient times came to an end.
The time between 476 A.D. and the discovery of America in
1492 is generally called the " Middle Ages " or " Medieval
Times."

The rise of the Franks. — After the fall of Rome, the
nations of Europe did not suddenly settle down and give
themselves the boundaries they possess to-day. There
was much fierce fighting among them. About the end of
the fifth century one of the new nations came to be stronger
than the others. This strong nation was that of the Franks.

Their first king was Clo'vis (an early form of the name
Louis). He united all the scattered Frankish tribes of
northern Gaul. Then he conquered the Gothic kingdom

of southern Gaul and some of the barbarian lands east of the Franks.

How the Franks became Christians. — Like all the Franks, Clovis still worshiped the old German gods, Woden and Thor. But his wife, Clotilde, was a Christian and urged him to accept her faith. During an important battle at Strassburg Clovis was converted; soon after, with more than three thousand of his soldiers, he was baptized amid great rejoicing. A historian of the time says: "The streets were shaded with embroidered hangings; the churches were adorned with white tapestries, giving out sweet odors; perfumed candles gleamed; the air was filled with heavenly odors" to celebrate the baptism.

CLOVIS PUNISHES A REBEL

After a victory won by Clovis and his army, a beautiful vase was found among the spoils. Clovis asked to have it added to his share; but a soldier, insisting on equal shares, destroyed the vase with his battle-ax. Clovis waited a year before he found a pretext for killing the soldier. This was before he became a Christian.

The conversion of the Franks to Christianity was a very important event in history. From that time, the Franks were united to Rome. The Franks and the Pope together were strong enough to subdue any troublesome neighbors.

When Clovis died, his kingdom was divided among his four sons, but later it was reunited. The kings after Clovis were cruel and often weak. Two hundred years after the death of Clovis, they had become mere "do-nothings." The real power was held by the "mayor of the palace," a kind of prime minister who ruled in place of the king.

THE USE OF GREEK FIRE IN SEA FIGHTING

From a fourteenth-century manuscript. The "fire" was shot through long copper tubes which were placed on the prow of the ship.

How Mohammedans conquered Christian lands. — In the seventh century, while the Frankish kingdom seemed to be on the point of going to pieces, a new and terrible power was rising in Arabia. About the year 570 Mohammed was born, at Mecca. When he was forty he said he had a vision of an angel who commanded him to found a new religion which should teach: "There is but one God, and Mohammed is his prophet." Mohammed considered himself a greater prophet than Jesus. Any one not a believer in Mohammed was an enemy who, he thought, should be converted or killed.

" The sword is the key to Heaven," said Mohammed. He also taught that a warrior who fell on the battlefield would be transferred at once to Heaven. So Mohammed and his Arabian followers, with sword in hand, converted the desert tribes of Arabia. In 717 A.D. the Mohammedans besieged Constantinople, the great capital of the Eastern Roman Empire. The defenders of the city fought bravely, and used " Greek fire," which was made by chemicals and could not be put out with water. Thus Christian Constantinople, at the eastern door of Europe, held off the Mohammedans. She preserved Greek and Roman learning until the rest of Europe was ready for it.

In less than one hundred years Mohammedan armies had conquered much of western Asia, Egypt, and northern Africa. In 711, Tarik, a Mohammedan general, crossed from Africa to Spain. He landed at the Rock of Gibraltar, named from him Gib-el-Tarik, or the mountain of Tarik. The Gothic kingdom in Spain was wiped out. The Goths found refuge in the mountains, and as a nation disappeared from history. The Mohammedan Moors took their place as the ruling race in Spain.

Southern France was next conquered. It seemed as if the Mohammedans would become masters of all Europe.

How Charles Martel saved the Christians. — Christians everywhere were in terror. They prayed in their churches for deliverance from the Mohammedans. Their deliverer came in the person of Charles Martel', a " mayor of the palace." Without asking the consent of the weak king, he and the Frankish army met the Mohammedans at Tours (tōor) in 732 A.D. and inflicted on them a crushing defeat. It was then that he received the name Martel', which means " the Hammer."

This battle is very important in the history of the world.
The Mohammedans were stopped from overrunning Europe
and wiping out the Christian religion. Gradually they
were forced out of France. Though Charles Martel was
not made king, his son Pippin was crowned king of the
Franks.

Mohammedans in Spain and the East. — The Moors
remained in Spain for more than seven hundred years.

CHARLEMAGNE'S EMPIRE

Cor'dova was the capital of the western part of the Mohammedan Empire.   During the Middle Ages it was the
greatest center of art and science in Europe.   The capital
of the eastern Mohammedan kingdom was Bagdad, on the
Tigris River.   One of its famous rulers, or " caliphs," was
Harun-al-Raschid (hä-rōōn'är-rȧ-shēd').   Many stories in
the *Arabian Nights* are about events in the reign of that
caliph (786–809); for example, *Aladdin* and *The Forty
Thieves*.   We owe all the stories of the *Arabian Nights* to
the Arabs or to more ancient peoples (p. 28).

Charlemagne's conquests. — Charlemagne (shär'lĕ-mān),
— from the Latin *Ca'rolus Magnus*, meaning Charles the
Great,— the grandson of Charles Martel, is called the
greatest hero of the Middle Ages.   He became king of the
Franks in 768.

A powerful tribe of barbarian Teutons called Saxons —
cousins of the Saxons who had settled in England — dwelt
next door to the Frankish kingdom and made war on it.
Charlemagne conquered these people, and forced them to
become Christians and to learn the ways of civilized life.
The conquest of the Saxons was one of the most important
things that Charlemagne did.   Ruinous invasions were
stopped for a time, and Europe had a chance to progress.

Charlemagne's wars against the Moors of Spain did not
accomplish much, but they gave to the world one of the
great hero stories, *The Song of Roland*.   Roland, a nephew
of Charlemagne, was leading the rear guard of the army
through a narrow pass in the Pyrenees.   Suddenly the
Moors swept down from the mountains upon them.   Roland and his men attempted to beat back their enemy, but
the struggle was useless.   Bleeding from a terrible wound,
Roland blew his horn for help.   Charlemagne, on hearing

the sound many miles away, hurried back to find Roland and his rear guard dead on the field of battle, and the Mohammedans in full flight.

How Charlemagne became emperor of the Holy Roman Empire. — By 800 A.D. Charlemagne united under his rule all the land from the Pyrenees in Spain to the Elbe River in Germany, together with northern Italy.   This was the first great union of states in western Europe since the downfall of the Roman Empire.   On Christmas Day in the year 800, while Charlemagne was in Rome, he was crowned "emperor" by the Pope.   The Pope was the most important person in European politics during the Middle Ages.   Charlemagne's empire was thus linked up with the strongest power of the time, the Christian Church. Because of this fact and because Charlemagne's great realm seemed to be a revival of the Western Roman Empire, it was later called the Holy Roman Empire.

How Charlemagne helped education. — In 800 A.D. learning was at a very low stage in the Frankish kingdom. Even the great emperor himself could not read.   He tried to learn how to write, and used to keep tablets under his pillow so that in his leisure hours he might practice forming the letters.   But he was never able to write any more than his name.   Charlemagne found that some of the priests could not read.   They simply learned the church service by heart from others. Many of the best men in the Frankish kingdom had little education.

Charlemagne ordered that "every monastery have its school, where boys may be taught the Psalms, music, arithmetic, grammar."   He also added this caution: "Let the books which are given them be free from faults."

The only books at that time were written by hand, and in the Latin language; the printing press had not yet been invented. Charlemagne knew that many of the books before his time had been incorrectly copied and badly written. He ordered that all books be clearly and accurately copied. Spelling and handwriting were thus improved. Charlemagne invited to his court men of learning from all parts of Europe to encourage education in his kingdom.

CHARLEMAGNE
Small bronze statue in Paris.

One of Charlemagne's outstanding qualities was his love of education. As a result of his efforts, learning never again fell so low as he found it in the eighth century.

In the disorderly times that followed Charlemagne's death, men remembered his empire as a golden age when the king was strong enough to keep order. Centuries later, poets sang of his deeds and of his greatness. He was selected as a model for true knights in the Middle Ages.

A king's estate in the ninth century. — Charlemagne's kingdom was an extensive one, but so rude were the times that this powerful king did not possess even the ordinary comforts of a poor working man of to-day. A list of the furnishings of one of Charlemagne's royal dwellings contains items such as these : coverings for one bed, one table cloth, and one towel ; two brass kettles, two drinking cups, one frying pan, one lamp, one ax, one chisel, one knife, two spades, and two sickles. The public health nurses in our towns would be alarmed if they found that a family had only one towel.

New European nations. — After several centuries, the people of western Europe were neither Teutons nor Romans. The mixture of the Teutonic Franks and the Romanized Gauls, for instance, made the French nation. The combination of the Teutons with the other peoples of Europe had formed other new nations, such as the English, Italian, and Spanish. The first settlers of America were from some of these nations. Most Americans to-day, therefore, are descendants of the ancient Teutons, who handed down to us what they inherited from the Romans.

Language, too, changed. The Latin language, as modified in different countries, produced the French, Italian, and other *Romance* languages, so called because they are descended from the language of the Romans (p. 121). Other modern languages of western Europe, such as the English, Dutch, Swedish, and German, are branches of the old Teutonic language. For centuries, however, Latin was the only *written* language.

Even the old Roman names of some countries were no longer used. For instance, Gaul became *France*, and Britain became *England*.

Things we should remember about the new European nations. — 1. Europe gradually became divided into many Teutonic kingdoms, which were often at war with one another.

2. The Franks were the first Teutonic nation strong enough to help restore order to Europe. They had accepted Christianity during the reign of their king, Clovis.

3. The Mohammedans threatened to sweep across Europe and wipe out Christianity.

4. Charles Martel and his Frankish warriors stopped the advance of the Mohammedans at the battle of Tours.

5. Charlemagne, the grandson of Charles Martel, conquered the barbarian Saxons beyond the Rhine.

6. Charlemagne united, in one great empire, northern Italy and all the lands from the Pyrenees to the Elbe River. In 800 A.D. the Pope crowned him emperor of this territory, which was later called the Holy Roman Empire.

7. Charlemagne aroused an interest in learning.

8. For several centuries after the reign of Charlemagne the various nations and languages of modern Europe were slowly being formed.

Things to do. — In Haaren and Poland, *Famous Men of the Middle Ages*, 61–70, read the story of Clovis's conversion.

Point out on the map the territory conquered by the Mohammedans.

Read Longfellow's poem, *Haroun Al Raschid*.

Tell to the class the story of Roland. Get more information by reading Baldwin's *Story of Roland* or any other account of this story.

Eginhard, or Einhard, a member of Charlemagne's court, has passed down to us the story of Charlemagne as he knew him. Read what Eginhard has to say of Charlemagne's appearance. See Ogg, *Source Bank of Medieval History*, 109–115, or Davis, *Readings in Ancient History*, Vol. II, 370–373.

Write some reasons why Charlemagne is called "the Great."

Draw a map of Charlemagne's empire.

Charlemagne was a powerful emperor. Tell why you would or would not change places with him.

References for Teachers. — Adams, G. B., *Civilization during the Middle Ages*, VII; Thorndike, *Medieval Europe*, X, XI; Einhard, *Life of Charlemagne;* Hodgkin, *Charles the Great;* Sergeant, *The Franks;* Harding, *New Medieval and Modern History*, 13–42; Ogg, *Source Book of Medieval History*, IV, IX; Emerton, *Introduction to the Middle Ages*, X, XII, XIV.

For Pupils. — Haaren and Poland, *Famous Men of the Middle Ages*, V, VII, X (Clovis, Mohammed, Charles Martel, Charlemagne); Van Loon, *Story of Mankind*, 138–149 (Mohammed, Charlemagne); Dutton, *Little Stories of France*, 20–24, 29–38 (Clovis, Charlemagne, Roland); Tappan, *European Hero Stories*, VI–IX (Clovis, Charlemagne); Harding, *Story of the Middle Ages*, VIII–XIII (Clovis, Charlemagne); Baldwin, *Story of Roland;* Holland, *Historic Heroes of Chivalry*, 9–71 (Roland); Creighton, *Heroes of European History*, 53–64 (Charlemagne).

Just as the Christians built fine churches, so the Mohammedans built many great mosques, or houses of worship, in the cities they conquered. Mohammedans are taught to pray seven times a day. At the proper hours the call to prayer is chanted from the tall minarets of the mosques.

MOSQUE IN CAIRO, EGYPT

CHAPTER XI

HOW THE ENGLISH NATION WAS FORMED

Why we shall now study about England. — We have seen (p. 109) that Britain was a Roman province. It included what are now England, Wales, and part of Scotland (maps following page 110 and on page 160). When compared with the other Roman provinces, Britain seemed rather unimportant. Yet this small island province was to become the home of the most powerful nation in the world. We shall give special study to England because some of her people were the founders of our own nation. We speak her language, and our ways of living have grown from what the early settlers brought here from England.

The fact that England is an island country helped to make her great. The water which separates her from the continent of Europe has served as a protection against enemies. Fertile soil, plenty of rainfall, and a temperate climate have made possible great crops of grain and vegetables. On the grassy hillsides fine sheep and cattle are raised. Excellent harbors have helped to make the English a great trading nation.

How Britain became England. — In Britain, as in all other Roman provinces, Rome built roads and cities, and introduced her ways of living. The city of Bath in England is so named because of the Roman baths that can be seen there to-day. When trouble with the barbarians came (p. 149), Rome withdrew her troops from Britain. The

ROMAN BATHS AT BATH, ENGLAND (RESTORATION)

Britons were without protection against the Teutons who entered the island. One king of the Britons who fought against the Teutons has become famous in song and story. This was King Arthur, who founded the Order of the Knights of the Round Table. His knights rode about fighting to protect the weak and to rescue those in danger. The Britons were finally conquered. Many of them moved over into Wales and are known as the Welsh.

The Angles and the Saxons were the most important of the Teutonic tribes that invaded Britain. Britain became known as "Angle-land" or *England*, and the language and the people were called *Anglo-Saxon*. The Anglo-Saxons were founding the English nation about the time when the Franks were making the beginnings of France.

The newcomers practically destroyed Roman civilization in the island. Many valuable things disappeared from use. For instance, coal had been used in Britain by the Romans, but was not known by the early English nor used again until the twelfth or thirteenth century.

How England was made Christian. — The story of how Christianity was brought to England begins in the Roman Forum. One day a monk, who afterwards became Pope Gregory I, was walking through the Forum, when he saw in the slave market some handsome boys with blue eyes, golden hair, and fair skin. Gregory was so struck by their beauty that he asked who they were. " They are called Angles," was the slave dealer's reply. " Well named," said he, " for they have angelic faces and ought to dwell with the angels in heaven." When he learned that the Angles were not Christians, he asked the name of their king. " Ælla " (ăl'la), was the reply. " Then," said Gregory, " must Alleluia be sung in Ælla's land."

When Gregory became Pope in 590, he remembered the fair-haired slave boys. In 596 he sent his friend Augustine and a company of monks to the land of the Angles and Saxons. The bishops of Gaul told Augustine such terrible stories of the savage Angles and Saxons that he and his men would have given up the undertaking, but Gregory commanded them to continue.

In the spring of 597 Augustine and his company landed in Kent on the south shore of Britain. Eth'elbert, the king, and Bertha, his wife, who was a Frankish princess and therefore a Christian, met them in the open air. Ethelbert did not trust these bringers of a new religion. But after he had listened to Augustine, he gave the Christians a lodging place in Can'terbury, his capital. At length the king was baptized, and Christianity soon became the religion of all England.

Monasteries (pp. 139–140) were founded, and they became centers of learning for England as in other countries. There the monks studied, taught, wrote, and copied books. They also showed the people how to cultivate their farms. The Christian church built in England the first almshouses for the poor and the first hospitals for the sick.

HOME OF AN ANGLO-SAXON NOBLE

Redrawn from an old manuscript. The central building, where the lord and his lady are standing, is the hall. To the left are bowers or sleeping rooms. At the right of the hall is the chapel. The lord and his lady are giving bread to the beggars.

The English thought of their heathen cousins in the forests of Germany across the sea. Just as Augustine was sent by Gregory to the Angles, Bon'iface was sent by the English to Germany. He converted many of the Germans.

Who the Danes were. — Across the North Sea, in what is now Norway, Sweden, and Denmark, lived the Danes. They were also called Northmen, Norsemen, Normans, or Vikings and were the fiercest of the Teutons. They had taken no part in the early invasions of the Roman Empire by their kinsmen. By the ninth century they were roaming the sea as heathen pirates. Wherever a river mouth invited them, they entered, robbed the towns, and then sailed away. Gradually the Northmen made settlements along the coast of Europe. The most famous, which included the region about the mouth of the Seine (sân) River in France, still bears their name, Normandy (North-man-dy).

The Northmen settled Iceland and founded colonies in Greenland which lasted several hundred years. One band, under the leadership of Leif Er'icsson, even visited the mainland of America, about the year 1000. The Northmen explored the coast of Labrador, Newfoundland, and Nova Scotia, and made a settlement in what they called Vinland. They traded red cloth for the furs of the Indians. Then the white men and the Indians quarreled, and many Northmen were killed. The survivors left the Vinland settlement and went back to Greenland. Nothing remains to mark the site of the Vinland settlement. Those in Europe who heard of the Northmen's story did not dream that they were hearing about a new continent.

Five hundred years were to pass before other Europeans settled on the American continent. They were to bring with them the higher civilization developed during that five hundred years.

How the Danes attacked England. — *The Anglo-Saxon Chronicle* tells us that the first visit of Northmen to England was in the year 790, and that they came in three ships. "The reeve [sheriff] rode to them to drive them away, for he knew not what manner of men they were, and they slew him." After that time the Northmen or Danes were frequent though unwanted visitors. When their long boats, decorated on the prow with the figure of a dragon, came in sight, the people along the coast were struck with terror. They knew that these tall, fierce strangers would ransack the churches and monasteries for gold, silver, and jewels; that they would rob the homes, kill the men, and carry off the women. In their prayers the monks and priests added: "From the fury of the Northmen, good Lord, deliver us." In the year 850 a fleet of 350 ships,

VIKINGS (DANES) MAKING A RAID ON A TOWN

The big ship with the dragon at the prow is anchored near the shore; the raiders use a smaller boat to bring them up to the shore.

carrying perhaps ten or twelve thousand men, entered the Thames (tĕmz) River and sacked London. Many other cities were plundered.

The monasteries, the chief schools of the time, were robbed of their treasures and were deserted by the monks. Learning came almost to an end. No one cared to study or write books when the Danes might swoop down upon him at any time. Such was the state of England when Alfred became king in 871, after the short reigns of his three older brothers.

The boyhood of Alfred the Great. — Alfred's father and mother loved him best of all their children. He was the favorite of the men at court. We see young Alfred at the age of four or five on his way to Rome with a company of nobles. The journey to Rome was a long, hard one for a grown man, and how much more so for this child! The Pope was so delighted with little Alfred's sweetness of face and manner that he made him his godson.

Alfred's mother was a fine, noble woman; long after her death, Alfred speaks of her patience and her great kindness. The following story is told by a man of Alfred's court:

" As Alfred grew into boyhood, he appeared more handsome than his brothers and pleasanter in face, in speech, and in manners. He had an earnest desire for learning and wisdom, but sad to say, through the shameful neglect of his parents and guardians, he could not even read when he was twelve years old or more. He listened night and day to poems that were recited and learned to repeat them.

" Now one day his mother showed to him a certain book of poetry which she had in her hand. She said, ' Whoever shall soonest learn this book, to him will I give it.' Alfred, attracted by the beauty of the initial letters in the book, answered his mother thus: ' Will you really give that book to him who understands and repeats it to you?' ' Yes, I will,' said she, with a happy smile. Whereupon he took the book from her hand, went to a master who read it to him, and then he took it back to his mother and recited it to her." The book was his. He studied hard and soon learned to read.

How Alfred governed England. — The first years of Alfred's reign were marked by fierce and continuous struggles with the Danes. Alfred knew that until the Danes were conquered, England could enjoy no peace or progress. He ordered his men to build ships larger than those of their enemies. Alfred has sometimes been called " the founder of the English navy."

To be a king in Alfred's day was no easy task. In the first place, he was expected to lead his army against the enemy and to direct the campaign. Alfred's skill as a general is seen in his wars against the Danes, which lasted several years. At last, after defeating them in a terrible battle, Alfred drove them into a fort which they had built. He laid siege to the fort for fourteen days. Then the Danes, driven out by hunger, cold, and fear, asked for peace. Their leader promised to accept Christianity. Alfred showed his wisdom by giving the Danes a part of eastern England, under an agreement that they would no longer molest his people.

The Danes settled down peaceably and after a time became one people with the Anglo-Saxons. The fact that the English became such fearless and successful traders and explorers is partly due to the sea-loving Danish strain in the English blood.

COIN OF ALFRED THE GREAT

Alfred collected all the laws of the Anglo-Saxons and selected those that " seemed good " for his kingdom. One law shows that Alfred tried to be a father to his people : " Injure ye not the widows and the step-children nor hurt them anywhere, for if ye do otherwise, they will cry unto me, and I will hear them, and I will slay you with my sword, and I will cause that your wives shall be widows, and your children shall be step-children."

People went to Alfred with their complaints. In settling troubles between the rich and the poor, he favored the poor, "because," he said, "the poor have no friend but the king."

What Alfred did for English learning. — Alfred's greatest work was encouraging learning in England. He tells us that when he came to the throne very few people in the south of England knew enough Latin to be able to understand the church service or to translate a letter from Latin into English. In order that his people might have books which they could read, Alfred himself set to work and translated four Latin books into English. This work has given him the title of " the father of English prose." The only English literature until Alfred's time consisted of a few ballads and one long poem, *Beowulf* (p. 149).

At his court Alfred set up a school for young nobles. He said : " Let every youth that is free-born and has wealth enough be set to learn as long as he is not fit for any other occupation till he knows well how to read the English writing." Boys who were to become priests were required to study Latin also.

The Anglo-Saxon Chronicle, the first English history written in Anglo-Saxon or Old English, was probably begun in Alfred's reign. It is a valuable record of events in early English history. An entry for the year 900 A.D. reads : " This year died Alfred, the son of Ethelwulf, six nights before the mass of All Saints. He was king over all the English nation, except that part which was under the power of the Danes. He held the government one and a half less than thirty winters."

Sometimes a strange entry appears. We wonder, for instance, what the writer really saw when he made this note in the *Chronicle*: "In this year dragons were seen flying in the sky."

ALFRED THE GREAT
Statue in London, made more than 500 years ago.

Why Alfred the Great is a hero to the English. — Alfred wrote, shortly before his death: "This I will say, that I have tried to live worthily while I lived, and after my life to leave to the men that come after me a remembering of me in good works." The English have never forgotten their debt to Alfred. One thousand years after his death, the English erected a monument at Wantage, Alfred's birthplace. These lines are engraved upon it:

> Alfred found learning dead,
>   And he restored it;
> Education neglected,
>   And he revived it;
> The laws powerless,
>   And he gave them force;
> The land ravaged by a fearful enemy,
>   From which he delivered it.

How the people of Alfred's time lived. — In Anglo-Saxon England people lived together in small villages and cultivated the land outside. Droves of pigs, belonging to the farmers, fed on the beechnuts and acorns in the forests near by. The cottages were built of wood and had thatched roofs. Even the homes of the wealthy nobles were generally of wood and protected by a kind of stockade of logs. The Anglo-Saxons seem to have seldom used stone for building. They called the stone walls and roads which the Romans had left in England " the work of giants." In one of the Anglo-Saxon poems a march over the old Roman roads is described thus:

> Manful they marched
> As far as ran the roads before them,
> Once built by giants.

ANGLO-SAXONS AT TABLE

Redrawn from an early manuscript. Notice the way in which the servants are serving the roast meats which they have brought to the table on the spits used for the roasting. Forks were unknown at this time in England. People ate with their fingers and used knives to cut meat and bread.

In Alfred's time, kings had no fixed capitals, but had instead royal estates scattered throughout their kingdoms. They traveled up and down their realms from one estate to another. Each estate was watched over by a caretaker or steward called a *reeve*. When a visit from the king was announced, the reeve collected taxes in the shape of cheese, salmon, beef, candles, eggs, honey, cloth, skins, and firewood from the tenants of the royal estate and from the neighboring villages. By the time the king and his followers arrived, the estate would be well stocked with all the food, cloth, and fuel they would need. They remained there until the provisions gave out, and then went to another estate.

Cities grew up at London, Chester, and York, — which had been Roman towns, — and at other places. The citizens were not farmers, but merchants and workers at various trades, such as shoemaking and weaving.

Even after Alfred's improvements, life was rude in England. A conqueror from across the English Channel was to bring to England some of the civilization which the continent of Europe was developing.

How the Normans conquered England. — The Normans or Danes who had settled in Normandy (p. 171) were, in 1066, no longer barbarians like their pagan forefathers. They had adopted the religion, the language, and the customs of their neighbors, the French. In fact, the Normans had become the *Norman-French*. But they still possessed the adventurous spirit of their Viking ancestors.

In 1066, at the death of the English king, Edward, the Wit'an, or council of wise men, gave the crown to Harold, a powerful English earl. William, the Duke of Normandy, said that Edward had promised him the English throne.

After a time the news went forth that William meant to cross the sea to fight Harold.

Harold met William on October 14, 1066, near Hastings. The battle raged for nine hours as the English stubbornly

DEATH OF HAROLD

Redrawn from the Bayeux Tapestry (p. 183). Harold is the second man from the left. He was shot in the eye with an arrow. The Latin inscription reads: "Harold the King was slain."

beat back the Normans. Only after the brave Harold fell dead, could William make himself the victor. He then marched on to London, crushing all who resisted him. On Christmas Day he was crowned king of England. Harold was the last of the Anglo-Saxon line of kings. William the Conqueror was the first of a new line of Norman rulers.

How the Norman Conquest changed England. — The Norman Conquest has been called one of the most important events in English history. Let us see why.

Many invaders of the new race, the Norman or Norman-French, came into England, and their children married Anglo-Saxons. The Anglo-Saxons possessed a great deal of common sense as well as the virtues of the Teutonic race (pp. 143, 153). The Normans had imagination and a spirit of adventure that led them to do things. The later English inherited the good qualities of both races.

England was now firmly united under one ruler. William had seized the estates of the English who rebelled against him. He turned these lands over to his Norman lords or barons. In each conquered district a great stone castle was built. One record tells us that sixteen English houses were torn down to make room for one castle.

STORMING A NORMAN CASTLE

From a manuscript Bible. Notice how the soldiers at the left protect themselves from anything that might be hurled down from the castle walls.

William introduced into England the feudal system, which he brought from the continent. This was a system whereby the lord gave land and protection to his vassals and in turn received service from them. The feudal system is described in Chapter XV. William saw to it that the lords or barons in England never became too powerful. He made every freeman of England, noble and common alike, swear he would be faithful to the king against all other men. If a lord started war against the king, his men were bound by their oath to fight for the king against their lord.

The good order that William established is not to be forgotten. The *Anglo-Saxon Chronicle* says: "It was such that any man might travel over the kingdom with a bosom full of gold and be unmolested, and no man dares kill another, however great the injury he might have received from him."

The peace and order which William's government brought helped England to progress. From France, the most highly civilized country on the continent, the Normans introduced into England more refined ways of living and acting. Then, too, the Norman nobles, traveling back and forth between England and Normandy, brought to England what France, Italy, and the rest of Europe were learning.

Things we should remember about the early history of the English. — 1. Britain was conquered by Angles, Saxons, and other Teutons. They were the founders of the English nation.

2. The Anglo-Saxons were converted to Christianity by Augustine and his missionaries from Rome.

3. The Danes or Northmen, a fierce Teutonic people from the north, ravaged the coasts of Europe and plundered English cities. Many Northmen settled in northern France in a region which came to be known as Normandy.

4. Alfred, the greatest ruler of Anglo-Saxon times, was crowned king in 871.

5. Alfred conquered the Danes and gave them a part of England in which to live.

6. Alfred made a collection of laws for his kingdom.

7. Alfred encouraged learning in England.

8. William, Duke of Normandy, conquered England in 1066 and was crowned king. This is one of the important dates in history.

9. William the Conqueror gave much of the land in England to his Norman-French nobles, and introduced the feudal system into England.

10. The Normans brought to England from France more refined ways of living.

Things to do. — Find the British Isles on the map of Europe. Draw a map of the British Isles.

Name on your map a body of water which separates them from France; from Norway and Sweden. Name a body of water west of the British Isles.

Point out and name the countries in the British Isles.

Read the stories of King Arthur and the Knights of the Round Table in Dutton, *Little Stories of England*, 24–32.

Dramatize the scene in the Roman Forum when Gregory saw the slave boys.

Read *The First Christmas Tree* by Henry van Dyke, a story which tells how the English brought the Christian religion to the Germans.

Imagine yourself to be a boy or girl living in an English seacoast town in the ninth century. Describe a Danish raid as you watched it from your hiding place.

Tell the story of Alfred and the book.

Write a composition on " Why Alfred is called *the Great.*" Read about Alfred in Haaren and Poland, *Famous Men of the Middle Ages*, 135–142.

Find the river Seine on the map. The lower Seine valley was in Normandy. Using the scale of miles, find how far William the Conqueror had to go in sailing from the mouth of the Seine to Hastings.

Imagine yourself to be one of Harold's men. Write a letter to a friend describing the battle of Hastings.

In early times the stories of important events were often woven into the designs of cloth. Such figured cloth is called " tapestry." The most famous tapestry in the world is the Bayeux Tapestry, which tells the story of the battle of Hastings. Look at the photographs of this Bayeux Tapestry in the *Encyclopædia Britannica*.

References for Teachers. — Munro, D. C., *Middle Ages*, 193–213 ; Mowat, *New History of Great Britain*, II–V ; Cheyney, *Short History of England*, 36–143 ; Traill and Mann, *Social England*, Vol. I, Ch. II ; Elson, *Modern Times and the Living Past*, 264–269 ; Stenton, *William the Conqueror;* Plummer, *Life and Times of Alfred the Great;* Pollard, *History of England*, 7–45 ; *Piers Plowman Social and Economic Histories*, Book I, Chs. VI–XIII ; Robinson, *Readings in European History*, Vol. I, 222–231 ; Bulwer-Lytton, *Harold, the Last of the Saxon Kings* (fiction) ; Kingsley, *Hereward the Wake* (fiction).

For Pupils. — Dutton, *Little Stories of England*, 20–63 (Arthur, Augustine, Alfred, William the Conqueror) ; Haaren and Poland, *Famous Men of the Middle Ages*, 126–142 (Vikings, Alfred) ; Dickens, *Child's History of England*, II, III, VII, VIII ; Abbott, *Alfred the Great* (Makers of History) ; Tappan, *European Hero Stories*, X–XVIII ; Tappan, *England's Story*, 12–63 ; Hall, *Viking Tales;* Luther, *Trading and Exploring*, 88–147 (Vikings) ; Stevens and Allen, *King Arthur Stories;* Lanier, *Boy's King Arthur; Piers Plowman Histories*, Junior Book IV, pp. 46–101 (life in England after the Norman Conquest) ; Tappan, *In the Days of Alfred the Great* (fiction) ; Tappan, *In the Days of William the Conqueror* (fiction).

CHAPTER XII

WHAT ENGLAND TAUGHT ABOUT GOVERNMENT

How people were tried for crime in early days. — Persons accused of crime have not always been tried by a jury as they usually are to-day. Let us glance at an English court of the first half of the twelfth century. It is held in the open air. It is presided over by an officer. The people of the neighborhood are present. A man accused of stealing sheep is brought before the court. He swears that he is innocent. The accused man may bring several men to swear that he is telling the truth. On the strength of the oath of the accused and his neighbors, the court may free the man.

But suppose the court is doubtful. The accused is then sent to the ordeal, or "judgment of God." A pit of water is blessed by the priest and told to receive the innocent and reject the guilty. If the accused, bound hand and foot, sinks when thrown in, it is considered a proof from God that he is innocent : he is quickly rescued and set free. If he floats, he is counted guilty. Instead of the ordeal by water, the court may decide on the ordeal by fire. A pound of red-hot iron blessed by the priest is placed in the hand of the accused, who carries it three paces. The hand is then bandaged and is examined after three days. "A blister half as large as a walnut" is accepted as proof that the accused is guilty.

There is still another form of trial. The accused and the accuser may fight each other with swords or clubs.

TRIAL BY BATTLE
Redrawn from a fifteenth-century manuscript.

If the accuser is beaten, his defeat is taken as proof that his accusation is false, and he has to pay a fine of sixty shillings. This " trial by battle " was introduced into England by the Normans.

How we came to have trial by jury. — About the middle of the twelfth century, a wise king, Henry II of England, thought of a better and fairer way of trying people. He sent his judges into all parts of England. In each district the judges picked about twelve men who were to bring to their notice any persons suspected of crime.

These men had to tell what they knew of each case and to decide whether the accused was guilty or innocent. As they swore to the facts which they related, they were called *jurors*, from the Latin *juro*, "I swear." The courts were trying to find out the truth, and we may guess that the guilty were usually punished and the innocent usually freed; but mistakes no doubt were still made. We can see how an innocent man might have been sent to the gallows because his neighbors would say he was just the kind of man who might kill or steal.

Later it was discovered that the jurors sometimes knew little or nothing of the case. Other persons acquainted with facts of the case were then called in as witnesses. Finally the twelve jurors became known as the *jury* and based their decision entirely on the facts the witnesses told them.

The beginnings of trial by jury were made on the continent of Europe before the Anglo-Saxons came to England, but it was England that developed this kind of trial in its present form. Most of the nations of Europe have borrowed trial by jury from England. Our English forefathers brought the jury system with them to America, and we use it to-day.

How the English guarded their liberty. — We have seen (p. 181) that William the Conqueror had, as the king of England, made himself stronger than the lords or barons. A bad king having too much power can easily become a tyrant. Such a king was John.

John quarreled with the French king. A war followed, and as a result John lost Normandy in 1204. This loss did not increase the barons' love for John. Then, too, the French war had proved a costly affair. To obtain money for the war and for himself, John had been taxing his subjects more and more heavily. No one was spared —

neither barons nor churchmen nor common people. He falsely accused many of his people, especially the wealthy, and made them pay heavy fines. People suspected of having money hidden were tortured until they handed over their gold to the king's officers. Enemies of the king, and even his friends, were thrown into prison and kept there for years without being brought to trial.

The barons grew angry at the king's tyranny. They knew that as Englishmen they should have certain liberties. The barons, accordingly, set down a list of these liberties in a document since known as *Magna Charta* (kär'ta), or the Great Charter. The king was asked to promise these rights to his people by signing the Charter (1215).

After the king read the Charter, he threw it aside, saying : " Why did not the barons ask for my kingdom also? " When he learned that the people were against him, he agreed to meet the barons at Run'nymede. Even then he might have refused; but the sight of the barons, clad in armor and accompanied by their thousands of soldiers, frightened the king into signing. The Charter provided for a council of twenty-five barons to see that John and later kings obeyed the promises of the Charter. " They have given me five-and-twenty over-kings," cried John angrily.

Ever since 1215, English kings have been forced to be true to John's promises to the people. One king, Charles I, was found guilty of treason and was beheaded (1649), because he tried to rule without obeying the Charter.

Why the Great Charter is important to the English and to Americans. — In the Great Charter the English people showed the king that he had to obey the law of the land, and that he could not rule as he pleased. By his promises in the Charter, the king was forced to respect the lives, liberty, and property of his subjects. He could not put to death, banish, or imprison any persons until they had been tried and judged. He could not seize any man's property

JOHN SIGNS THE MAGNA CHARTA

except for a lawful reason. If he wished to lay taxes on his people, he first had to obtain the consent of his council of barons.

If we examine the Constitution of the United States, we notice that certain articles like the following are based on Magna Charta: "No person shall be deprived of life, liberty, or property without due process of law." "The accused shall enjoy the right to a speedy and public trial." "Congress [representatives chosen by the people] shall have power to lay and collect taxes."

How the English Parliament developed. — In order to protect the rights of the English people, the Great Charter provided that a council of barons should meet with the king. All the chief barons who held large grants of land from the king were members of the council. This body became known as the "Parliament" (from the French word *parler*, "to talk"). Parliament was at first a meeting in which the king "talked" over government matters with his council.

King Henry III, the son of King John, tried many times to lay taxes upon the people without the consent of Parliament. When the people were at the height of

SIMON DE MONTFORT

From a window in the Cathedral of Chartres, in northern France. De Montfort held estates in France as well as in England.

their anger, Simon de Mont'fort, a baron, gathered together an army composed of a few barons and great numbers of churchmen and common people from the towns and country districts. He met the king and his followers in battle. Henry was defeated and imprisoned, and for more than a year Simon was master of the kingdom.

In 1265 Simon called together a new kind of Parliament, a Parliament that was to bring about great changes in the government of most nations of Europe. He realized that besides the barons there were in England many other wealthy landowners and rich merchants in the towns. They were paying heavy taxes, but they had no chance to vote for or against taxes proposed by the king. Therefore, in addition to the barons and the bishops, Simon summoned two lesser barons, called " knights of the shire," from each county. He also asked each town to send two representatives to Parliament. This was the first time that the towns were permitted a voice in the government.

The important facts to remember are (1) that people of less importance than the great lords were added to Parliament, and (2) that towns elected members to Parliament. Thus Parliament became in part a representative body elected by the people or by part of them. The election of representatives is important because our colonial ancestors asked for the same right as the English had to elect a few men to speak for all.

After a time, Parliament was separated into two bodies: (1) the House of Lords, composed of the chief barons and the bishops, and (2) the House of Commons, made up of the knights of the shire (lesser barons) and citizens. In the course of time Parliament gained the right to make all the laws for the kingdom. The English Parliament has served in some ways as a guide to the United States, which has also divided its Congress or lawmaking body into two parts.

The representative system of government. — The English had taken a great step forward in government. The invention of the representative system was better than any invention in government the Greeks or Romans had made. Instead of sending several thousands or millions of citizens from their shops, their farms, their offices, and their schools to go to Parliament, the English elected a few men to represent them. These representatives were expected to vote as the majority of their fellow citizens wished. America and nearly all European nations have copied the representative system from England.

What we should remember about early English government. — 1. The ordeal and trial by battle were early forms of trial for crime in England.

2. In later times a jury decided an accused person's guilt or innocence on the testimony of witnesses.

3. The Great Charter, which King John was forced to sign, is a safeguard of the liberty of the English people.

4. Some clauses in the Constitution of the United States are like parts of the Charter.

5. The early English Parliament was a meeting of higher nobles and churchmen to talk over government matters with the king. This body afterwards became the House of Lords.

6. English government took a great step forward when the common people obtained the right to elect men to represent them in Parliament. Later these representatives came to be the House of Commons.

7. Parliament gradually became a lawmaking body.

8. The representative system, which Americans brought with them from England, and which many other countries have copied from England, makes it possible for millions of men through their representatives to have a voice in making the laws of their country.

Things to do. — Read about three kinds of ordeals, the Judgment of the Glowing Iron, the Judgment of Boiling Water, and the Judgment of the Morsel, in Davis, *Readings in Ancient History*, Vol. II, 355–357.

If you were wrongly accused of a crime, which form of trial would you rather have to prove your innocence, trial by ordeal or trial by jury? Why?

Imagine your class to be the council of barons. Hold a discussion to show why John should be forced to sign the charter.

Write a composition on " Why Magna Charta Is One of the Great Documents in History."

Read some extracts from the Great Charter. See Ogg, *Source Book of Medieval History*, 298–310.

Show that Simon de Montfort's Parliament was a great step forward in government.

How are the members of the Senate and of the House of Representatives at Washington elected?

Make a list of some of the things England taught about government.

References for Teachers. — Mowat, *New History of Great Britain*, VI–VIII; Cheyney, *Short History of England*, VIII, IX; Traill and Mann, *Social England*, Vol. I., 411–423, 566–573; Elson, *Modern Times and the Living Past*, 270–278; Pollard, *History of England*, 45–60; Larson, *History of England and the British Commonwealth*, IV, V; Scott, *Ivanhoe* (fiction); Scott, *Talisman* (fiction).

For Pupils. — Dutton, *Little Stories of England*, 85–104 (Robin Hood, Great Charter, Simon de Montfort); Dickens, *Child's History of England*, XII–XV; Tappan, *European Hero Stories*, XXII (Magna Charta); Tappan, *England's Story*, 64–102 (Magna Charta, Simon de Montfort); Gilman, *Magna Charta Stories*, 7–22; Marshall, *Island Story*, 171–188 (Magna Charta); Pyle, *Merry Adventures of Robin Hood;* Yonge, *Prince and the Page* (Simon de Montfort) (fiction).

CHAPTER XIII

HOW WE GOT OUR LANGUAGE

How language grows and dies. — The English language which we speak was not always as it is to-day. Language grows and dies like everything else. You can look in old books and find words that we no longer use, as, for instance, *eke*, meaning " also," and expressions like *methinks.* If a person who lived a hundred years ago should return to-day, he would not understand some things you say. Suppose you told him to " switch on the electric light " or to " telephone for a taxicab." So far as he is concerned, you might be speaking a foreign language. In his lifetime he never saw an electric light, a telephone, or an automobile. Words to fit these inventions are newcomers in the language.

The earliest English. — If you could go back to the court of Alfred the Great, you would hear Anglo-Saxon or Old English. This language sounds more like German than like English. However, Anglo-Saxon may be called the parent of the English language. In the following lines from the American poet Longfellow, each word comes directly from the Anglo-Saxon:

> The day is cold, and dark, and dreary;
> It rains, and the wind is never weary.

The endings *-ton, -ham,* and *-bury* or *-burg* are Anglo-Saxon. *Ton* and *ham* both mean a village. Thus Allington or Allingham was the village of the Allings. A *burg* or *byrig*

was generally a walled town. Canterbury was formerly
Cant-wara-byrig, the walled town of the people of Kent.
The names of many American towns bear these Old English
endings.

**The effect of the Norman Conquest on the English
language**. — When the Normans conquered England, they
made Norman-French the language of the court and of the
castle. They scorned Anglo-Saxon because it was the language of their English servants.

A NORMAN SCHOOL

From an old English Psalter, or Book of Psalms. The bench on which the pupils sit forms
a complete circle. The teacher at the right is probably giving a lecture. Note the two
at the left writing on manuscript rolls.

An Englishman of the time complains : " The children
in school are compelled to leave their own language and to
study their lessons in French and have done so since the
Normans came first into England. Countrymen, wishing
to act like gentlemen, try to speak French in order to be

more highly thought of by their neighbors." Like this man, most of the English believed the Anglo-Saxon language good enough for themselves and stubbornly continued to use it. The Normans, unlike some conquerors, were not able to force their language upon the conquered English people.

Even as late as the thirteenth century, two languages, Anglo-Saxon and Norman-French, were spoken side by side in England. The English language was finally to be a combination of these two.

How Norman-French words entered the English language. — The Normans were not able to dislodge the Anglo-Saxon words for everyday things and acts. *Father, mother, sister, brother, home, sleep, sing, weep, horse,* and many other words from the Anglo-Saxon remained in the English language. In general, the Norman-French words that entered the language were those belonging to French customs introduced into England by the Normans. Let us see how this came about.

An historian who lived about the time of the Norman Conquest tells us that the Anglo-Saxons cared about nothing but eating and drinking. They lived in dirty wooden houses and bothered little about dress. They showed no love for books and religion, and " a person who understood grammar was an object of wonder and astonishment." This same historian says that the Normans dwelt in handsome stone houses and were " proudly dressed." They did not want great quantities of food so much as delicate and appetizing dishes. For this reason they brought their own cooks with them to England.

Through these Norman cooks the English language received many words that the Anglo-Saxons had not known. *Cook* is Anglo-Saxon, but the various kinds of cooking that make foods taste different, such as *fry, roast, broil,* and *boil,* come from the Norman-French. The Anglo-Saxon peasants on the Norman estates probably learned these words

NORMAN COOKS IN ENGLAND

From an old manuscript. At the left a pot is boiling. Two geese are being roasted on the spit. The cook is catching the juice as it drips from the fowl. The boy is turning the spit. At the right is an inn

from the Norman cooks along with the new ways of cooking.

The Saxon would say that he was going to sit down at the *board* and *eat.* The Norman seated himself at the *table,* and *dined* or *supped.* He called the meals *dinner* and *supper.* These more polite words from the French became a part of our language We still use the term *breakfast* from the Anglo-Saxon. You can see how just in the names of the meals our language is part Norman-French and part Anglo-Saxon.

Sir Walter Scott, in his novel *Ivanhoe*, very cleverly explains why we have one name for the animal and another for its meat. He says that when the animals are tended by a Saxon peasant they are called by their Saxon names, as *calf*, *cow*, *pig*, and *sheep*. But when the animals are served as meat at the Norman table, they are called by the Norman-French names. *Pig* becomes *pork*, *calf* is *veal*, *cow* is *beef*, and *sheep* is *mutton*.

Some of the names of our clothing are Norman-French: others, Anglo-Saxon. *Cloth*, from which clothes are made, is from the Anglo-Saxon, as are also *hat* and *shirt*. The Normans spent much time on dress and introduced new garments into England. One of these was the cloak. The Norman horseman wore a cape which had the shape of a bell. He called it a *cloche*,

DRESS OF AN ANGLO-NORMAN LADY
Redrawn from an old manuscript.

the French for "bell." This garment became known in English as *cloak*. The fashionable new word *tailor* came from the Norman-French.

The Saxons wore beards, but the Normans had theirs shaved off by the *barber* (from the French *barbe*, "beard"). Thus a new occupation with its French name came into England. *Mason* is also from the French because the Normans needed masons to build their stone castles.

The Anglo-Saxon names for the important occupations such as *goldsmith*, *weaver*, *baker*, and *fisher* were kept in the language. But the clumsy Anglo-Saxon word *gemwright* gave place to the Norman-French *jeweler; treewright* was replaced by *carpenter*.

Why we have pairs of words of similar meaning. — The Normans and the English realized that they had to live together. They were constantly meeting in the marketplace, in the church, in the shops, in the courtyard of the castle, and on the roads. Each had to make the other understand. Each had to learn something of the other's language.

When a Norman said he wanted to " purchase " a cow, the Englishman came to know that he meant " buy " it. When the Englishman spoke of a " bloom," the Norman learned that he meant " flower." For this reason we find in our language pairs of words that mean about the same thing, as the Norman-French *branch* and the Anglo-Saxon *bough*, Norman-French *gentle* and Anglo-Saxon *mild*, and many like pairs.

By the fourteenth century a language that was neither Anglo-Saxon nor Norman-French but a combination of both was being spoken in England. This language, which is called " English," keeps its Teutonic foundation.

How English became the language of England. — The Normans, of course, had taken over the English law courts. Cases were tried and judged in Norman-French, from which come words like *court*, *suit*, *judge*, and *justice*. In 1362, nearly three hundred years after the Norman Conquest, an important law was passed. It stated that great mischief had come to people because the laws of the realm were not known, and because lawsuits were pleaded, shown, and judged in the French tongue, which was much unknown;

CANTERBURY PILGRIMS DESCRIBED IN CHAUCER'S POEM
Redrawn from an early manuscript. Notice the walled town at the right.

people did not know what was said for or against them. It was therefore ordered that all cases in court should be debated and judged in the English tongue.

After this time, English, instead of French, was taught in the grammar schools. An Englishman writing in 1385 tells us that "the children learn in English and know no more French than their left heel knows."

Before English could be recognized as the national language, it had to be used in the writing of great books. Geoffrey Chaucer (1340–1400), one of the greatest poets of England, thought English better than Latin or French when he wrote his famous poem, *The Canterbury Tales*, which we enjoy reading to-day. He describes the twenty-nine pilgrims who ride to Canterbury to visit the tomb of a martyr. The band of pilgrims is led by a knight. Chaucer tells us that

"He was a verray parfit gentil knight"
(He was a very perfect gentle knight) —

The words describing the knight, *very*, *perfect*, *gentle*, are from the French; the others, from the Anglo-Saxon. You can see how the two languages are blended in this

simple sentence. Since Chaucer's time, English has been the language in which English-speaking people have written their stories, plays, poems, and histories.

How printing helped settle the English language. — Before the fifteenth century, books were written by hand on parchment which was made from the skin of lambs and goats. Books were scarce and very expensive. Until they

EARLY PRINTING PRESS
From an engraving used on title pages of some books printed in the sixteenth century.

could be turned out in large quantities and sold cheaply, common people could not own them.

In the twelfth century paper was introduced into western Europe by the Moors in Spain. A material cheaper than parchment was thus secured. Then in the fifteenth century the printing press was invented. Instead of writing one copy of a page at a time, the printer could strike off five hundred copies of each page if he wished, when once his type was set. William Caxton set up the first printing press in England. From his time on, books began to grow more and more plentiful and much cheaper. The art of reading became common.

Printed books helped to fix the form of our language. The early English writers had hardly any models of writing to follow. Each made up his own spelling as he thought it should be. One writer, for instance, doubled almost all the consonants in words. He spells "named," *nemmnedd*. In writings made from 1340 to 1490, "English" is spelled *inglis, engliss, englysch, englysche,* and *englysshe.*

Not only did the readers of the time find different spellings for the same word; they heard different words used for the same thing in various parts of England. Caxton tells the following story: A merchant and his friend left their ship to buy food in a town on the Thames River. The merchant asked the mistress of a house to sell him some *eggys.* She answered that she spoke no French. The

And the marchaũt was angry.for he also coude speke no frensshe. but wolde haue hadde egges/ and she vnderstode hym not/ And thenne at laste a nother sayd that he wolde haue eyren/then the good wyf sayd that she vnderstod hym

SAMPLE OF CAXTON'S PRINTING

Part of the story in which Caxton tells of the differences in English dialect. From Caxton's edition of the *Prologue to Vergil's Æneid.*

merchant grew angry and said he could not speak French either, but wanted some *eggys.* The friend, who knew the kind of English spoken in that part of England, said that the merchant wanted *eyren*.   Says Caxton, " The good wyf sayd that she vnderstod hym wel."   Out she went and brought back some eggs.

Caxton then asks: " What should a man in these days write, *eggys* or *eyren*?   Certainly it is hard to please every man because of the difference in the language."   Evidently *eggys* was printed more often then *eyren*, and so *eggs* remained in our language.

You can see how unsettled the English language still was in 1491, the date of Caxton's death and the year before America was discovered.   However, people all over England had begun to use the English in books as a model for their own speech and writing.

How new words come into the language. — New words are constantly being added to the language.   The names for new inventions are sometimes made up of old words that describe the invention, as *steamboat*, from *steam* and *boat*. Sometimes we use Latin and Greek words or parts of words.   Thus, *automobile* is a combination of the Greek *auto*, which means " self," and the Latin *mobile*, which means " moving."   *Telephone* is made up of two Greek words: *tele*, " far," and *phone*, " voice."

New words creep into our language from other countries. From Germany we got the words *pretzel*, *waltz*, and *kindergarten*.   From Italy we have borrowed many terms of art, such as *piano*, *opera*, *studio*.   To the Indians we owe the words *potato*, *tobacco*, *persimmon*, *hickory*, plants and trees which were new to the white men who first came to America. Spain has contributed the words *cigar*, *mosquito*, *cork*, *vanilla*.   These are only a few examples of many such borrowings.

The Arabs in the Middle Ages knew much more science

and mathematics than the western Europeans. We use to-day in these branches of learning a number of words from an Arabic source, such as *alcohol, sirup, algebra, zero*. We also have from the Arabic such common words as *sofa, cotton, coffee*.

We have from the Arabs another very important gift, the Arabic numerals 1, 2, 3, 4, 5, 6, 7, 8, 9, 0. You probably do not realize what a wonderful contribution this is. Suppose in looking for a telephone number you had to read numbers like MMCCLXXVIII and CCCXXXIII instead of 2278 and 333. Until the twelfth century the people of Europe had been using these awkward Roman numerals. Then Europe borrowed the Arabic system of numbering. The Arabs themselves had borrowed these numerals from the Hindus, who invented them. The zero was the last and most valuable addition to the Arabic numerals. Before the invention of the zero, 208 was written 2 8. Finally the sign 0, which was called a *cifr* (meaning "empty"), was invented to fill the empty space. We get our words *cipher* and *zero* from French forms of *cifr*.

Some reasons for the difficulties in English spelling. — Foreigners who study our language find the spelling very difficult, as we also do. We say that our words have many silent letters. Instead of writing *nee* we spell *knee;* instead of *nite* we write *knight*. We say that *k* and *gh* are silent in these words. Once these letters were pronounced. The Anglo-Saxons and the English of Chaucer's time said, " *ke-nee*," and " *ke-night*." The *gh* in *knight* or *night* was pronounced like the German *ch* — a deep sound made in the throat. Though the sound of the words changed, the spelling did not, and so we still write *laugh, brought, night*, and *knee, knock, knife, knight*.

On the other hand, many letters once pronounced and spelled have disappeared entirely. In early English, *leap, ring,* and other such words were *hleap, hring,* and the like, the *h* being pronounced. You see that our spelling is not so hard as it would be if our ancestors had not lopped off some of the unnecessary letters.

The richness of the English language. — Our language is very wonderful and remarkable among languages. As a result of the mixture in our language, we have several words for the same thing, as *house, habitation, dwelling, home;* we can, therefore, make our meaning very clear. Many adjectives, also, mean nearly the same thing and yet have slight differences, for example, *great, big,* and *large.* A *big* man is not always a *great* man.

The English language, based on the old Anglo-Saxon and Norman-French mixture and enriched by the contributions of many peoples, is one of our greatest inheritances.

What we should remember about the history of the English language. — 1. Anglo-Saxon, the language of England before the Norman Conquest, is the foundation of modern English.

2. After the Norman Conquest, Norman-French became the language of the court and of fashion in England, but Anglo-Saxon continued to be spoken by most of the English.

3. Many Norman-French words gradually entered the English language.

4. In the fourteenth century English became by law the language of the English courts. It also took the place of Norman-French in the schools.

5. Writers, such as Chaucer, and printers, such as Caxton, helped to fix the form and spelling of English.

6. English includes many words borrowed from other languages.

7. The English language is still constantly changing.

Things to do. — Mention some words that your great-grand-fathers would not know the meaning of.

Name some cities or towns in America that end in *-ton*, or *-ham*, or *-burg*. See if you can discover how these towns received their names.

Imagine yourself to be a Norman in England and give your opinion of the Anglo-Saxons.

Imagine yourself to be a Saxon and give your opinion of the Normans. Find more information in some of the earliest chapters in Scott's *Ivanhoe*.

Consult a large dictionary to see if the following words are from the Anglo-Saxon or from the French: *cup, house, tree, library, bed, excellent, perfume, bottle, shoe.*

From what language did we borrow *garage* and *chauffeur?*

See if you can find why your city and the streets of your city were named as they are.

References for Teachers. — Smith, L. P., *English Language;* Halleck, *New English Literature*, II; Krapp, *Modern English;* McKnight, *English Words and Their Background;* Cheyney, *Readings in English History*, 272–273; Traill and Mann, *Social England*, Vol. I, 628–640; Bateson, *Mediæval England;* Greenough and Kittredge, *Words and Their Ways in English Speech; Encyclopædia Britannica*, article on "English Language."

For Pupils. — *Piers Plowman Social and Economic Histories*, Book II (social life in England after the Norman Conquest); O'Neill, E., *Stories That Words Tell Us;* Warren, *Stories from English History*, 156–165 (English language, Caxton); Dutton, *Little Stories of England*, 140–145 (Caxton); Dale, *Landmarks of British History*, IV (Normans and what they did in England); Darton, *Story of the Canterbury Pilgrims;* Smith, D. E., *Number Stories of Long Ago.*

CHAPTER XIV

HOW THE CHURCH INFLUENCED THE LIFE OF THE MIDDLE AGES

The Christian church during the Middle Ages. — For a long time the only Christian church in western Europe was the Catholic Church. As late as five hundred years ago nearly all of our Christian ancestors belonged to this church. In western Europe, only the priests of the Catholic Church baptized the children, performed the marriage ceremony, and read the service over the dead.

The head of this church was the Pope at Rome. Under him were different ranks of the clergy, — such as cardinals (who elected the Pope), archbishops, bishops, and parish priests. The church had also religious orders of monks and nuns, who lived apart from the world in monasteries and convents (p. 139). There were also friars (from the French word meaning " brother "), who traveled about the country, usually on foot, preaching to the people and trying to be brothers to them. They particularly cared for the poor and the sick. Saint Francis (1181–1226), the founder of the order of the Franciscan friars, was the most loved of all the friars. His own life was a sermon of love for all creatures. He called even the birds and the animals his brothers.

How the church took part in governing nations. — The Pope was the ruler of the central part of Italy, and Rome was his capital city. The church had much influence also in the government of other Christian nations. We have seen that Charlemagne was crowned by the Pope (p. 162). The Pope became a very powerful person. At times he used his influence to decide who should be crowned king and who should be deposed from his kingship. Sometimes archbishops and other church officials in a country were political statesmen; that is, they helped the king to govern the nation.

Church courts. — The church had courts of its own which tried all the clergy. In the Middle Ages few could read except those connected with the church. England gave the privilege of trial by church courts to all who could read the first verse of Psalm LI. This was usually called the "neck verse," because the ability to read it saved the accused from being hanged. The decisions of the church

A THIRTEENTH-CENTURY BISHOP
From a thirteenth-century manuscript Book of Prayers.

courts were not so severe as those of the king's courts, for church courts would not punish any one by mutilation or death.

Sanctuary. — The church also gave protection to any person who reached its bounds and claimed the protection of its altar. Those who visit Durham Cathedral in England may still see the knocker which a fleeing person used to gain entrance. If any one took the fugitive away from

KNOCKER ON THE SANCTUARY DOOR OF DURHAM CATHEDRAL

the altar, the church might "excommunicate" him. Excommunication meant cutting off from all protection of the church, and the people thought that the soul of an excommunicated person would be forever lost.

The fugitive might be either a person threatened with violence or a person accused of crime. A criminal might keep his sanctuary for forty days. He could then safely leave the country if the crime could not be atoned for in some other way. The early church gave the right of sanctuary to check bloodshed, to give time for passions to cool, and to show that the Christian church stood for mercy.

Gothic architecture. — The churches in England built in the Middle Ages are so beautiful that it is a pleasure to enter them to-day. People were taught to serve God by building beautiful structures for worship. Gothic architecture is the great art creation of the Middle Ages and one of the great art creations in the history of the world. Gothic architecture appears at its best in the cathedrals which were built in western Europe between 1100 and 1400. A cathedral is the church of a bishop.

NAVE OF A GOTHIC CATHEDRAL — EXETER, IN ENGLAND

Notice also the side aisles, and the windows in the clerestory, or upper part of the nave.

So beautiful are many of the Gothic cathedrals that they may be called poems in graceful stone and colored glass.

There are more than twenty-five Gothic cathedrals and abbeys (monastery churches) in England. One of the most wonderful is Westminster Abbey in London. Here the kings are crowned and many noted men are buried.

The architects made the cathedrals appear varied and beautiful (1) by the new creation of the flying buttress, which gave greater support to the side walls and thus allowed larger windows in them; (2) by the graceful pointed Gothic arch instead of the round Norman arch; (3) by the most wonderful large stained glass windows that the world has ever seen, windows that were a story book for the people because they showed scenes from the Bible and the lives of saints; (4) by heads and figures in stone outside the walls; (5) by the wood carving in the choir. Sometimes the vaulted ceiling of stone is almost as delicately carved as lace work. No two cathedrals are alike.

FLYING BUTTRESSES

Part of the cathedral of Bayeux, France. The weight of the slanting roof would push over the light upper side walls if they were not supported by the flying buttresses. Notice three flying buttresses near the middle of the above picture.

What the carvings show us about the people. — The varied work on these cathedrals gave all the craftsmen a chance to express themselves. The wood carvers often

BUILDING A CATHEDRAL

From an old drawing, probably by Matthew Paris. The king and the architect are on the left, and the builders are at work on the right.

showed humor. One made for a seat in the choir an excellent carving of a cat with its head in a cream pitcher and a housewife rushing toward it with a broom. Another carved graceful vines with an imp's head peering out from them. Most of these carvings are under the hinged seats in the choir and may be seen when the seats are raised. Francis Bond, a writer familiar with the wood carving in the English Gothic cathedrals, says: "They present to us a picture realistic and true of that history which

WOOD CARVING IN WORCESTER CATHEDRAL, ENGLAND

The cook and the dog are warming their feet at the fire under the pot. At the right of the picture two pieces of bacon are hanging. This wood carving is on the bottom of a choir seat which may be lowered for use.

does not find its way into books. They give an honest transcript of what went on every day in the cottages and on the streets." On the water spouts, or "gargoyles,"

COMIC FIGURES ON THE CATHEDRAL OF NOTRE DAME

there were often carved queer figures. The gargoyles and other comic figures on the cathedral of Notre Dame in Paris are especially famous.

Influence of the monasteries. — One of the great things the church did was to keep education alive for a thousand years, from 500 A.D. to 1500. It kept western Europe from going back into barbarism after the fall of the Roman Empire.

The monasteries (p. 139) were one of the great agencies of the church for education. For a long time they and the cathedral churches furnished the only schools.

In an age of fighting, men who wanted to study or teach had to retire from the world, join the order of monks, and live in a monastery where the calls to fight could not reach them.

The buildings of the monastery were surrounded by a strong wall. The monastery often served as an inn and therefore it had guest chambers. The monastery was also in some ways like a manual training school. It had good workshops where the monks made the various things

needed.   They learned how to work in wood.   They made
chairs, tables, beds, wooden bowls, platters, and spoons.
They also hammered out copper kettles and made horse-
shoes and nails.   They tanned leather, out of which they
made coats for men and harness for animals.

The most interesting room in the monastery was the
scripto'rium, or writing room.   The monks prepared parchment out of the skins of
sheep.   This was used
instead of paper.   Even
to-day parchment is used
for the diplomas which
college students often call
" sheepskins. "   Monks
made their pens out of
goose quills or reeds.
They scraped soot from
the chimneys as the basis
for their ink.   They made
paints from flowers, ber-
ries, gold leaf, and white
of egg.   On their parch-
ment they copied the
Scriptures, prayers, songs,
and other books.   The
initial letter at the be-
ginning of a chapter

MONK AT WORK IN A SCRIPTORIUM
Before the invention of the printing press monks
carefully copied many books by hand.

was often a beautiful little painting in blue, crimson, and
gold.

Monks sometimes kept a parchment diary of what seemed
most important.   Some monks wrote histories of their
time, such as the *Anglo-Saxon Chronicle* (p. 175), which

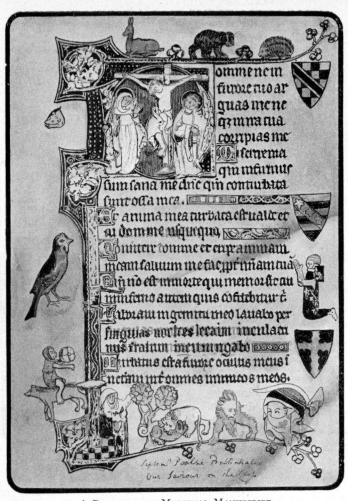

A PAGE FROM A MEDIEVAL MANUSCRIPT

A leaf from a Book of Hours made in England. This shows how the monks sometimes ornamented their manuscripts. The writing is in Latin.

historians consult to-day. The monastery took the place of a modern printing and publishing house.

Outside the walls of the monastery lay its fields and woodlands. Here the monks raised their food and kept their cattle, sheep, and pigs. Sometimes the monks received grants of land from the king or from a noble on condition that they should pray for the donor's soul.

The monks were skillful farmers. They showed the peasants how to raise larger crops. If the land was covered with a tangle of shrubs and vines, they cleared it; if it was marshy, they drained it. We have seen (p. 140) that Saint Benedict taught monks the gospel of work.

Pilgrimages. — Religion led to much travel in the Middle Ages. Many went on pilgrimages, which were journeys to some holy place.

The first Christian pilgrimages were made to places connected with the life of Jesus: to Bethlehem, his birthplace; to the Garden of Gethsemane; to the hill of the Crucifixion; and to the cave in Jerusalem where the body of Jesus was laid. Later, pilgrims also went to the graves of martyrs, saints, and holy men in Rome and other places in Europe. One of the great English poems, Chaucer's *Canterbury Tales* (p. 200) tells the stories which a company of pilgrims related on the way to the tomb of a martyr, Thomas à Becket, whose grave was at Canterbury in southeastern England.

People in the Middle Ages thought that visiting the Holy Land or other sacred places would cause their sins to be forgiven, cure their diseases, and bring them good fortune. Sometimes cripples threw away their crutches at the shrines of the saints, and the sick became well. A story is told of how two sick beggars were tricked into going near the bones of a saint and how both were healed against their will and had to work for a living.

The Crusades. — We have seen (p. 158) that Mohammed, an Arab born about 570 A.D., founded the Mohammedan religion. The Holy Land was held a long time by Mohammedan Arabs, who were a well-educated race with many good qualities. Had the Arabs remained in possession of

A PRIEST URGING A CRUSADE
Redrawn from an old engraving.

the Holy Land, there might have been little trouble for Christians visiting it. But it was taken by the Turks, a barbarous race of Asiatics. Like the Arabs, they were Mohammedans, but they were ruder and more cruel.

It had long been the custom of Christians to visit the sepulcher of Christ and other sacred places in the Holy Land. Some time after the coming of the Turks, Pope Urban II, the head of the Roman Catholic Church, said before a vast throng (1095) that the Turks were insulting Christians at the tomb of Christ and even selling some into slavery. He urged the people to rescue " the holy sepulcher of our Lord and Savior from the wicked race." The people answered with the battle cry: " It is the will of God!"

Men of all classes from Christian Europe joined armies that fought not only the Turks but also other Moham-

medans in western Asia at various times (beginning 1096)
for nearly two hundred years. These attempts to drive
the Mohammedans out of the Holy Land are called the
Crusades, from the Latin word meaning "cross." The
church showed its great influence in starting the Crusades.
The crusaders, to show their respect for the cross on which
Christ died, wore a cross of red cloth. They captured
Jerusalem (1099) and held it for nearly a hundred years.
The crusaders failed in their real purpose, for the Mohammedans took Jerusalem from them (1187) and kept it for
more than seven hundred years. The Christians then
recaptured it (1917) in the World War.

If the crusaders did not keep the Holy Land from the
Mohammedans, they helped change the history of the world
in other ways. We shall see later (Chapter XVII) how the
Crusades, which began as pilgrimages, affected the trade
and knowledge of Europe and proved to be a step toward
the discovery of America.

**Things we should remember about the Church of the Middle
Ages.** — 1. There was only one Christian church during the
Middle Ages, — the Catholic Church.

2. The church had great power and influence.

3. The church was merciful in an age of cruelty.

4. Religion led the people of the Middle Ages to build great
Gothic cathedrals which rank among the most beautiful things
man has made.

5. The monasteries belonging to the church were centers of
education, and they took the place of modern printing and
publishing houses.

6. Many people made religious pilgrimages.

7. The Crusades were not only pilgrimages but wars to
wrest the Holy Land from the hands of the Mohammedans.

Things to do. — Tell how Europe was improved by the Christian religion. (See pp. 133, 134, 140, 170, 208-215.)

Find out more about Saint Francis.

Explain how the church took part in governing nations. Look up in a cyclopedia or in Haaren and Poland's *Famous Men of the Middle Ages* why Henry IV of Germany went to Canossa. Tell the story.

What were the differences between a church court and a state court of the Middle Ages?

What was a sanctuary? What is excommunication?

Collect pictures of Gothic cathedrals. Point out the flying buttresses, pointed arches stained-glass windows, clerestory.

Are there any Gothic churches or cathedrals in your city?

Why did men go on pilgrimages in the Middle Ages?

Find the Holy Land (Palestine) on the map following page 110.

Find or draw a picture of a crusader. Imagine yourself to have been a crusader. Describe your adventures.

References for Teachers. — See pp. 131-141 of this book; Seignobos *History of Medieval and Modern Civilization*, VII; Bateson, *Medieval England*, III, IV, IX, X, XV, XVI; Harding, *New Medieval and Modern History*, V, VI, VIII; Robinson, *History of Western Europe*, XVI; Adams, *Civilization during the Middle Ages*, III; Cutts, *Parish Priests and Their People*; Gasquet, *Parish Life in Medieval England;* Jessopp, *The Coming of the Friars;* Ogg, *Source Book of Medieval History*, XXII (Saint Francis); Sabatier, *St. Francis of Assisi;* Traill and Mann, *Social England*, Vol I, 425-426 (sanctuary); *Encyclopædia Britannica*, articles "Crusades," "Sanctuary," "Monasticism," "Ecclesiastical Law"; "Clergy, Benefit of"; any English history, account of reign of Henry II (for church courts); Monroe, *Text-Book in the History of Education*, 243-276 (education in monasteries); Thompson, *English Monasteries;* Power, *Medieval English Nunneries;* Archer and Kingsford, *The Crusades;* Munro, *Middle Ages*, XXI, XXV.

For Gothic architecture, see Parker's *Introduction to the Study of Gothic Architecture;* Bond, *English Cathedrals;* Singleton, *How to Visit the English Cathedrals;* Munro, *Middle Ages,* 385, 386; Adams, *Mont-Saint-Michel and Chartres;* Davis, *Life on a Medieval Barony,* XXIV (cathedral and its builders).

For the temporal power of the church, see Munro, *Middle Ages,* XV; Harding, *New Medieval and Modern History,* VI, VII; Thorndike, *Medieval Europe,* XV.

For Pupils. — Marshall, *Island Story,* 277–285 (sanctuary); Terry, *Lord and Vassal* (History Stories of Other Lands), 117–120; Lang, *Book of Saints and Heroes* (Saint Francis); Warren, *Stories from English History,* 62–78 (Henry II); Van Loon, *Story of Mankind,* 162–167 (temporal power of the church); Harding, *Story of the Middle Ages,* XXII (life in the monastery), XXIII (temporal power of the church), XVII, XVIII (Crusades); Tappan, *Old World Hero Stories,* 136–156 (Crusades); Church, *The Crusaders;* Stein, *Our Little Crusader Cousin of Long Ago;* Stein, *Gabriel and the Hour Book* (fiction); Hewes, *Boy of the Lost Crusade* (fiction); Scott, *The Talisman* (Crusades, fiction).

DURHAM CATHEDRAL

CHAPTER XV

THE FEUDAL SYSTEM AND CHIVALRY

A WRITER in the Middle Ages said that men were divided into three classes: (1) the priests to serve God, (2) the knights or lords to protect society, (3) the peasants or villeins to till the soil and support the other classes. We have seen what the priests accomplished through the church. In this chapter we shall see what was done by the lords or knights.

How land was held. — The king of each country in western Europe claimed to own all the land in his kingdom.

A LORD'S CARRIAGE

From a lord's fourteenth-century Psalter, or Book of Psalms. When a lord owned more than one estate and had eaten up his provisions on the first, he traveled to another. Transportation was so difficult that it was easier for him to go to the provisions than to have them brought to him. Notice the dog under the wagon.

He could not manage it all, so he gave large parts of it to important men in return for service to him. Such men were called knights, nobles, or lords, and part of their service to the king was to fight in his army.

Suppose one lord, whom we will call " Q," should receive so much land from the king that he could not manage it all. Suppose " Q " gave parts of this land to lesser lords or nobles, called " X " and " Y"; and suppose " Y " gave some of his land to lesser knights.   Every one who received land would have to promise to aid and defend the giver. Land was given only in return for service.   " Q " was called a *vassal* of the king; " X " and " Y " were vassals of " Q "; and the lesser knights were vassals of " Y." " Vassal " means one who owed service.

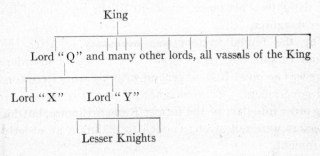

The king and every lord or knight owned and managed some land — one or more estates — for himself.   The work on each estate was done by villeins, whose life is described in Chapter XVI.

What the feudal system means. — The feudal system was a kind of government based on the holding of land.   The agreement between each lord and his vassal called for duties both ways.   The vassal had to fight in his lord's army, and the lord had to protect his vassal.   When necessary, the lord gathered an army to fight off invading enemies.   He also acted as governor and judge to keep order among his vassals, conduct trials, and settle disputes. A vassal was subject to call to sit in his lord's court and to advise his lord. All vassals were required to pay money to their lord on special occasions, such as for a ransom (price for setting a prisoner free) if the lord should be captured by an enemy, or for a dowry (large wedding gift) when the lord's daughter was married.

When a lord died, his place, with its powers and duties, was taken by his oldest son. When a vassal died, his place was taken by his oldest son; but the new vassal was required to make a new promise of service and might also have to make a payment of money or goods. If a man left only daughters, his place would go to the first son of his oldest daughter.

Why the feudal system was necessary. — After the Roman Empire fell, there was a long period of disorder. There was no great Roman general with his army to restore good government. Charlemagne (pp. 162, 163) helped to bring order into part of the former Roman Empire, but his successors were not strong enough to maintain an orderly government.

The feudal system grew up as a way to keep order and make life and property safe in a district owned by a lord and his vassals, when no king was strong enough to control the entire nation. It began in the tenth century and lasted about five hundred years.

Let us suppose that a man owned a thousand acres and that he did not want to be anybody's vassal. What would happen? Some neighboring lord of ten thousand acres, with a large number of fighting men, might swoop down on him, perhaps kill him, and add that thousand acres to his own estates. Every small landholder who was without protection would find it to his interest to become the vassal of some more powerful lord and receive protection from him.

ARMOR OF A FEUDAL WARRIOR

Photograph of a model clothed in armor of the fifteenth century. Metropolitan Museum of Art, New York.

We to-day think that the feudal system was a bad form of government. So it was, but it was better than no government.

Private wars. — One trouble with the feudal system was that the king and the lords too often were unable to give their vassals the protection that was due them. One lord often quarreled with another and waged war on him in spite of anything the king could do. The victor would seize new estates to add to his own. A powerful lord who was summoned to come with his vassals to the king's aid might even bring them to fight against the king instead. It was a common thing in some countries for lords to fight against lords whenever they liked; but William the Conqueror (p. 181) and other strong kings would not allow such private warfare.

The church tried to limit war by making a rule known as the "Truce of God." This forbade the nobles to fight with each other from Wednesday evening until Monday morning of each week. Lent and certain sacred days were also set aside as a time of peace. This effort of the church did not entirely stop war on the forbidden days.

The castles of the lords. — The warfare of the Feudal Age made it necessary for the nobles to live in stone castles built in places that were hard to reach or attack. The bend of a river, an island in a lake, solid ground in the middle of a marsh, and the top of a hill were favorite sites for castles. Where possible, the castles had deep trenches, called "moats," dug around them and filled with water. The castle was always built where drinking water could be had, either from a well inside or from a lake or river that could be safely reached when an enemy laid siege to the castle.

The castle had an outer wall of stone with slits at the top through which bowmen could shoot arrows. If an attacking enemy tried to fill the moat or undermine the walls, the defenders would drop stones or boiling pitch on them. Men entered the castle over a drawbridge which could be pulled up at a moment's notice. Behind the drawbridge was a heavy gate, called a "portcullis," that slid up and down. This could be dropped instantly. Beyond this was the first courtyard, where the horses could be kept and where the villeins who tilled the soil could stay during a siege.

Beyond the first courtyard was another stone wall protecting a second court and buildings inside. The most important of these buildings was the "keep," which had stone walls from eight to ten feet thick. If all the rest of the castle was taken, the keep might withstand assault. Beneath the keep were dungeons where no ray of sunlight ever entered. Prisoners captured in war were often kept there. A prince engaged to marry some fair princess was sometimes a captive in such a prison. She might try to raise an army to rescue him or might give a large sum of money for his ransom.

A FEUDAL CASTLE (RESTORED)

The castle of Coucy-le-Château, on a hill in northern France, was built in the thirteenth century. Notice the moat in front. The drawbridge is at the right. On three sides the castle is protected by steep slopes, without any moat. The round tower in the center front is 100 feet in diameter and over 200 feet in height. The lord's residence was at the far end of the inner court. This castle was destroyed during the World War.

The lord of a castle usually feared that some other lords might become too strong for him, and so he tried to get as many vassals and fighting men as he could. When he captured an enemy's castle, he would give it to another vassal who could help him in war. There was thus a constant temptation to fight. The lord's men welcomed fighting because it relieved the dullness of life in the castle. They would not remain loyal unless he gave them a chance for adventure and for getting plunder.

How people lived in the castle. — The lord and lady of a castle had many people to work for them. When the lord

EARLY FIREPLACE WITHOUT A CHIMNEY
From the hall at Penshurst in Kent. A fireplace like this was in the center of the great hall in the houses of many lords.

was tired of salted meat, he could send his men into the forest to hunt deer, hares, wild boars, and wild fowl. The savory venison roasting over the large fireplace, the swans and ducks and geese turning on their spits over the coals (picture, p. 196), must have been very tempting to the appetite. He could have warm fires in the winter because his villeins would cut the wood. There were, however, few chimneys to carry away the smoke, even in castles, until the latter part of the Middle Ages. Before chimneys were made, the clothes of the lord and his guests must often have had the odor of smoked hams.

The lord and lady and their many guests did not need so

much heat as we have to-day. Wool was cheap then, and people wore the heaviest woolen clothing. They also had deerskins for covering, and lambskins in place of furs. There were plenty of feathers of ducks and geese for the beds. In very cold weather people sometimes slept between feather beds.

Only the lord's family and his special guests enjoyed these comforts. When enemies appeared and besieged the castle, life was very uncomfortable. The castle was then crowded, because the field workers came in for protection. Food was given out sparingly for fear it would not last.

How the sons of knights were educated. — When boys of the upper class were about seven years old, they might be sent to the castle of some high lord to be educated to become knights, as the well-trained noble warriors were called. These youths remained in the castle until they were young men. Their presence made the castle more interesting. Many castles were schools of chivalry. This means that they taught the boys to be polite, to serve the nobles, to have the right kind of manners for every occasion, to ride a horse, and to fight in armor.

1. *The page.* — From the age of seven to fourteen or fifteen, the boy was a page. He waited at first on the ladies and learned politeness and manners. Next he waited on the table of the lord and lady and their guests. The page was specially taught to honor women. Chivalry helped the world in its progress by raising women to a position of greater honor than they had ever before held.

2. *The squire.* — After the boy had learned good manners and had become strong enough, he was made a squire. The squire continued to be chivalrous to women and to

serve them, but he waited more specially on his lord. He cleaned the lord's armor and saw that his horses were

A SQUIRE
From an early manuscript copy of Chaucer's *Canterbury Tales.*

kept in good condition. The squire also learned how to ride and how best to use his armor, sword, and spear. He went with his lord to battle, ready to replace a broken spear or a crippled horse. War was the great business of the feudal age, and the squire learned how to fight.

3. *The knight.* — The next step was knighthood. None could become a knight unless he was approved for knighthood by another knight. The knight had to take an

oath to defend the church, to protect women, and to fight for his country and for his brother knights. The English poet Alfred Tennyson tells in his *Idylls of the King* how King Arthur made his knights swear:

> To break the heathen and uphold the Christ,
> To ride abroad redressing human wrongs,
> To speak no slander, no, nor listen to it,
> To honor his own word as if his God's,
> To lead sweet lives in purest chastity,
> To love one maiden only, cleave to her,
> And worship her by years of noble deeds
> Until they won her.

The knight was an important person during the Crusades (p. 216) and afterwards until the fourteenth century, when warfare was much changed by the introduction of firearms. The time when knighthood flourished was called the Age of Chivalry. Schools and churches are to-day trying to teach the new spirit of chivalry, which means courtesy, kindliness, and helpfulness in everyday life. Modern chivalry applies as much to girls as to boys, for it means service to all classes. The old-time knight thought that he was chivalrous if he was kind to his equals and superiors. He took good care of a knight captured in battle, but he often rode his horse over wounded peasants.

Tournaments, or mimic war. — Tournaments were as much liked in the Feudal Age as football games are to-day. Tournaments were more dangerous because the knights who took part in them were more often killed or crippled. A tournament meant playing the game of war of the Feudal Age. During the Crusades, knights often practiced holding their spears in position while they ran their horses toward a dummy dressed like a Mohammedan. The object was to strike the dummy squarely between the eyes. The figure was suspended in such a way that if it was struck elsewhere it would turn and strike the knight a blow.

When the knight thought himself skillful enough, he might challenge another knight to meet him in a tournament. We should read chapters VII, VIII, and XII of Sir Walter Scott's *Ivanhoe* to catch the spirit of a tournament. He shows the throngs coming to see it, like crowds to a modern football game. We hear the trumpets blow and see five English knights gallop their horses toward their Norman opponents. A moment later four Normans are rolling on the turf. Their spears did not strike the shields of their opponents firmly in the center. Two knights then enter the lists and dash at each other like thunderbolts.

Each has his lance splintered.   Both horses are thrown back on their haunches, but both skilled knights keep their seats.

KNIGHTS JOUSTING IN A TOURNAMENT

Redrawn from the Louterell Psalter, a fourteenth-century manuscript.   Notice the elaborate suits of armor worn by the knights, the shields held in the left hand, and the long spears used as weapons.

Last comes the most exciting contest between two companies of knights.   When the armor-clad men and horses dash against each other in the center of the field, the crash is heard a mile's distance.

If poor students have skill enough, they may in these times play on a football team.   In the Feudal Age only a knight could take part in a tournament.

What we should remember about the feudal system. — 1. The feudal system was a system of landholding by which a vassal received land and protection of a lord in return for service.

2. The feudal system was also a kind of government — a way of keeping order in a disorderly world.

3. Wars between rival lords led to the building of castles.

4. Chivalry taught the knights to be courteous and helpful to the men and women of their own rank.

5. Chivalry, which was first taught in the castle, has come now to mean courtesy toward all kinds of people.

Things to do. — Compare our way of holding land with that of the feudal system.

Imagine yourself to be a small landowner of the Middle Ages and tell why you like or dislike the feudal system.

Collect pictures of castles.

Construct a castle on the sand table. Show the moat, the drawbridge, the wall, the courtyard, and the keep.

Collect or draw pictures of knights in armor.

Imagine yourself to be a boy in training in a castle. Write three letters to your mother: in the first, tell her about your training as a page; in the second, of your training as a squire; and in the third, of your activities as a knight.

Read and tell to the class the story of Gareth, one of King Arthur's knights. (See Lanier, *The Boy's King Arthur*.)

Ask your teacher to read to you the description of the knight and the squire in the *Canterbury Pilgrims* by Katharine Lee Bates.

Read Tennyson's poem *Sir Galahad*, and learn its first stanza.

References for Teachers. — Munro, *Middle Ages*, XXVI ("The Nobles"); Bateson, *Medieval England*, VIII, XIII, XIV; Davis, W. S., *Life on a Medieval Barony;* Harding, *New Medieval and Modern History*, 160–168; Cheyney, *Readings in English History*, 131–136; Robinson, *Readings in European History*, Vol. I, pp. 399–405; Seignobos, *History of Medieval and Modern Civilization*, VI; Adams, G. B., *Civilization in the Middle Ages*, IX; Thorndike, *Medieval Europe*, XIII; *Encylopædia Britannica*, articles "Castle," "Feudalism."

For Pupils. — Tappan, *When Knights Were Bold;* Tappan, *European Hero Stories*, XXIII; Van Loon, *Story of Mankind*, 155–161; Harding, *Story of the Middle Ages*, XIV, XIX (feudalism, life of the castle); Dale, *Landmarks of British History*, 88–107; Creighton, *Heroes of European History*, 99–105; Stein, *Troubadour Tales* (fiction); Pyle, *Otto of the Silver Hand* (fiction); Scott, *Ivanhoe*, VII–XII (description of a tournament).

CHAPTER XVI

HOW THE COMMON PEOPLE LIVED

For a long time the principal classes of people were priests, lords and knights, and peasants (p. 220). Lords and knights and churchmen of high rank, such as bishops, were together called the upper class. This upper class has always formed a small part of the people.

How the villeins lived. — The largest class was the peasants, who tilled the soil on the estates of the lords, high churchmen, and monasteries. They were called *villeins* from *vil* (Latin *villa*), which means a country manor or estate. "Villein" meant at first simply a rustic or worker in the country.

The villein, like the fences, belonged to the land, and he could be sold with it. He had, however, risen a step above

VILLEINS PLOWING

From the Louterell Psalter, a fourteenth-century manuscript book.

slavery. His lord could not sell him apart from the estate. The villeins had for many years held strips of land, including from ten to thirty acres, on which to raise their

VILLEINS BREAKING CLODS

From the fourteenth-century Louterell Psalter. Note that one of these workers is a woman. Women generally worked in the fields with the men.

food. The force of custom was so great in England that the lords dared not take this land away from them. For the privilege of its use, the villeins had to work nearly half their time on the lord's land, and they also had to give him part of their produce. The villein was not completely a slave but he was not free. He and his children after him were forced to remain in this same unfree condition on the lord's estate. The villeins were really of great importance in the feudal system, for they made it possible for the lords and knights to live and fight. They cultivated the land and raised food for the lord and his fighting men. The lords and knights, however, thought that work was disgraceful; hence they gave a bad meaning to the word *villein*, which later came to be spelled *villain*.

The poor homes of the villeins made a little village near the castle or home of the lord for whom they worked. If there was war, the lord housed them in the outer courtyard of the castle. War fell most heavily on them, for their homes and crops were destroyed when their lord's castle was besieged. Lords were seldom killed in war because it was more profitable to capture them alive. If a lord was captured, he usually made his vassals pay a large ransom for his release. While the villeins were not expected to go to war, they were killed without mercy because no one would think of ransoming them.

The villeins usually lived in little one-story cottages made of sticks and mud and thatched with straw. They had no chimneys and no glass windows. If we could enter a villein's cottage, we should notice the smoke from the open wood fire finding its way out of a hole in the roof. We

A SMALL FARMER'S HOUSE WITH THATCHED ROOF

This house, on a Scottish island, is occupied to-day. It is much better than the houses of the villeins in the Middle Ages.

might stumble over a chicken, a duck, or a pig. As our eyes grew used to the smoke, we might see bacon hanging from poles, a pot for cooking, a window covered with oiled linen, a wooden trough for kneading bread, wooden cups, bowls, and plates, stools, a table on trestles, a straw mattress with a log for a pillow, the wife's spindle for flax and wool, and the villein's ax, sickle, and hoe.

A MEDIEVAL COUNTRY CART
Redrawn from the Louterell Psalter.

For company the villeins had the domestic animals, the cows, pigs, and chickens. Sometimes the friendly ducks and other fowl would pass the night with the family to escape being caught by wild animals.

The villeins had to work out of doors in rain and cold and heat. The manager of the lord's estate rose early and watched them plowing, manuring, planting, digging ditches, reaping, threshing, carting, cutting wood, and caring for the animals. Sometimes one villein might be the blacksmith for the castle, and another the carpenter, but most of them did all kinds of work.

How the villeins improved their condition. — There were two ways in which villeins might hope to better their condition. (1) If they could escape to a town and live there for a year and a day without being caught, they were free. (2) They might save enough from working their land to pay rent for it, and then be allowed to work entirely for themselves. The lord could then use the rent money for hiring labor. Both lord and villein would get more in this way. It took the lords a long time to learn that a free worker for wages would do more work and be more profitable. Learning this lesson was a great step forward in human history.

Why the struggle for better conditions was hard. — An Asiatic plague, called the Black Death, killed about half of the population of England (1349). There were then fewer workers, and wages rose fifty per cent for men. But the English Parliament, made up of landowners, passed a law that all laborers should work for the same wages as were paid before the Black Death. Another law ordered that no boys or girls who had worked on the land before they were twelve years old should leave it for any other occupation.

These laws were only partly successful. Wages rose in spite of them, but they would probably have risen much higher if no laws had been made. Attempts to enforce these laws made the laborers so angry that they rose against the nobles in what is called the Peasants' Revolt (1381). When a certain villein was taken prisoner, his lord promised to save his life if he would persuade his comrades to disperse; but the villein, a true hero, replied: " If I die for the cause of liberty, I shall think myself happy to end my life as a martyr."

The Peasants' Revolt was put down and seemed at the time to be a failure, but in the long run it had its effect in bringing villeinage to an end. More and more lords accepted rent, sometimes seven pence an acre, in place of labor service. By the time America was discovered, there was not much villeinage in England. When the descendants of many of these villeins settled later in America, they came as free men. In France, however, there were villeins or serfs as late as the French Revolution (1789).

Villages and towns. — " Village " means a small settlement of a few houses. The villeins lived in villages, usually near a castle or a lord's house. These villages seldom had more than one street. From fifty to one hundred and fifty or more people lived in them, according to the size of the estate on which they worked. A " town " or " city " was larger, and was the home of people many of whom did not work on the land. Towns often sprang from growing villages that were well situated for trade, usually on a river or a harbor.

How trade caused the growth of towns. — In the early part of the Middle Ages there were few towns. The Teutonic conquerors of the Roman Empire did not like towns. They preferred to live in the country. In England they destroyed the Roman towns.

Gradually the Teutons developed a desire for things which they did not produce on their own land, such as jewelry, silks, fine woolen cloths, and many things made from metals. They also often wished to sell the produce of their land and buy produce of a different kind from the lands of other lords. Because of these wishes, centers of trade and manufacturing sprang up and were called *towns*.

The work of English craftsmen. — Let us imagine ourselves taking a walk in an English town in the thirteenth century. We notice the shops of many craftsmen. A craftsman is one who lives by his craft or skill. We see four signs on adjoining houses: R. Bladesmith, J. Locksmith, J. Wainsmith, and W. Arrowsmith. The men who practice the craft of " smith," in making knives, locks, wagons, and arrows, live on the same street. We find that those of the same craft in any trade live side by side, each working in his little shop and selling his own goods. We see such streets as Bread Street, Wine Street, Goldsmith's Lane, Tanners Row, Fleshmarket. The craftsmen are very friendly and call each other " brother."

Blacksmith

Potter

MEDIEVAL CRAFTSMEN
Redrawn from contemporary drawings.

In a goldsmith's shop we watch the gold melted, mixed
with alloy, and poured into molds for rings, which are
polished when they are cold. In another goldsmith's shop
we see a man making a string of beads for a rosary out of
a piece of amber. While he is at work, a buyer enters and
buys a rosary of white amber joined with silver rings.

We see a whole street of workers in wool. Men are
combing the fibers out straight. A woman spins them into
yarn. A man weaves the yarn into cloth. We wonder
what is the matter with another man's arms until we see
him plunge them up to his elbows in a red dye and pull out a
piece of cloth. His name is John the Dyer. The grease is
removed from the cloth with fuller's earth, and we know
where the " Fullers " got their name. A man next walks
up and down on the cloth in a trough of soapy water. His
name is Thomas Walker. When we see a shearman clipping
the nap of the cloth to make it smooth, we wonder if he
gave his name to the " Shermans. " As we look at other
signs, we know where the Potters, Tanners, Taylors, Turn-
ers, Carpenters, Coopers, Shoemakers, Weavers, and Masons
got their names. We feel that they ought to be proud
to trace their descent from such wonderful craftsmen.

Tailor   Shoemaker

MEDIEVAL CRAFTSMEN
Redrawn from contemporary drawings.

Perhaps we think that the Smiths ought to be proudest of all because they did skillful work that few to-day can equal.

We see in the shops boys who must work for seven years as apprentices to learn the craft. They then become " journeymen " for a time before they can be masters.

The work of the guilds. — Craftsmen made things to sell. They could not have earned their living by their crafts if trade had not increased. Increase of trade made it necessary for some one to see that buying, selling, and making things were carried on fairly. The merchants and craftsmen had societies, called guilds, to do this. A merchants' guild would get the right to carry on the trade in one town and for a certain distance outside its walls. Any profit made from a good bargain by one member of the merchant guild was shared by all the members. Each craft guild would get the right to make the particular thing produced by that craft. For instance, the guild of tanners in each town had the sole right to make leather in that town.

The first purpose of the guilds was to have things well made. Leicester (lĕs'ter), England, had a reputation for making good cloth. The weavers were distressed to find (1377) that some cloth was woven out of bad yarn. The mayor summoned all the weavers and they decided to fine " William Martin with the Bald Head and James French " for weaving bad cloth.   The guilds had regular searchers or

THE GAME OF BOB APPLE

Redrawn from a fourteenth-century manuscript.
The game was to see how much the men could get
at one bite.

inspectors of the things which each craft made. They fixed wages, the time of apprenticeship, and the number of apprentices.   They helped members that were sick or in need.   They built beautiful Gothic guild-halls where they ate together and played games and grew more social.

The guilds in certain English towns (York, Coventry, Chester) took pride in giving plays that are known as Mystery or Miracle Plays.   They presented the chief miracles in the Scriptures, beginning with the Creation.   Each guild selected its best actors to give its play.   The craftsmen showed much humor in choosing plays for special guilds. They gave to the carpenters the building of the ark.   The fishmongers and mariners played the part of Noah in the ark with his family and the animals.   The bakers gave the last supper; the butchers, the Crucifixion.   The guilds in York gave forty-eight plays, beginning with the Creation.

How goods were sold. — English towns had, and still have, market days once a week.   The markets usually sold goods produced in the vicinity.

A number of towns in England had fairs every year, lasting a week or more. Things of all kinds, many brought from foreign countries, were offered at these fairs. Every measure and weight was tested before the fair opened, — pints, quarts, gallons, pounds, and cloth yards. If a baker,

A DISHONEST LONDON BAKER

Redrawn from a thirteenth-century manuscript in the London Guildhall. The baker is being drawn to the pillory with a short-weight loaf tied to his neck.

for instance, sold a loaf of bread underweight, he might be dragged on hurdles through the town with the loaf tied to his neck.

If we had walked around the fair, we might have seen a man fastened in the pillory. This was made of adjustable boards or planks to inclose the neck and sometimes also the hands of a culprit. The pillory had " Forestaller and regratter of markets and fairs and victuals " written above it. The man in the pillory, we might be told, had waited at the river to buy all the fish that the fishermen had caught. Then he had sold them for more than the fishermen would have charged. He was called a " forestaller." The people of the Middle Ages thought it was dishonest for him to get an extra profit because he had bought up all the fish. A " regratter " was a man who bought things in one part of the fair and sold them at a higher price in another part of the same fair.

Every nation and every age has had its problem of how to obtain honest products at honest prices. As late as the early part of the twentieth century, manufacturers in America were advertising " fruit " jellies that were made without fruit, and were selling " pure " pepper and spices mixed with flour or other things. A law was finally passed (1906) to end such dishonest labeling.

Health conditions in the towns. — The manager of a king's household bought at an English fair in 1300 one

EARLY ENGLISH JUGGLERS

Redrawn from a thirteenth-century manuscript. Jugglers often joined the crowds on their way to tournaments or at country fairs and received coins for amusing the people.

hundred and twenty towels. Think what an advance in cleanliness this showed over the single towel on one of Charlemagne's estates (p. 164). In 1319 the best inn-keeper in a certain English town was known to have two towels and two tablecloths.

Towns were usually inclosed by stone walls for protection (picture, p. 199). London had a wall twenty-two feet high built around it on all sides except the river front. The walls cost much to build, and space inside the city was precious. The streets were narrow; in some of the old cities in England, like York, the people in the upper stories could almost shake hands across the street. The houses were as a rule so crowded that it was hard to keep the cities clean. Plagues often broke out in them and killed large numbers. For a long time cities had no means of cleaning the streets except by rain and the work of crows, other birds, and pigs.

The people of the Middle Ages knew nothing about germs and little about the causes of disease. The dyers and walkers (p. 238) poured their waste water out of their front doors. The butcher threw anything that he chose into the street. "Dirt is healthy" was a common saying. However, more than a hundred years before Columbus discovered America, the English Parliament forbade refuse to be thrown in front of the doors in certain cities, and ordered that pigs should no longer be allowed in the streets.

The rise of the middle class. — The rise of the middle class is one of the important facts of the Middle Ages. The " middle class " was mostly the craftsmen (p. 237) and the merchants who made their living from buying and selling things at home and abroad. Villeins who had been freed often came to towns, learned a craft, and belonged to the middle class. Craftsmen and traders gradually became the most influential men in the town. The rise of the middle class added a fourth class to the three named on page 220.

The towns and the middle class grew (1) because there was a chance to gain wealth through trade, and (2) because the towns became free.

How towns became free. — In the beginning a town, like a village, was under the feudal government of some lord.

A GLIMPSE OF LONDON ABOUT 1480

From a fifteenth-century French manuscript of poems by Charles, Duke of Orleans. The building at the right is the Tower of London, where many famous prisoners have been held, among them the Duke of Orleans, the author of this manuscript. He is shown here seated at a table, writing. The French words under the picture mean: "Tidings from England, if it pleases you to hear, my brother and my companion."

Trade brought the townspeople wealth. The king or lord who controlled the town was sure at some time to need money. The town would give it in return for certain rights. Three rights that towns specially wanted were: (1) the right to collect a reasonable tax or fixed sum themselves instead of having the king's sheriff come and take an unreasonable amount, (2) the right to elect their own officers, (3) the right to have their own courts of law. Sometimes towns would want other special privileges for which they were willing to pay. A good time for towns to buy freedom and privileges was when king and lords wished to raise money for the Crusades.

By the end of the Middle Ages most English towns had a large share of freedom. Other countries in Europe, such as Italy, France, the Netherlands, and Germany, also had many free towns.

We must look back to the English towns for the foundation of some of our liberties in the United States. Colonists who came to America from these towns had taken part in local government. We may find the background of New World self-government in those Old World towns that enjoyed it before nations as a whole knew what it was.

Things to remember about the common people of the Middle Ages. — 1. The unfree villeins formed the largest class in the Middle Ages.

2. The work of the villeins made it possible for the lords and their vassals to live and fight.

3. The lords finally found that free labor was more profitable and allowed their villeins to pay them rent instead of service.

4. Trade led to the growth of towns.

5. The towns were the homes of merchants and craftsmen.

6. Merchants and craftsmen formed guilds to see that work was well done and to protect themselves from competition.

7. Towns in the Middle Ages were dirty and unhealthful because the people knew little about the causes of disease.

8. The rise of the middle class was very important.

9. The wealth from trade enabled the towns to buy their freedom to manage their own affairs.

Things to do. — Imagine yourself to be a villein. Compare your life and your home with those of your lord. (See Chapter XV.)

Give reasons why the labor of a free man would be more profitable to the lord than that of a villein. What did the lords accept in place of the forced labor of the villeins?

Write a short dialogue between two members of different crafts in the Middle Ages, having each explain his own craft to the other.

Talk for three minutes on the subject, "The Source of Some of Our Common Surnames." Get additional help from O'Neill's *Stories That Words Tell Us*.

Show how the guild protected buyers and craftsmen.

Find out how the measures used in the markets of your city are tested to see if they are honest.

Talk to the class on some of the differences between your city and a medieval town.

References for Teachers. — Munro, *Middle Ages*, XXVIII, XXIX; Bateson, *Medieval England*, V, VI; Cheyney, *Industrial and Social History of England*, II–V; Gibbins, *Industry in England*, V–XIII; Traill and Mann, *Social England*, Vol. II; Waters, *School Economic History of England* (villeins, villages, towns, guilds, trade, decay of villeinage); *Piers Plowman Social and Economic Histories*, Books II and III (village life, merchants, market days and fairs, industry, internal trade); Green, *Town Life in the Fifteenth Century;* Davis, *Life on a Medieval Barony*, XVI, XXI, XXII; Zimmern, *Hansa Towns;* Harding, *New Medieval and Modern History*, 169–182; Thorndike, *Medieval History*, XVII; Robinson, *History of Western Europe*, XVIII; Pollard, *English Miracle Plays*.

For Pupils. — Van Loon, *Story of Mankind*, 174–197 (medieval city, life, and government); Harding, *Story of the Middle Ages*, XX, XXI; Tappan, *European Hero Stories*, XXV; Tappan, *When Knights Were Bold;* Dutton, *Little Stories of Germany*, 72–78 (a medieval town).

CHAPTER XVII

CHANGES IN THE OLD WORLD LEADING TO THE DISCOVERY OF THE NEW

How wants come. — We have seen in the preceding chapter how trade grew in England. The townspeople saw more things and wanted more than the people living in small villages. To see is often to want.

Knowledge brings wants. If we had never seen or heard of an automobile, we should not know enough to want one. Negroes who have not left their homes in Central Africa could not know what to want in cities. Neither could the European toilers who had never left the country estates on which they worked. If the people of the Middle Ages had not learned what the East had to offer, they could not have been interested in the trade with the East, which led to the discovery of America.

How the Crusades taught Europeans to want things. — Tens of thousands of Europeans went to Asia Minor and the Holy Land in the Crusades (p. 216). Most of them had never before been outside their own neighborhood. They saw for the first time such wonderful cities as Ven′ice and Constantinople, and many things, new to them, which the people enjoyed.

During the Crusades many Europeans settled in Syria, north of the Holy Land, and engaged in trade. They sent ships to Europe loaded with carpets, rugs, silks, fine cloth,

AN ARMY OF CRUSADERS

pepper, ginger, cloves, nutmegs, sugar, citron, figs, melons, steel mirrors, glass, and vases. Thus trade grew between the East and Europe.

What the Arabs taught Europe. — When the Crusaders reached the Holy Land, they found that the Arabs were more civilized in many ways than the Europeans. They were surprised to find that the Arabs could teach them many valuable things. We have already seen (p. 203) that the Arabs gave to Europe the figures that we use to-day, and some common words.

The Arabs taught the Crusaders the use of baths. European Christians in the Middle Ages did not take frequent baths. An eastern traveler astonished Europe with the story of a city that had three thousand baths. In the second century of the Crusades a town crier might have been heard at dawn in Paris calling: "The water is hot and the baths are open." It took the Christians a long time to form the habit of bathing, but the example of the Arabs during the two hundred years of the Crusades had its effect.

Europeans learned also to replace the filthy rushes on their floors with eastern rugs and carpets. They bought soft cloth made of camel's hair in place of coarse European woolens which scratched almost like briers. Pretty yellow, red, and blue dyes were brought from the East. People became interested in making their dress and homes more pleasing. Europeans also began to take more care in the preparation of their meals. Their food could be seasoned with eastern pepper, ginger, and nutmegs.

How the Crusades hastened the discovery of America. — The Crusades are important in American history for two reasons :

(1) They showed Europeans new things from the East which people liked and wanted. As we shall see in the next chapter, America was discovered in an effort to find a new trade route to the East.

(2) The Crusades caused Europeans to build better and larger ships. The vessels of all nations came to rely more and more on sails. Galley slaves, often more than a hundred of them

VESSEL ROWED BY GALLEY SLAVES

in one ship, chained to their seats, had for hundreds of years rowed vessels in the Mediterranean. Straining all day and often all night at heavy oars was a cruel task.

An overseer whipped the men to keep them at work even when they were tired or sick. Sails were used at first only when the wind came from nearly astern. Gradually, however, the shape of the sails and the way of using them were so improved that if the wind came from the north, the vessel could sail either east or west as well as south. It could even sail first northwest and then northeast and so make progress toward the north. America was discovered by the use of sailing ships.

Trade between nations. — The latter part of the Middle Ages saw more trade between nations. Venice was sending each year to London two ships loaded with goods from the East. People were more anxious to get them after the Crusades. The Hanseatic (hăn-sē-ăt′ĭc) League was a union of towns, mostly in Germany, that wished to sell goods abroad. It had warships to protect its trading vessels from pirates, and to compel nations to treat it fairly. This League had one of its depots for goods in London.

Trade routes from the East. — Goods from the East usually reached Europe by way of three chief trade routes. The northern route began in China, joined with one from India, continued overland to the Black Sea, and ended at Constantinople. The middle one led from India to the port of Antioch (ăn′tĭ-ŏk) in Syria on the eastern shore of the Mediterranean. The southern one came from the Spice Islands and India. This route was mostly by water, through part of the Indian Ocean and up the Red Sea. As there was no Suez Canal, the goods were taken by land to the Nile River, thence by water to the Mediterranean Sea.

The Mediterranean was very important in Old World

history. After the goods reached the shore of that sea or a body of water flowing into it, they were taken in ships, usually to Venice or Genoa (jĕn'ō-a). These two cities distributed the goods to buyers in various countries.

All the goods from the Far East were carried part of the way on the backs of animals. The increase in wants caused a greater demand for eastern goods than could be brought over the old trade routes. The Turks shut off the northern route by the capture of Constantinople (1453). Even if they had not interfered, men would soon have sought for some other way of bringing more goods from the Far East.

The Revival of Learning. — The desire for a better way of bringing things from the East did not mean that the way would be found at once. More knowledge was necessary before that could be accomplished. The movement which history calls the "Revival of Learning" began in Italy in a feeble way as early as 1250. It worked slowly westward and it is shown at its height in Shakespeare's work in the sixteenth century.

The teaching and the writings of the Middle Ages dealt mostly with religion and the life to come. An increasing number of people, however, were seeking for joy in this life as well as in the next. They wished more interesting books to read, and they wanted wider knowledge.

We are especially interested in two facts about the Revival of Learning: (1) It helped to make possible the discovery of America. (2) We are still using the results of its advance in knowledge which our ancestors brought to our country.

What Roger Bacon did for science. — Roger Bacon (1214–1294) was an English priest who became a famous scientist. He showed the new spirit which helped to bring in the age of the Revival of Learning.

In the Middle Ages people commonly believed whatever was said by men of authority. If such a man had said that a certain bird hatched butterflies, most people would have believed him. Roger Bacon would have wanted to see the bird, the eggs, and the hatching. He would thus have shown the way in which future ages would study science.

Bacon was a scientist because he tried to learn the laws of nature from his own experiments and observation and not from what others told him. Bacon experimented with a mixture of saltpeter, charcoal, and sulphur. The explosion which followed made those who saw it believe that he was in league with Satan. He was, however, merely trying to learn by experiment what was the right proportion of those articles to make the best gunpowder. Gunpowder had been made before, but Bacon left the first written recipe for making it, after he had experimented with it.

Roger Bacon was put in prison partly because people did not understand his experiments and did not approve of them. His kind of work in our times would bring a man honor and rewards.

Why the progress of science was delayed. — The feeling that it was not wise to pry into God's mysteries, and the belief of the Middle Ages that anything unusual or hard to understand might be the work of the devil, hindered progress. An Italian who saw Roger Bacon experimenting with the mariner's compass, wrote home : " This discovery, so useful to all who travel by sea, must remain concealed until other times because no mariner dare use it, lest he fall under the imputation of being a magician, nor would sailors put to sea with one who carried an instrument so evidently constructed by the devil."

Universities. — The new desire for education brought about the founding of universities. When some teacher learned more about a subject than others knew, students would come from all over the country to hear him lecture.

© *Galloway*

MERTON COLLEGE, AT OXFORD

Oxford University is made up of a number of separate colleges, each with its own professors and group of students. Merton College is the oldest in the University.

Other well-known teachers might come to the same place and lecture on other subjects. Universities began in this way and increased in number. Before Columbus discovered America, there were many universities in western Europe, from Italy to England. Oxford and Cambridge (kăm′brĭj) universities in England were founded more than a hundred years before the discovery of America. They gave to the English colonists the idea of founding colleges in America.

The classics. — Men were eager for writings that dealt with this life and its interests. Such a literature was found in Grecian manuscripts that had been almost forgotten. Grecian literature was not widely known until Constantinople, the capital of the Eastern Roman Empire, was captured by the Turks (1453). Many men then fled from Constantinople to Italy, bringing Greek manuscripts. Italian students learned the Greek language and read Greek literature. They also began to read more of the great Roman authors.

The best writings of Greece and Rome were called the " classics." They were better literature than the Middle Ages had produced. The classics told of the joys of this life, of the beautiful things which one might see in nature. The Greek poet Homer in his *Iliad* and *Odyssey*, and the Roman poet Vergil in his *Æneid*, told exciting stories about the adventures of gods and heroes, — about Jupiter, Mars, and Apollo, and about Ulysses and Æneas.

How the reading of the classics affected literature. — Whole books have been written to show how the myths of Greece and Rome affected English literature. Our American poet Longfellow read the stories in Homer's epic poems, the *Iliad* and the *Odyssey*. He knew the Greek myths and Æsop's *Fables*. They taught him how to weave from American materials the story that he has given us in his epic *Hiawatha*.

All our great writers studied the classics. Nathaniel Hawthorne, one of our great prose writers, has in his *Wonder Book* retold Greek stories, such as " The Golden Touch." From a translation of Æsop's *Fables*, Abraham Lincoln learned how to tell a story and make an argument in a few words to drive home his point.

The revival of art. — Some of the world's greatest artists did their work under the stimulus of the Revival of Learning. Three who were born in the last half of the fifteenth century, before Columbus discovered America, were Raphael (răf′a-ĕl), Leonar′do da Vinci (vēn′chē), and Michelan′gelo.

One of Raphael's great paintings is the Sistine (sĭs′tēn) Madonna (p. 257). Da Vinci painted a famous portrait that is called "Mona Lisa." Michelangelo was painter, sculptor, and architect. His frescoes (paintings on plaster) on the ceiling of the Sistine Chapel in Rome, and his statues of "The Thinker," "Night," and "Day" in Flor-

"THE THINKER," BY MICHELANGELO

This statue really represents Lorenzo de' Medici, Prince of Florence, and is part of the sculpture on his tomb. "The Thinker," however, is the name by which the statue is commonly known.

ence, are masterpieces. As an architect he helped build the Church of St. Peter in Rome, one of the greatest structures in the world.

The work of these men and of other great artists of that time continue to influence our country. American painters, sculptors, and architects go abroad to study the masterpieces of the fifteenth and sixteenth centuries. We may find copies of some of these statues and paintings in our schools and art stores.

How the first modern school was managed. — Our schools to-day owe a debt to Vittorino da Feltre (vēt-tŏ-rē'nō dä fĕl'trä), the first modern schoolmaster. " Da Feltre " means "from Feltre," which is a little hill town in northern Italy. We may learn much about the new education from knowing how he taught. The modern school which he founded (1423) at Man'tua in northern Italy showed the

influence of the Revival of Learning. He called his school building "Pleasant House." It was large and airy and decorated with beautiful frescoes. Everything around was beautiful. Most of the teachers of the Middle Ages had taught in ugly surroundings, for fear that anything pleasant would take the minds of pupils away from their tasks.

CORPORAL PUNISHMENT IN A MEDIEVAL SCHOOL

From a fourteenth-century manuscript. The head master is wielding a bundle of birches while his assistant holds the boy. Such aid to learning was much used.

Vittorino taught Greek culture in two ways : (1) He had his pupils learn the Greek language and translate Greek classics. (2) He knew that athletics and healthy bodies were just as much a demand of Greek culture as anything else. He used the meadow around the school as a playground. He made the pupils play games to keep healthy just as much as he made them study. When he found

THE SISTINE MADONNA

Painted by Raphael in 1518 for the Benedictine monks at Piacenza, Italy, for their church of San Sisto. (Hence the name Sistine.) Since 1754, however, this painting has hung in the Dresden Gallery, Germany.

two boys bent over a book outside of study hours, he ordered them to the meadow to join in the games, which might be riding, running, jumping, or playing ball. He was wiry and active and walked long distances with his pupils.

Vittorino's aim was threefold: to train the mind, the body, and the character. He used both study and play to develop character, and taught his pupils never to cheat in the schoolroom or on the playground. Character with him as with George Washington in later times meant doing the right thing one hundred times out of one hundred.

Vittorino thought clearness of speech was necessary in all business with one's fellow men. He had the pupils recite passages from the classics or read aloud every day to show whether they understood what they were reading. He would not allow his pupils to talk in a loud tone, which he found unnecessary if they spoke distinctly.

Drawing, surveying, arithmetic, and science were modern subjects taught by Vittorino. Latin also was carefully taught, because it was then the common tongue of the educated world. The service of the church could not be understood unless one knew Latin. Authors had their books printed in Latin so that men in all lands might read them.

How printing helped to distribute knowledge. — It is hard to think of anything that has had greater influence on education than printing. A hundred years before the invention of printing, a copy of the Bible, in manuscript, cost about as much as $300 would buy to-day. A short time before the printing press was started, an amount equal to the wages of a workman for 266 days was paid for a manuscript copy of the Bible. When a wealthy book lover in Florence, Italy, wished a library, he sent for a book contractor, who secured forty-five copyists. By working hard for nearly two years, they copied in handwriting two hundred volumes. If these copyists could see a newspaper printed in a fraction of a second, might they not think that the printers were using magic?

We do not know the name of the man who invented printing, nor the exact year when a book was first printed. Probably Holland should have the credit for printing the first European book with movable metal type. The art of printing was developed between 1440 and 1450. The city of Mainz (mīnts) in Germany was an early center of printing, from which the art spread over Europe.

A FIFTEENTH-CENTURY WRITER

From an old tapestry. Note the book which he may have copied, also pen case and ink bottle on the table. Drawings showing an early use of spectacles are rare. Spectacles had been used some time before the invention of printing, but they were valuable enough for a man to make special mention of them in his will when he left them to a monk.

Fifteen years before Columbus discovered America, William Caxton, the first English printer, began to print books in London. The most famous book that he printed was Chaucer's *Canterbury Tales* (p. 200). Caxton's work has been considered so important for the English people that collectors have paid as much as $10,000 for a book printed by him and once sold for a few shillings.

The mariner's compass. — Our ancestors brought with them to America five of the most valuable discoveries or inventions that the world had made. Four of these were the use of fire (p. 4), alphabetical writing (p. 47), Arabic numerals (p. 203), and the art of printing. The fifth was an aid to sailors.

No ship could have safely sailed thousands of miles out of sight of land unless she had something to show the direction of her course in storm and fog and cloudy weather. The instrument which answered this need is known as the mariner's compass. We do not know who first found that a piece of iron or a needle that has been touched by a lodestone will point in a nearly north and south direction if placed on a floating cork. It must have been a long time after this fact was known before such knowledge was applied in sailing ships. We know that many sailors had proved the worth of the mariner's compass before America was discovered.

EARLY MARINER'S COMPASS

Notice the needle in the center. The chief directions are indicated by names of winds: Levante (east), Sirocco (southeast), etc.

How the Portuguese explored the way to India. — Prince Henry of Portugal (1394–1460), known as the Navigator, was one of the great explorers to use the mariner's compass on long voyages. He was the son of an English mother and a Portuguese father. He had two very strong wishes: (1) to take the gospel of Christ to the heathen, (2) to explore the coast of Africa and, if possible, to find a sea route to India. If successful in this aim, he hoped to load his vessels with spices and other products of the East, and thus solve the problem of finding a better way of bringing such things to Europe.

Prince Henry went to live on the seashore near Cape St. Vincent, Portugal. Here he had sailors taught all that was known of geography and of sailing ships. He sent his sailors on voyage after voyage down the coast of Africa and studied the accounts of what they found. For a long time they feared to go as far south as the equator because they had been told that the ocean boiled there. But Prince Henry, like Roger Bacon (p. 252), believed in testing the truth of such stories by experiment. The Portuguese sailors, encouraged by him, kept up their voyages and safely crossed the equator (1470), ten years after Prince Henry's death.

Seventeen years later, Bartholomew Diaz (dē'äs) discovered the Cape of Good Hope (1487) and the ocean beyond. Vasco da Gama (väs'kō dä gä'mä) continued his voyage beyond the Cape of Good Hope and reached India (1497). He brought back enough spices to Portugal to astonish the world. This discovery changed the route of eastern commerce and solved the problem of bringing goods from the East in large quantities at a much lower cost. But meanwhile had come the great discovery made by Columbus, as we shall see in the next chapter.

Things to remember about changes which led to the discovery of America. — 1. Wants come because of knowledge of new things which we can use.

2. The Crusades caused people to want many new things which they saw in the East.

3. Increasing trade with foreign nations was a long step toward discovering America.

4. More knowledge was needed before long voyages to the East could be made by sea.

5. The age of the Revival of Learning developed knowledge and invention.

6. Some of the causes of progress in this age were: (1) Roger Bacon's teaching that science must be based on seeing things and experimenting with them, (2) the influence of Greek and Latin literature, (3) the revival of art, (4) better education, (5) invention of printing and the mariner's compass.

7. Prince Henry the Navigator's interest in discovery led to finding a sea route to India.

Things to do. — What wants do you and your family have that your great-grandfather did not have?

Be able to talk to the class for two minutes each on (1) What the Crusades taught people to want and (2) What the Arabs taught Europe.

Is it better for a city, a state, or a country to trade with others, or to produce everything that it wants and to buy nothing abroad?

Explain clearly to the class how Roger Bacon shows the new spirit in science and why the Middle Ages had not made more progress in science.

Have you noticed the influence of the Greeks in any books that you have read? What Greek myths do you know?

Collect pictures of buildings and paintings which belong to the period of the revival of art.

Be ready to talk for three minutes on the work of the first modern schoolmaster.

What rank among the great inventions would you give printing?

Be able to explain the mariner's compass and tell why it was needed for long voyages.

Give a short talk on the work and influence of Prince Henry the Navigator.

References for Teachers. — Munro, *Middle Ages*, XXIX, XXXI; Thorndike, *Medieval Europe*, XX, XXI, XXXI, XXXII; Seignobos, *History of Medieval and Modern Civilization*, XVII, XIX; Adams, *Civilization during the Middle Ages*, XII, XV; Harding, *New Medieval and Modern History*, XVI; Robinson, *History of Western Europe*, XIX, XXII; Zimmern, *Hansa Towns;* Gibbins, *History of Commerce in Europe*, 68–123; Day, *History of Commerce;* Elson, *Modern Times and the Living Past*, XXII; Woodward, *Vittorino da Feltre*, 1–92; Aldis, *The Printed Book;* Beazley, *Prince Henry the Navigator;* Gayley, *Classic Myths in English Literature and in Art; Encyclopædia Britannica*, articles on "Bacon, Roger," "Universities," "Printing," "Caxton," "Compass," "Renaissance," "Henry of Portugal," "Painting"; Reade, *The Cloister and the Hearth* (a novel giving a wonderful picture of medieval Europe in the fourteenth century).

For Pupils. — Van Loon, *Story of Mankind*, 206–229; Harding, *Story of the Middle Ages*, XXVIII; Tappan, *European Hero Stories*, 157–169; Terry, *Lord and Vassal* (History Stories of Other Lands), 115–117; Hale, *Stories of Invention*, 36–57; Holland, *Historic Inventions;* Haaren and Poland, *Famous Men of the Middle Ages*, 257–262; Piercy, *Great Inventions and Discoveries*, 15–29, 92–126; Fryer, *Book of Boyhoods* (Leonardo da Vinci); Holland, *Historic Boyhoods*, 21–34 (Michelangelo); Terry, *The New Liberty* (History Stories of Other Lands), 18–31.

CHAPTER XVIII

HOW THE NEW WORLD WAS DISCOVERED

How Columbus was educated. — Christopher Columbus was born about 1450 in the Italian city of Genoa, then one of the world's great trading seaports. He belonged to the middle class (p. 243), which was rising in importance and helping to make a modern world. His father was a weaver, and he sent the boy to a school which the weavers supported for their children. It is possible that Christopher went also for a short time to a university near Genoa, to study the sciences needed for sailing a vessel.

Astronomy was then a necessary study. From the position of the stars a sailor could tell the latitude and the direction in which the ship was sailing. Columbus, in order to fit himself to be a sea captain, also needed to know the instruments that aided in sailing a vessel. The most important of these were: (1) the mariner's compass, which told in what direction the vessel was sailing, even in fog or cloudiest night, and (2) the as'trolabe, an instrument for measuring the distance of the sun or of the North Star above the horizon. The latitude of the vessel could be told in this way. He did not have the instruments for telling longitude exactly; but he could make an estimate of the speed of his ship by tossing a chip overboard at the bow and noting how long it took to reach the stern. If he knew the longitude of the port of departure and about how far west he had gone each day, he knew something of his longitude.

In order to learn as much as possible about the sea, Columbus began at the age of fourteen to take trips in vessels sailing from Genoa. He made many voyages in the Mediterranean Sea and in the Atlantic Ocean. He went to Portugal, where he married the daughter of a governor of Porto Santo, one of the Madeira (ma-dē'ra) Islands. While he was living in Portugal, Columbus must have been told many stories of the sea by the sailors of Prince Henry the Navigator. In all these ways Columbus was educated for his great task.

A TERROR OF THE UNKNOWN SEA

From a thirteenth-century book of stories about beasts. The Latin begins: "There is a monster in the sea." The story, believed by some in the Middle Ages, is that a huge whale slept on the surface of the ocean until sand gathered on its back and shrubs grew there. Sailors, thinking they had found an island, would land on it to cook their food. The whale would awake and dive down into the sea, sinking ship and crew.

What idea did Columbus have of the world? — Columbus either learned from other sailors, or went far enough down the coast of Africa to find out for himself, that the heat near the equator did not melt the pitch between the planks of the vessel and allow the water to run in and sink the ship, as was commonly believed. He had read in a book that the torrid zone was so hot that it could not be inhabited. He wrote on the margin of that book: " I have seen inhabitants there." He saw none of the sea monsters reported to be so large and so hungry that they swallowed ships at a mouthful. Unlike ignorant men, Columbus had no fear of sailing over the edge of the ocean and dropping into bottomless space. Ancient Grecian men of learning had believed that the world is round. Columbus and educated people of his time had the same belief. The ignorant thought that if this were true, a man on the side of the world opposite them would have to walk like a fly on a ceiling, and that a ship would have to sail uphill to return.

Columbus and the men of his time believed the earth smaller than it really is, but they thought Asia larger than it is. If we draw a map to show their idea of the world between the west coast of Europe and the east coast of Asia, we must leave out America and place China where California is. The islands southeast of Asia would then be located where the West Indies are. The Atlantic Ocean would be shown washing the shores of both Europe and Asia. Columbus thought that Japan was only 4000 instead of 12,000 miles from Spain.

While the Portuguese were slowly sailing long distances down the coast of Africa (p. 261), Columbus believed that a western route to India and China would be shorter and more pleasant.

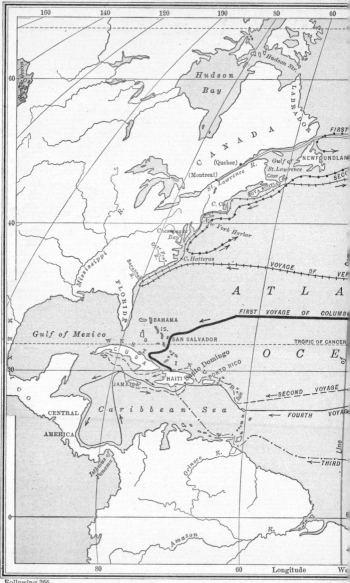

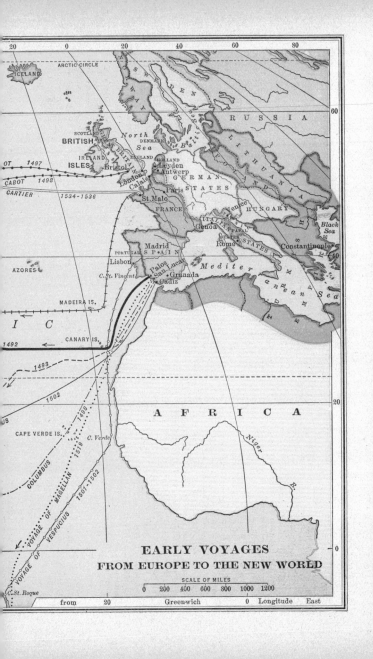

EARLY VOYAGES
FROM EUROPE TO THE NEW WORLD

SCALE OF MILES

0   200   400   600   800   1000 1200

from   20   Greenwich   0   Longitude   East

Others besides Columbus had dreamed of sailing around the world. Why do we consider Columbus the greatest of all sailors? It is because (1) he was the first to act on the belief that men could find the East by sailing west, and (2) his great voyage across the Atlantic led to the discovery and colonization of a New World, which soon began to change human history.

What kind of man was Columbus? — He had patience. Until he was more than forty years old, he tried first in Portugal, and next in Spain, to get some one to furnish him ships for his voyage across the ocean. He asked aid of Ferdinand, king of Spain, and especially of the queen, Isabella, who was partly of English descent. They turned Columbus over to a council headed by a priest. This body kept him waiting for four years and then decided against him.

CHRISTOPHER COLUMBUS

Painting in the Marine Museum, Madrid. This was probably painted in the nineteenth century, and based on imaginary likenesses found in early engravings. There are no portraits of Columbus painted during his lifetime.

Columbus had will power, determination. He was not easily discouraged. He kept on trying to get the ships and men for his voyage.

He had imagination. He could dream great dreams, and then work to make them come true. It is probable that nothing he ever read influenced the dreams and actions of Columbus more than the *Book of Marco Polo*. This tells of Marco Polo's travels in Asia and along its coasts; of buildings roofed with gold, of plentiful rubies and sapphires, of trees that bore enough spices to load ships. In this book Columbus read of the ocean that washed the shores of China, Japan, and the Spice Islands. He thought that this must be the Atlantic Ocean.

Columbus was religious. His first name, Christopher, means " Christ-bearer," and he wished to take the religion of Christ to the dwellers in the East. A recent historian says that the objects of Columbus as a discoverer were five: gold, religion, spices, Cipanzu (Japan), and Cathay (China). This author then adds that the *Journal* of Columbus mentions religion almost as much as gold.

Columbus was tall and had a handsome figure. He looked like an actor who could take a leading part in some great play. He was careful to wear becoming garments. He specially liked a scarlet robe and cap and yellow beads.

How Columbus secured his ships. — The king and queen of Spain would not then listen to Columbus because they were busy waging war to drive the Moors (p. 159) out of Spain. In January, 1492, the Moors were at last conquered, and Queen Isabella listened to Columbus. He told her that he wanted (1) three ships for his voyage, (2) the title of Admiral of the Ocean, (3) the position of governor of all lands discovered, (4) ten per cent of all gold, jewels, and spices found, and (5) the rank and privileges of a Spanish nobleman.

Isabella's advisers thought he wanted too much, and she at first declined to aid him. He left the court, but she soon sent a messenger after him, and the king and queen accepted his terms.

The town of Palos (pä'lōs) was ordered to furnish him ships and men. Criminals were released from jail to help man the ships. When enough seamen did not volunteer, a Palos sea captain of influence said to them: "Come with us, for according to accounts you will find the houses covered with roofs of gold, and you will return rich and prosperous."

Three little ships, the *Santa Maria* (sän'tä mä-rē'ä), the *Pinta* (pēn'tä), and the *Niña* (nēn'yä),

THE *SANTA MARIA*, THE FLAGSHIP OF COLUMBUS

were secured with eighty-eight men to sail them. One Irishman and one Englishman were among the number.

What Columbus discovered. — The first entry in the log of Columbus as the vessels started on the great voyage is: "In the name of our Master, Jesus Christ, Friday, August 3, 1492, at eight o'clock we started from the bar. We went with a strong sea breeze sixty miles." The *Santa Maria*, with Columbus on board, led the way. The ships stopped at the Canary Islands for repairs and then on September 6 headed due west.

The log tells us that on September 26 the ocean was covered with seaweed. This hindered the ships and scared the sailors, who feared that the seaweed would hold the vessels prisoners. They were more than a week struggling in this tangle.

The compass, instead of pointing a little to the east of

the North Star, as in Europe, one night pointed directly to the north and afterwards began to point a little to the west of it.   The sailors thought the sea bewitched.   As they sailed on, day after day, they came to the point of mutiny. Some wanted to shove Columbus overboard at night and then turn back.   His will power mastered them, and he forced them to sail on and on until October 12, 1492, the thirty-sixth day after leaving the Canaries, when he discovered land.   This day is now in more than half of the states a holiday, called Columbus Day.

Columbus named the island on which he first landed " San Salvador " and took possession of it in the name of Spain.   He thought that he had come to the Indies, or southeastern Asia, and so he gave the name of " Indians " to the people whom he found there.   The savages believed that the strangers had come down from the sky and that the ships were large sea birds.

While searching for the mainland of Asia, Columbus found Cuba and Haiti (hā′tĭ).   He tried in vain to have the Indians show him the land of gold of which Marco Polo had written.   One night the *Santa Maria*, his largest vessel, struck a reef and was wrecked.   Columbus had to leave half of his men, including the Englishman and the Irishman, on Haiti to form a colony.

Columbus reached Spain on his return voyage in March, 1493, and was received as a hero.   Ferdinand and Isabella had him sit as an equal in their presence.   The people were interested in the Indians, parrots, and strange animals that he brought with him.   Columbus became a famous man, for everybody believed he had reached Asia by sailing west.

Columbus made three more voyages to the west and

COLUMBUS AT HAITI

Redrawn from an engraving in a history published in 1601. The natives are offering gifts to Columbus. Some of his men are planting a cross.

explored the shores of the Caribbean Sea in trying to find India. He discovered Central America and the continent of South America (map following page 266).

He died (1506) without knowing that he had found a New World. He was neglected at the time of his death because Spain had not then profited much from his discovery. Meanwhile the new sea route leading east to India (p. 261) was bringing great wealth to Portugal.

Why the New World was called America. — In comparison with what Columbus did, he received very small returns.   Even the land which he discovered was not named after him.   It was called America from the name of Amer'icus Vespu'cius, an Italian in the service of Portugal. Americus explored the coast of Brazil, which was thought to be a new continent. It was not known at the time that Columbus had reached the same land. An early geographer suggested that this continent be called "America" after its supposed discoverer. The name was printed on the map of South America. Men got in the habit of calling this land America and later applied the name to North America also. But most of the people in the United States honor Columbus Day (p. 270), while few know who Americus Vespucius was.   Columbus is one of the very few men of all time whose name and work are known in every civilized land.

© *Keystone*

MONUMENT TO COLUMBUS

In Columbus Circle, at the southwest corner of Central Park, New York. There are few spots in America where more vehicles pass every day. This statue is decorated on Columbus Day, especially by Americans of Italian descent.

How England became interested in exploration. — After Columbus had made his great discovery, England became interested in the trade and wealth which might be gained from westward voyages to Asia. John Cabot, an Italian born in Genoa, afterward a citizen of Venice, was the first explorer to cross the Atlantic for England. For the same reason that Columbus went to Spain, Cabot went to Henry VII, king of England (reigned from 1485 to 1509), and asked to be sent on a voyage of discovery. The English king gave permission and promised rewards. Cabot started from Bristol in May, 1497, with one ship and a crew of eighteen men. He sailed west, and on June 24 saw land in the New World, perhaps Nova Scotia or New'foundland. Early in August of the same year, he was back in Bristol.

An Italian living in England wrote as follows to his brothers in Venice soon after Cabot returned : " The Venetian, our countryman, who went with a ship from Bristol in quest of new lands, is returned, and says that 700 leagues hence he discovered land, the territory of the Grand Khan [China]. He coasted for 300 leagues and landed ; saw no human beings, but he has brought hither to the king certain snares which had been set to catch game, and a needle for making nets ; he also found some felled trees. The discoverer of these places planted on his new found land a large cross with one flag of England. Vast honor is paid him ; he dresses in silk, and these English run after him like crazy people."

Importance and extent of Cabot's discovery. — The English later made John Cabot's discovery the basis of their right to settle in America. Henry VII gave Cabot a yearly pension worth as much as $1500 is to-day, but England received vastly more from Cabot than she gave to him.

John Cabot, with his son Sebastian, made a second voyage

(1498) and sailed south along the American coast. He was probably the first European to see our coast as far south as Cape Hatteras. A Spaniard drew a map in 1500 which shows that the English had discovered a large part of the eastern shore of North America.

Like Columbus, Cabot thought that he had found the eastern shore of Asia. The English at first expected to send many ships to the land which they supposed to be the Indies, and to have in London the greatest storehouse of spices in the world.

The English said nothing about discovering precious metals or jewels. They did, however, find the valuable fishing banks near Newfoundland. In a few years, more than a hundred fishing vessels crossed to this part of the Atlantic every year. Sometimes baskets were dropped overboard and pulled in full of fish.

French exploration. — Spain and England had laid the basis for claims in the New World by the explorations of two Italians, Columbus and Cabot. The French king employed a third Italian, Verrazzano (věr-rät-sä'nō), to sail for France. Verrazzano explored parts of the east coast of North America (1524). He was the first European to enter New York Harbor.

Ten years after Verrazzano's exploration, a Frenchman, Jacques Cartier (zhȧk kär-tyā'), began to explore the St. Lawrence River, thinking that it was a passage to China. He could go no farther than the Lachine (lȧ-shēn', which means " the China ") Rapids. He gave the name of Mont Réal (Royal Mountain) to a hill at the site of the present city of Montreal (mont-re-ôl'). He also built a fort on the site of Quebec'. In this way France got her title to Canada.

Why Italy and Germany did not explore the New World. — Italy, as we have seen, furnished the men who first discovered and explored the New World. It would seem natural that she should have led all nations in making discoveries for herself. There were two reasons why she did not :

(1) Italy was not a united nation. It was a collection of separate states that were often at war with each other. Italy did not become a united nation until the last half of the nineteenth century.

(2) Both Venice and Genoa were interested in having the Mediterranean the center of the world's trade. They did not wish an ocean route to India to be discovered by sailing either west or east, because the ships bringing spices or other articles would then go direct to England, France, and other ports in northern Europe. Venice and Genoa saw that they would lose much of their trade in this way.

CARTIER AND THE INDIANS NEAR LACHINE RAPIDS

The Indians believed Cartier to be a god. They are shown here bringing their sick to him to be cured. Notice the palisade which incloses the Indian village.

Before the new trade routes were discovered, the Mediterranean was the most important body of water in the world. After the New World was found, the Mediterranean gradually became less important. The European nations on the Atlantic rose to first place in the world's trade. Venice and Genoa declined. Spain, Portugal, France, England, and Holland made the Atlantic play a new part in commerce. The ships of these nations carried things to all parts of the world. The discovery of America thus led to a change in the world's trade and history.

Germany had in part the same reason as Italy for not sharing in the exploration of the New World, because there were then many German states but no united Germany. The different German states were often fighting each other. Some agreed to give four days' notice before beginning war, but some gave no notice. The separate states out of which Germany was formed did not combine until the latter half of the nineteenth century.

Magellan's plan. — Ferdinand Magellan (ma-jĕl'an) was born in Portugal. As a sailor he was so brave and skillful that he was made a captain. The king of Portugal afterward became unfriendly to him. In those days the king had so much influence that Magellan saw that he must go to Spain if he would be a great discoverer.

Portugal was claiming all the trade of the Indies because Vasco da Gama (p. 261) was the first to reach them by sailing east around Africa. The Pope (p. 206), to prevent a contest between Spain and Portugal, had divided the newly discovered lands between them; and the two countries then made a treaty to settle the "line of demarcation" (map following p. 266). Spain received all the new lands west of a meridian running through Brazil. Portugal

claimed all of those lying east of this meridian and all
that she could reach by sailing east. Magellan told Spain
that she ought to claim all the new lands that she could find
by sailing west. The king of Spain employed Magellan
to reach the Spice Islands and India by sailing in the
opposite direction from the route of the Portuguese.

What Magellan did. — Magellan started on the second
greatest voyage in history with five vessels (1519), twenty-
seven years after the greatest
voyage by Columbus. Coasting
along South America, Magellan
thought that the Plata was a
passage to India, and he sailed
up it for three hundred miles
before he learned his mistake.

The Strait of Magellan through
which he sailed has since borne
his name. To the ocean beyond,
he gave the name of " Pacific "

FERDINAND MAGELLAN
Redrawn from old engravings.

because it was so calm. No one had any idea of the size
of this ocean. After Magellan's men had sailed it for two
months, some of them thought that the world was flat and
that it extended on without end. Their provisions gave
out, and they nearly died of starvation. They sailed for
more than three months before they landed on an island,
probably Guam (gwäm), in the western part of the Pacific
Ocean. They next stopped at the Philippine Islands, which
Spain claimed, along with Guam, by right of discovery.
Spain held them until 1898, when the United States took
them during the Spanish-American War. Magellan was
killed in the Philippines in a little war between natives who
had accepted Christianity and others who rejected it.

End of the voyage; what it proved. — Of the five ships and 270 men that sailed from Spain, only one ship, the *Vittoria*, with eighteen men, finished the voyage. She reached Spain by way of the Cape of Good Hope three years after she had sailed.

This wonderful voyage proved (1) that it is possible to sail entirely around the world, (2) that there is a vast body of water between the Indies and the lands found by Columbus.

Things we should remember about the discovery of the New World. — 1. Columbus is the world's greatest discoverer.

2. From his earliest boyhood he prepared himself to become a sailor. He studied geography, astronomy, and mathematics, and learned to use the mariner's compass and the astrolabe.

3. Columbus believed the world to be round, and thought he could reach India and China by sailing west.

4. In August, 1492, Columbus set out from Spain with three ships given him by the king and queen of Spain.

5. Columbus found land in the west on October 12, 1492. His discovery gave Spain a claim to the New World.

6. The new continent was named for Americus Vespucius.

7. John Cabot's discovery gave England a claim to the New World.

8. The explorations of Verrazzano and Cartier gave France a claim.

9. Magellan's ship was the first to sail around the world.

Things to do. — Find Genoa on the map. Why did it become an important seaport?

If there is a compass in your school, see if you can find different directions by using it.

Write one hundred words on "How Columbus was Educated to Become a Sailor."

Read from the *Book of Marco Polo* some descriptions that Columbus must have liked.

Dramatize the scene in which Columbus asks Queen Isabella to aid him.

Imagine yourself to be one of the sailors of Columbus. Write a letter giving an account of your voyage.

Read or ask your teacher to read to you Joaquin Miller's poem *Columbus*.

Explain how America got its name.

Point out on the map Cabot's discovery. Why was his discovery important?

Explain how the Lachine Rapids got their name.

Trace Magellan's voyage on the globe. What did the voyage prove?

References for Teachers. — Richman, *Spanish Conquerors* (Chronicles of America), II; Markham, *Life of Christopher Columbus;* Fiske, *Discovery of America;* Young, *Christopher Columbus and the New World of His Discovery* (has a valuable Appendix "On the Navigation of the First Voyage of Columbus" by a modern sea captain, the Earl of Dunraven). Williamson, *Maritime Enterprise, 1485–1558*, III, IV (the Cabot Voyages); *Encyclopædia Britannica*, articles on "Columbus," "Vespucci, Amerigo," "Cabot," "Gama, Vasco da," "Magellan."

For Pupils. — Van Loon, *Story of Mankind*, 232–240; Tappan, *Old World Hero Stories*, XXXIII–XXXV (Columbus, Vasco da Gama, Magellan); Johnson, *World's Discoverers*, 18–92 (Columbus), 93–116 (Vasco da Gama), 119–176 (Magellan), 177–188 (Verrazzano); Gordy, *Stories of American Explorers*, 1–21 (Columbus); Holland, *Historic Boyhoods*, 9–20 (Columbus); Haaren and Poland, *Famous Men of Modern Times*, 16–30 (Columbus), 40–52 (Vasco da Gama); Butterworth, *Story of Magellan;* Towle, *Magellan.*

CHAPTER XIX

HOW THE SPANISH EXPLORED AND COLONIZED THE NEW WORLD

The Spanish West Indies. — The first Spanish settlements in America were made in Haiti while that island was supposed to be part of the Indies belonging to southeastern

SPANISH EXPLORATIONS IN AMERICA

Asia. The little colony which Columbus left in Haiti after the wreck of the *Santa Maria* (p. 270), was destroyed by the Indians. On his second voyage (1493), however, Columbus planted in Haiti a large colony, which was strong enough to conquer the Indians there. He thus gained the honor of planting the first permanent colony in the New World which he had discovered. Other Spanish colonies were soon founded in Cuba, Porto Rico, and smaller islands.

Spain called these islands the Indies even after it was known that they were not part of Asia. They soon came to be called the West Indies, while the islands of southeastern Asia were known as the East Indies.

The Spaniards made an important gift to the New World when they brought the sugar cane to the West Indies. Its early introduction there was important for three reasons : (1) It increased the world's supply of sugar, which was still a rare luxury, used only by the rich and in medicine. (2) The Spanish colonies grew prosperous because they could raise sugar cheaply. Cuba became the world's largest producer of sugar. (3) Sugar plantations needed a large number of laborers and caused the introduction of negro slavery. When Columbus came, the West Indies had a large population of Indians, but they did not make good slaves, and most of them were soon killed off. So many negroes were brought to the sugar plantations as slaves that in some of the West Indies they outnumbered the white men.

Darien and Florida. — From the West Indies the Spaniards set out to explore and conquer the mainland of North and South America. Their first successful colony on the mainland was Darien' (1510), on the Isthmus of

Panama'. From Darien, Balboa crossed the isthmus in 1513 and was the first explorer of the New World to see the Pacific Ocean, which he called the " South Sea."

In the same year (1513) Ponce de Leon (pōn'thā dā lå-ōn'), a wealthy planter, sailed northwest from Porto Rico on a voyage of exploration. On Easter Sunday he came to a land which he named Florida. He wanted to found a colony and to find the fountain of youth which he had been told was in that land. He hoped to become a young man again by bathing in that fountain; but his search was in vain, and he did not succeed in founding any colony.

How the Spanish conquered Mexico. — While Magellan was making his voyage around the world, Hernando Cortes (kôr'tĕs) went to Mexico (1519) with a small Spanish force and founded the town of Vera Cruz (vā'rä krōōs') on the coast. The Aztecs were semi-civilized Indians who ruled a large part of Mexico. Their capital was on the site of the present city of Mexico. This ancient Aztec city was surrounded by a lake, and was reached by roads and bridges built across the water. It had many large houses and temples, built of red stone covered with white plaster. The largest temple was a hundred feet high. Great numbers of human beings were killed every year in this temple as sacrifices to the war god. The Aztecs thought that it was necessary to keep the favor of this god in order to conquer the surrounding tribes. The conquered tribes were kept almost as slaves to raise corn, fruit, and other food to support their victors. The Aztecs loved flowers, especially roses. They could make gold and silver ornaments and pottery, and could weave fine garments. They built aqueducts to supply the city with water.

While Cortes was at the coast, Montezuma, emperor of the Aztecs, was greatly troubled by the news brought him. The white strangers had death-dealing firearms and rode horses — an animal unknown in America. Montezuma sent Cortes many presents, among them two large wheels, one of gold and the other of silver, and a peck of gold dust. These presents made Cortes wealthy and roused his desire for more. They were sent as a bribe to cause Cortes to leave Mexico, but they had the opposite effect. Cortes made up his mind to visit Montezuma and get the rest of the Aztec treasures. He boldly marched into the Aztec capital and even took Montezuma prisoner. After several months, however, the Aztecs began to fight under a new emperor.

MONTEZUMA

From an engraving in a Spanish book published in 1715.

Cortes was joined by a few more Spaniards, and also by tribes of Indians who had been forced to labor for the Aztecs. In less than two years he conquered the country and made it a Spanish province. He sent to the Spanish king an immense quantity of gold and silver that proved to Spain the value of Columbus's discovery.

The conquest of Peru. — The Incas, who were more civilized than the Aztecs, lived in western South America. Their country was called Peru, but it was much larger than the Peru of to-day. The Aztecs levied tribute on Mexican tribes living in an area about the size of Massachusetts.

The Incas ruled over a country as large as that of the United States east of the Mississippi. They were artists in weaving and in making ornaments of gold. They had dramas and poems, in spite of the fact that they could not write.

The Incas worshiped one god, the Sun. To them, everything that was good seemed to be a gift of the Sun. He gave them all their food, their corn, potatoes, and fruits.

PERUVIANS WORSHIPING THE SUN

Redrawn from an old sketch in a book of 1572. Four festivals were held during the year to celebrate the worship of the Sun in early Peru. Animals were sacrificed at these times.

He warmed the earth and called forth the flowers and the grass which fed the creatures that furnished wool for clothing. The very color of their abundant gold seemed to prove that it was a child of the Sun. Their temple of the Sun had many thrones of gold—one for every Inca emperor that had reigned. The statue of the Sun was a great disk of gold. The temple contained seven hundred plates of gold. The Inca emperors wore golden sandals and ate from golden dishes.

The Spaniards heard of this gold and came to Peru (1531) to find it. They were led by Francisco Pizar´ro. He and some of his soldiers rode horses, which the Incas had never before seen. They, like the Aztecs, at first thought that the horse and rider were one animal and were as much terrified by them as by the guns which the white men had.

Pizarro took the Inca ruler captive. The Inca offered to give the Spaniards enough gold to fill a large room if they would set him free. Pizarro accepted the offer. Gold to the value of more than fifteen million dollars was brought to that room. Nothing like this had happened before in the history of the world. The dreams of Columbus fell short of the truth. In causing such a vast treasure of gold to be brought together, the Inca had done in reality such a deed as could be matched only in the tales of Aladdin in the *Arabian Nights*. Pizarro took the gold and afterward killed the Inca.

All the land of the Incas passed under Spanish control. The conquerors found so much gold and silver there that Spain became the wealthiest nation in the world. She used this gold to try to conquer countries like Holland and England and to build a navy to keep other nations away from the New World.

Early explorations in the north. — The king of Spain gave one of his subjects, Narvaez (när-vä′āth), the right to colonize the country from Florida to Mexico. Narvaez landed on the coast of Florida (1528) with three hundred men. They wandered westward until many became sick and all were nearly starved. They fared worse than Robinson Crusoe on his island. Their problem, like his, was how to escape by sea, and so they tried to build boats. They had no tools, no nails, no rope. They had nothing fit for men to eat while at hard labor. They killed their horses for meat and used strips of horsehide for ropes. Nails and tools were made from the iron in their stirrups, spurs, crossbows, and swords. Fibers from the palm tree and pitch from the pine were used to stop the leaks between the planks. Five boats were thus built to carry fifty men each, and were launched on the Gulf of Mexico. The men almost died of hunger and thirst when they were blown far from the shore. Once they " took fresh water from the sea, the stream entering it in freshet." They must have been at the mouth of the Mississippi River, and they were the first white men to drink of it.

Nothing was heard of this expedition for eight years after it landed in Florida. Then (1536) four survivors appeared on the Pacific coast of Mexico. All of the others had been drowned, or had been killed by the Indians, or had died from starvation or disease.

The story of De Vaca. — The attempt of Narvaez to plant a colony would not have affected our history if a written account of the expedition had not been left by De Vaca (dä vä′kä), one of the four surviving members. Just as Columbus was the first to cross the broad Atlantic, De Vaca was the first white man to go from shore to shore across the wide part of the North American continent. By writing a most remarkable story of his travels during those eight years, he caused other Spaniards to explore North America.

From De Vaca's account we learn something of the country through which he passed. He gives the first written account of the buffalo, which he said provided the Indians with food, blankets, and shoes. He tells how the Indians lived and what food they ate, how they could run all day without tiring, and how they sometimes chased a deer, giving the animal no rest until it could go no further. He is the first white man to describe how North American Indians boiled their food without kettles: " They fill the half of a large gourd with water, and throw on the fire many stones such as are most convenient and readily take the heat. When hot they are taken up with tongs of sticks and dropped into the gourd until the water boils from the heat of the stones. Then whatever is to be cooked is put in, and until it is done they continue taking out cooled stones and throwing in hot ones. Thus they boil their food."

The tale of De Vaca interested Hernando de So'to and Francisco Coronado (kō-rŏ-nä'thō), two Spanish explorers. They set forth at about the same time from opposite sides of the continent to explore parts of what is now the United States. The object of both explorers was to find gold.

De Soto's expedition. — De Soto had gained a fortune under Pizarro in Peru, and was now governor of Cuba. He landed in Florida (1539) with six hundred men. He took many hogs and horses with him. When his men could find no other food, they killed the hogs. Much of their trouble was to find food for the animals as well as for themselves. They depended most on corn, which the Indians raised in large quantities in fertile places. Around one Indian village they got enough corn to last them and their animals three months. Other articles of food were beans, walnuts, and roasted pumpkins. For meat, the Indians sometimes sent De Soto 150 rabbits at a time. One Indian village gave him 700 wild turkeys, more than one apiece for all his men. Sometimes, however, the Spaniards suffered for lack of food.

The expedition crossed the Mississippi River and passed one winter in what is now western Arkansas. One chief brought a present of many buffalo skins, under which the soldiers slept warm in the cold weather.

De Soto captured many Indians and put them in chains to serve as slaves for his party. The Indians long remembered how he treated them, how he took their corn which they needed for food, and how he sometimes cut off their hands when they took his hogs.

After traveling for three years, De Soto died and was

DE SOTO DISCOVERING THE MISSISSIPPI
From a famous painting by William Powell.

buried in the Mississippi River. His men built boats to take them down the Mississippi to the Gulf, on which they sailed to Mexico. Half of their number had died since they began their journey in Florida.

De Soto's journey was considered a failure because he found no gold. The story of the expedition, written by one who was with him, gave the world its first lesson in the geography of what is now Florida, Georgia, South Carolina, Alabama, Mississippi, Tennessee, Arkansas, and Louisiana. It told about the life of many North American Indians. We learn that farming, especially the raising of corn, was their chief industry. This story also gave the first knowledge of the mighty Mississippi, so broad that a man could not be distinctly seen on the opposite bank.

Coronado's expedition. — Coronado started north from Mexico (1540) about the time that De Soto landed in Florida.

At one time he and De Soto were near each other. An Indian woman left De Soto's expedition and in nine days stumbled on Coronado's. The journeys of these two explorers nearly covered the distance from sea to sea.

Coronado had been told of Seven Cities where gold was as plentiful as the stars in the Milky Way and where there were streets in which only goldsmiths dwelt. He found that these "cities" were really only the poor stone houses of the Zuni (zoo'nye) Indians in what is now New Mexico. Coronado then fell in with an Indian who said that in the city of Quivira (kwe-ve'rä), farther north, "the lord of that country took his afternoon nap under a large tree on which were hung a great number of little gold bells, which put him to sleep as they swung in the air." He said also that the jugs and bowls there were of gold. This "city" turned out to be a cluster of poor Indian villages in what is now central Kansas, where no gold was found.

Like De Soto, Coronado failed to find the gold for which he searched, but his expedition greatly strengthened the claim of Spain to large parts of our country. He and his companions were the first to see the Grand Canyon of the Colorado. They furnished a first-

EARLY AMERICAN BUFFALO
Redrawn from sketches made by Spanish explorers in the sixteenth century.

hand description of the vast herds of buffaloes in what became later the central United States. The account says that the men chased a herd toward a ravine. "So many of the animals fell into this that they filled it up, and the rest went across on top of them." Coronado saw great tents made of buffalo skin. He watched the Indians cutting the buffalo meat " thin, like a leaf," and then drying it in the sun and grinding it into meal. He took a supply of this for his homeward journey.

Coronado discovered the Great Plains, which are to-day an important part of the United States. The Spaniards, used to trees, hills, and mountains, thought these nearly level, treeless plains the strangest of all that they had seen. They said : " The country is like a bowl, so that when a man sits down, the horizon surrounds him all around at the distance of a musket's shot. Even if a man only lay down on his back, he saw nothing but the sky."

Why Spain colonized the New World. — The three motives which led Spain to colonize the New World have been called " gospel, glory, and gold." " Glory " meant the honor which came to Spain from increase of territory and wealth. It also meant the fame which men like Cortes and Pizarro gained from their explorations and conquests. The story of these two Spaniards, and of De Soto and Coronado, shows what power gold had in drawing men to the New World.

As we have seen, Spanish conquerors did not hesitate to steal the red men's corn and to enslave them. It is also true that Spanish priests faced danger and death to go among the Indians to teach them the Gospel and help them to live better. It was a great priest, Las Casas (läs kä′säs), who at last persuaded the Spanish king to stop Indian slavery in the New World (1542). The order from the king came after slavery had killed most of the Indians in the West Indies, but it saved those on the mainland from destruction.

The Spanish priests brought the Indians to live in villages around a religious mission house as a center. The old mission buildings are still to be seen in many places. The missions were schools as much as churches. The priests taught Indian children and their parents how to live in a civilized way. The Indians learned how to raise food and

SPANISH MISSION, SAN GABRIEL, IN CALIFORNIA

to make what things they needed. They were taught farming, carpentering, cooking, weaving, dyeing, and how to make clothes, leather, saddles, bridles, and shoes.

Extent of the Spanish colonies in America. — Spanish missions and settlements were founded in New Mexico, Texas, and California. Florida also was occupied by a small Spanish colony. Large parts of our country were thus held by Spain for many years, and we still use many names given by the Spaniards, as Florida, California, Rio Grande (" Great River "), Colorado (" Red ") River, San

Francisco (" Saint Francis "). Some of our people are descended from Spaniards, and numbers of words in our language have come to us from Spain (p. 202); some from the Spaniards in the Southwest are *canyon, corral, ranch.*

In the lands to the south of our country, the Spanish influence was greater. Spain colonized the West Indies, Mexico, Central America, and nearly all of South America except Brazil, which was settled by the Portuguese. There are to-day in that part of the New World eighteen nations which are called Spanish-American. Most of the white people there are of Spanish descent, and most of the people — Indian and negro as well as white — now speak the Spanish language. These countries were governed by Spain for about three hundred years, but all are now republics.

Things we should remember about Spanish colonies in America. — 1. The Spaniards planted the first permanent European colonies in the New World.

2. The Spaniards, under Cortes, conquered Mexico, the home of the Aztecs.

3. Pizarro and his army of Spaniards conquered the Incas of Peru and took possession of their land and treasures.

4. De Vaca, a Spaniard, made the first coast-to-coast trip across the wide part of North America.

5. The explorations of De Soto and Coronado in the southern part of what is now the United States gave the world an idea of the geography and inhabitants of that part of the New World.

6. The main reason for Spanish explorations and conquests in the New World was the desire for glory and gold.

7. Spanish priests built missions, where they converted the Indians to Christianity and taught them the industries of civilized races.

8. Spain colonized the West Indies, Mexico, Central America, and nearly all of South America except Brazil.

9. Most of the white people of these countries to-day are of Spanish descent and speak the Spanish language.

Things to do. — Draw a map showing the extent of Spanish colonies in the New World.

Write one hundred words on the importance of the Old World's gift of sugar.

Take your choice of Ponce de Leon, Cortes, De Soto, Coronado, De Vaca, and Pizarro. Talk to the class for three minutes about the Spanish explorer you have chosen. As you talk, trace the explorer's route on the map. Get more information about these explorers from the reference books mentioned below.

Imagine yourself to be an Indian in an early Spanish colony. Tell how the missions helped the Indians.

References for Teachers. — Richman, *Spanish Conquerors* (Chronicles of America), 64–215; Bourne, *Spain in America* (American Nation Series); Hodge, F. W., *Spanish Explorers in the Southern United States, 1528–1543* (Original Narratives of Early American History); Shepherd, *Latin America;* James, *In and Out of the Old Missions of California; Encyclopædia Britannica*, articles on " Central America," " Mexico," " Peru," " South America," " Florida," " Balboa," " Cortes," " Pizarro," " Soto," " Coronado."

For Pupils. — Johnston, *Famous Discoverers and Explorers of America*, 63–186 (Ponce de Leon, Balboa, Cortes), 219–276 (Pizarro, De Soto); Shaw, *Discoverers and Explorers*, 68–91 (Cortes, Pizarro, De Soto); Higginson, *Young Folks' Book of American Explorers*, VI (De Soto); Griffis, *Romance of Discovery*, XV–XVII (Ponce de Leon, De Vaca, Coronado); Towle, *Pizarro;* Gordy, *Stories of American Explorers*, 52–107 (Cortes, Pizarro, Ponce de Leon, De Soto); Foote and Skinner, *Explorers and Founders of America*, 42–80 (Cortes, De Soto, Pizarro, Ponce de Leon).

CHAPTER XX

STEPS TOWARD ENGLISH COLONIZATION
OF AMERICA

Why England was late in planting colonies. — The English people, whose language we speak, did not plant a lasting colony in America until more than one hundred years after the first Spanish settlement in the New World. England was at war most of the one hundred and thirty

SIEGE OF A FORTRESS DURING THE HUNDRED YEARS' WAR

From an old print. The movable tower at the left enables the besiegers to shoot over the wall of the fortress. Notice the early form of cannon in the center. Some of the people who are defending the walls are hurling down stones on the archers. Notice the moat around the fortress which makes it difficult for the besiegers to reach the wall.

years before the discovery of America. One of England's wars with France, known as the Hundred Years' War (1337–1453), lasted a little more than a century. The most heroic figure in this long war was the patriotic French maid, Joan of Arc, who has been called the creator of modern France. Next came civil war, called the Wars of the Roses, between two parties of English nobles. These wars weakened England.

Peace came with the reign of Henry VII (p. 273), the first of the great line of Tudors who ruled England from 1485 to 1603. They were called Tudors because

JOAN OF ARC

Statue by Chapu (nineteenth century) in the Louvre, Paris. This represents Joan as a peasant girl before she left home to inspire and lead the French armies.

they were descended from Owen Tudor, a Welshman. During a century of peace England slowly grew strong.

We shall see in this chapter how a change in religion, increasing trade on the seas, and daring English sailors prepared the way for the English colonization of America.

The Protestant Reformation. — The Middle Ages end with the discovery of America. Soon after that event came several important changes, so that 1492 may be taken as the beginning of Modern Times. One of the first great events in modern history was the change in religious belief called the Protestant Reformation.

Until the first part of the sixteenth century, the Roman

Catholic Church had been the only church in western
Europe (p. 206). The Pope, the head of the church, had
been powerful enough to punish wicked kings and to forbid their subjects to obey them. Once a disobedient king,
in danger of losing his throne, crossed the Alps in winter
and waited barefoot for three days outside the castle where
the Pope was staying. When the king was admitted, he
promised obedience to the church. The Pope then ordered
the king's subjects to obey him.

In the century following the discovery of America there
was a widespread revolt against the Pope and the Catholic
Church. This revolt is called the Reformation because it
was a re-forming or changing of religious belief. Martin
Luther, a German friar, began this new movement by pro-
testing (1517) against some things that the Roman Catholic
Church believed and did. The Pope summoned Luther to
appear at Rome, but Luther did not go. He began to
preach and to write in defiance of the Pope. Those who,
like Luther, disobeyed the Pope and insisted on choosing
their own religious belief, became known as Protestants.
Many people in northern Germany became Protestants.
Large numbers of the German Protestants settled in our
country about the end of the next century.

John Calvin was a French Protestant leader who had to
flee to Switzerland for safety. The Huguenots (hū'gē-nŏts),
or French Protestants, and many of the Scotch and English
people followed his teaching. Many of the early English colonists in America were Calvinists. Luther and
Calvin were the chief leaders of early sixteenth-century
Protestants.

How the Reformation began in England. — The Reformation did not start in England in the same way that it did

in Germany.   Henry VIII, king of England (reigned 1509–1547), had married Catherine, the widow of his brother and a daughter of Ferdinand and Isabella (p. 267).   Catherine was older than Henry, but he married her to keep the friendship of Spain.   When he tired of her, he asked the Pope for a divorce but was refused.   Henry then declared that the Pope should have no more power in England.

Parliament (1534) made Henry instead of the Pope the supreme head of the English Church. This was a long step toward Protestantism, although England still considered herself Catholic.

Henry VIII did not like Protestants.   If we had lived in England at that time and had called him a Protestant, we should have been in danger of having our heads cut off.   The king had Protestants burned for teaching their new beliefs.   On the other hand,

CHAINED BIBLE IN A CHURCH

Bibles were chained to stands in the church so that they could not be carried away.   In Henry VIII's time very few were owned by individuals.   Indeed, there were laws forbidding people of certain classes to read the Scriptures.

he had Catholics beheaded for treason if they denied that he was the head of the Church of England.   He also seized the property of the monasteries throughout England. Before Henry's time, the Latin Bible had been used in English churches.   He ordered an English Bible to be put in every church.

Henry had three children, all of whom became monarchs of England. Mary, the daughter of his first wife Catherine, was a Catholic. His other two children, Edward and Elizabeth, were Protestants.

How England became Protestant. — Edward VI (reigned 1547–1553), the son of Henry VIII, came to the throne when

Brown Bros.

HENRY VII'S CHAPEL IN WESTMINSTER
ABBEY

This Gothic chapel contains the tomb of Henry VII. Other rulers also are buried there, among them Edward VI and Queen Elizabeth.

he was ten years old. Edward Seymour (sē'mōr), the uncle of the boy king, was his protector and guided his rule. England still had the Roman Catholic form of worship when Henry VIII died. Both the young king and his uncle, however, were Protestants. Under their rule the Church of England became Protestant in many ways and adopted an English Prayer Book.

Edward VI died at the age of sixteen and was buried in the chapel of his grandfather, Henry VII. This chapel, which is a part of Westminster Abbey, is one of the most beautiful pieces of Gothic architecture in the world. If we could have been present at the two funerals, that of Henry VII (1509) and that of Edward VI (1553), we should have wondered at the difference. At the first funeral there were many candles burning on the altar and around the king's bier. The king had ordered that ten thousand masses or prayers should be said after his death for " the remission of his sins and the weal of his soul," and had left money to provide for them. Less than fifty years later the body of Edward VI was brought from the palace to the chapel the night before the funeral " without cross or light." Only the simple burial service of the Church of England was read at his funeral. No provision was made for candles or masses. Edward VI was the first English king to have a Protestant funeral service.

Queen Mary, the half sister of Edward VI (p. 298), succeeded him. She married the Roman Catholic king of Spain. During her short reign (1553–1558) she did all that she could to make England and the English Church again Roman Catholic. Protestant leaders were burned.

Mary was followed by her half sister Elizabeth (reigned 1558–1603). Elizabeth made the Church of England Protestant, and it has remained such ever since. Most of the English people continued to be members of the English Church and became Protestants. Some English Protestants did not like the service of the Church of England (Protestant Episcopal Church), but the laws ordered all the people to attend the service of that church. Elizabeth punished severely those who refused.

The Pope excommunicated Elizabeth and said that her subjects need not obey her. English Protestants remained loyal to Elizabeth, and Catholics who wanted to be loyal to both the Queen and the Pope had a hard time. The Protestants in France and Spain also had a hard time because the rulers there were Catholic.

Religious persecution. — In many countries of western Europe the period of the Reformation was a period of

civil wars, wars between nations, and imprisonment, behead-
ing, and death by torture on account of religious opinions.
Catholics and Protestants would not allow each other to
worship in peace. Religious persecutions lasted for more
than a hundred years. Even different groups of Protestants persecuted each other.

One result, as we shall see, was the founding of several
English colonies in America by those who were determined
to worship God as they chose.

Religious persecution gradually became less and less in
civilized countries. In our country we have the protection
of two clauses in the Constitution, ordering (1) that no
religious test shall ever be required for holding any office
under the United States, (2) that Congress shall make no
law prohibiting the free exercise of religion. The Constitution of the United States protects any religion which does
not teach people to break the laws.

How reading and education increased. — The Protestants said that all their beliefs had their foundation in the
Bible; the Catholics said that the Bible was a source of
the Catholic faith. Many people learned how to read because they wished to find out for themselves what the Scriptures really said. In the Middle Ages the ability to read
was uncommon outside of the church. An English translation of the Bible was printed for the first time in 1535 and
was eagerly read.

People also wished to read other things besides the Bible
and to learn what many books could tell them. The demand
for reading led men to write and print more books. It
also led to more education.

The number of schools in England increased, although
some of the new schools merely took the place of Catholic

schools that had been closed. People began to think of education for girls as well as for boys. A schoolmaster asked: "Do not children for the most part prove like their mothers?" A teacher living at this time said: "Every one desireth to have his children educated." The parents of William Shakespeare made their mark when they signed

WHERE SHAKESPEARE WENT TO SCHOOL

Latin room in the grammar school in Stratford-on-Avon. This school is one of the oldest buildings now standing in Stratford. It was built at the end of the fifteenth century.

a deed, because they could not write their names; but they sent their son to a grammar school.

Spain's world empire. — Spain became the great fighting champion of the Roman Catholic religion. Spain was the most powerful nation in Europe, because of (1) her discovery of the New World, (2) her colonies planted there, (3) the shiploads of gold and silver which she received from her colonies. Her vast wealth enabled her to build strong fleets and to support a large army.

The emperor who is known in history as Charles V

(reigned 1520–1556) inherited from his father and mother the crown of Spain, the territories of the Netherlands (modern Holland and Belgium), Austria, and parts of what are now Italy and France. He was elected emperor of Germany to succeed his grandfather. He was also ruler of many colonies in America and claimed all of America except Brazil (p. 276). The lands over which he ruled were broader in extent than those under the rule of Charlemagne (map, p. 160) or even those in the Roman Empire (map following page 110). Charles V was a Catholic. He tried to conquer the German Protestants but failed because he had to carry on other wars at the same time.

Charles V gave most of his dominions to his son Philip II, king of Spain (reigned 1556–1598). Philip was not elected emperor of Germany, but he tried to increase his power by marrying Queen Mary of England (p. 299). When she died, he offered to marry Queen Elizabeth " at great sacrifice to himself " and to protect her if she would uphold the Catholic religion. She surprised him by refusing his offer.

How Spain used her power: 1. *In Florida.* — French Protestants (Huguenots) tried to settle in Florida after the middle of the sixteenth century. Spanish soldiers were quickly sent to destroy the French colony. Spain took this step for two reasons: (*a*) She desired to keep all North America for herself. (*b*) She was determined to stop the growth of Protestantism in all her dominions.

2. *In the Netherlands.* — The northern part of the Netherlands is now known as Holland (or the Netherlands), and its inhabitants are called the Dutch. In Philip's time there were many Protestants in Holland. In the southern part of the Netherlands, now named Belgium, most of the people were Catholics. Philip tried to put down the Protes-

tants in the Netherlands. His rule there was so cruel that some of the native Catholics joined the Protestants to oppose him.

William, Prince of Orange, became the leader of Holland. He was called " William the Silent " because he kept still when he heard a Spaniard tell how the Protestants were to be hunted down. " From that hour," he said, " I resolved with my whole soul to drive the Spanish vermin from the land." He was often defeated, but he was patient, honest, and brave. Once he had to cut the dikes and let in the sea to help drive away the Spanish army that was besieging the city of Leyden (li'den).

Philip offered a large reward for any one who would kill William, thinking that Holland would then end the struggle. William was killed in his home by an assassin (1584), but his followers continued to fight until they became free.

What the struggle of Holland meant to America. — (1) The Dutch made their country a republic and gave the world an inspiring example by winning their independence. (2) They wisely granted all people the right to worship as they chose. (3) They upheld the freedom of the press to print books when other governments were keeping all printing presses under lock and key. (4) They set the example of supporting common schools by taxation. (5) Holland's independence led to her founding a colony in America, which later became one of the important English colonies — New York. (6) The revolt of Holland used up much of Spain's energy and thus helped to prevent her from extending her power over all North America.

Elizabethan seamen and commerce. — England became a school for sailors. English merchants found that they could get wealth by going on long voyages to trade. They sailed into the Arctic Ocean and opened up trade with Russia from the north. They traded far down the coast of Africa on the south.

Two famous English sailors of Elizabeth's time were born in southwestern England and traded with America.

AN ELIZABETHAN GALLEON WITH FOUR CONNING TOWERS
From an engraving published in Holland in 1588 to illustrate the defeat of the Armada.

They were John Hawkins and Francis Drake. Both were Protestants who disliked Spain. English sailors had been ill treated in Spain, and they hated the Spanish.

Hawkins made three voyages to the coast of Africa, where he caught negroes and sold them in the West Indies. The laws of Spain allowed only Spanish vessels to trade with her colonies, but the owners of sugar plantations were eager to buy slaves from any ship. Hawkins and others of his time did not think that slavery was wrong. One of his ships that carried slaves was named the *Jesus;* another, the *Grace of God*. His rules for his sailors were: "Serve God daily; love one another, preserve your victuals, beware of fire." His coat of arms showed a negro in chains.

Francis Drake was one of the most skillful and daring of all English sailors. While on a trading voyage, he and Hawkins stopped at Vera Cruz in Mexico. A Spanish fleet entered the harbor and made a truce with the English. When the English went ashore, the Spanish in spite of the truce killed most of them and destroyed the larger English ships. Drake and Hawkins barely escaped in two small vessels. Drake lost all that he had, and he made a vow that Spain should repay him.

He soon sailed again for the West Indies with his two little vessels. Before he returned to England, he overhauled two hundred Spanish ships and took their treasure from them. When he wanted better vessels than his own, he took Spanish ships. His daring and success were the wonder of England when he returned in 1573.

Drake's voyage around the world. — In 1578 Drake passed through the Strait of Magellan in a small vessel, the *Golden Hind*. He sailed into Spanish ports on the western coast of South America and took what gold and silver he could find in Spanish vessels. Going north, he overtook a large Spanish ship carrying gold and silver to Panama, where it was to be taken across the isthmus and shipped to Spain. Drake seized all her treasure.

Drake sailed across the Pacific, through the Indian Ocean, and around the Cape of Good Hope to England. His was the second ship to sail around the globe (p. 278).

When Drake returned, Elizabeth and her court visited him on the *Golden Hind*. She bade him kneel, and said: "Spain hath demanded Drake's head. Here is a gilded sword to strike it off." As the sword touched him, she exclaimed: "I bid thee rise, *Sir* Francis Drake." She thus made him a knight and defied Spain.

After Drake had sailed around the world, the Spanish name for him became " the Dragon." King Philip of Spain was preparing a fleet, the great Armada, to attack England. Drake sailed into the harbor of Cadiz, Spain, and destroyed so many Spanish ships that the sailing of the Armada was delayed for a year.

The Spaniards accounted for the superiority of the English sailors by saying that Drake was a magician. They said he had the power to look into a glass in his cabin and see all the fleets of his enemies and what they were doing. When Spanish mothers wanted to quiet their crying children, they said : " Hush ! or the Dragon will get you."

Why Spain fought England. — Philip had three reasons for fighting England : (1) He was a champion of the Catholic religion, and England was the foremost Protestant nation. (2) Englishmen had helped the Netherlands in their struggle against Spain. (3) Drake and other English sailors had plundered his ships.

The men of both nations felt like the old Crusaders who went to attack the Mohammedans (p. 216). Every Spanish ship in the Armada showed a red cross as the sign of a holy crusade.

How the Armada was defeated. — A battle that changed the history of the world was fought (1588) in the last half of Elizabeth's reign. Philip sent against England a fleet which the Spaniards called the " Invincible Armada " because they were sure it could not be defeated. There were about one hundred and thirty vessels in this fleet as it entered the English Channel. Twenty-one thousand soldiers were on board, and more were to be added from the Spanish army in the Netherlands. The combined force was to be landed in England to conquer it and annex it to Spain.

The Spanish ships stood high above the water. They made easy marks for the English guns. The English could sail much faster than the Spanish and fire their cannon three times as quickly. A running fight, lasting eight days, took place while the Armada was making its way through the English Channel toward Antwerp to join the army. The Spanish had lost several ships but were not defeated. The English lacked powder, and victory for them was not at all sure.

The admiral of the English fleet was Lord Howard, a capable officer. Sir Francis Drake was vice admiral.

BATTLE OF THE ARMADA

The Spanish anchored off Calais in good order on the night of the eighth day of fighting. The Armada was within a short distance of Antwerp, its goal. That night the English set eight blazing fire ships adrift among the vessels of the Armada. The Spanish ships cut their cables to avoid the danger. A naval critic says: " It was the hour for which Drake had been born, and without a glance at his commander, he led the fleet onward." He attacked the Spanish ships while they were in disorder. The English guns disabled and sank so many of them that the rest fled into the North Sea. They tried to get back to Spain by sailing around the north of Scotland and west of Ireland. Storms then wrecked more than the English had destroyed. Only fifty-two ships of the Invincible Armada returned to Spain.

Philip had relied on the help of the English Catholics to aid him in conquering England, but they loved England and showed their patriotism by fighting beside the Protestants against the Spaniards.

The defeat of the Armada by English seamen made it possible for the English to plant permanent colonies in America.

Things to be remembered. — 1. The Protestant Reformation began (1517) early in modern history. Martin Luther and John Calvin were the chief leaders of the Protestants in the sixteenth century.

2. Henry VIII took a decided step toward Protestantism in England when he became head of the English Church in place of the Pope.

3. The Church of England became Protestant in the reigns of Edward VI and Queen Elizabeth.

4. The Spanish king ruled over more territory than the Romans had ever held. Spain became a world power.

5. Holland gained its independence and helped break down Spain's power.

6. Trade made Elizabethan seamen skillful, and they helped prepare the way for the English colonization of America.

7. The defeat of the Spanish Armada was one of the decisive battles of the world, because it made possible the planting of English colonies in America.

Things to do. — Tell something about the two leaders of the Protestant Reformation.

Tell the class how most of the English people became Protestant.

Memorize the clause in the Constitution of the United States (Amendment I) allowing freedom of (1) religion, (2) speech, (3) the press. Which of these did Holland have?

Find in some book the story of William Prince of Orange and be able to tell it to the class.

Read some book about Hawkins and Drake and tell their story.

Trace on the map the progress of the Armada to Calais, its flight into the North Sea, and its route back to Spain.

References for Teachers. — In any good English history read about Henry VII, Henry VIII, Edward VI, Mary, and Elizabeth; Robinson, *History of Western Europe*, XXV–XXVIII; Lindsay, *History of the Reformation;* Elson, *Modern Times and the Living Past*, XXIII–XXVI; Halleck, *New English Literature*, IV; Corbett, *Sir Francis Drake* (English Men of Action Series); Wood, *Elizabethan Sea-Dogs* (Chronicles of America); Froude, *English Seamen in the Sixteenth Century;* Payne, *Voyages of the Elizabethan Seamen* (Payne's accounts of the voyages of Hawkins and Drake are taken from Hakluyt's *Voyages*, which has been called the " Elizabethan *Odyssey*, the great prose epic of the English race ");*Encyclopædia Britannica*, articles on " Reformation," " Luther," " Calvin," " Charles V," " Huguenots," " Philip II (of Spain)," " William (of Orange)," " Henry VIII," " Edward VI," " Mary I (of England)," " Elizabeth," " Mary Queen of Scots," " Hawkins," " Drake "; Orczy, *Leatherface* (fiction).

For Pupils. — Terry, *The New Liberty* (Reformation); Dutton, *Little Stories of Germany* (Martin Luther, Charles V); Haaren and Poland, *Famous Men of Modern Times* (Charles V,

Drake); Van Loon, *Story of Mankind*, 251–278 (Reformation, William Prince of Orange); Warren, *Stories from English History*, 188–198 (Reformation), 152–171 (Henry VIII), 227–239 (Drake and the Armada); Banks, *Boys' Motley;* Griffis, *Young People's History of Holland;* Seaman, *Jacqueline of the Carrier-Pigeons* (William Prince of Orange, fiction); Tappan, *England's Story*, V, VI; Dale, *Landmarks of British History*, VII, VIII; Bacon, *English Voyages of Adventure and Discovery Retold from Hakluyt;* Bacon, *Boy's Drake;* Tappan, *Old World Hero Stories*, XLVI (Armada); Holland, *Historic Heroes of Chivalry* (Drake); Fryer, *Book of Boyhoods* (Drake); Griffis, *Romance of Discovery* (Hawkins).

CHAPTER XXI

HOW THE ELIZABETHAN AGE LEFT ITS MARK ON OUR HISTORY

Two great ages. — The Age of Pericles, when Athens was at the height of her achievements (p. 66), was one of the great times in the world's history. About 2000 years later came another great age, that of Queen Elizabeth, one of the greatest monarchs that ever sat on the English throne (1558–1603). The times of Pericles and of Elizabeth were days when the world was very wide awake. There are long periods of time when the world appears to do nothing unusual. Then comes an age when it shakes off its sleep and does something that will always be remembered. We should take pains to learn of the heritage which we have from the Elizabe'thans.

The early English settlers who came to America in the first part of the seventeenth century, were

QUEEN ELIZABETH

From a portrait printed soon after her death. The Latin reads: "Elizabeth, by God's grace Queen of England, France, Ireland, and Virginia." Notice the Elizabethan style of dress with the large sleeves, small waist, and full skirt. The queen here holds the symbols of her power, and at her side are shown the arms of England, the sword of Justice, and the Bible.

born in the age of Elizabeth or soon after it. They brought to our country the Elizabethan way of doing things. In the early chapters of this book we have been learning of our heritage from far-off times and peoples. We are now to see what special gifts our nearer ancestors gave us.

What the Elizabethan Age gave us. — We are specially interested in the Elizabethan Age. (1) It left us as a heritage the work of William Shakespeare, one of the greatest writers of all time. (2) Our theater has sprung from the Elizabethan theater, which Shakespeare helped to make. (3) The Elizabethans had the qualities that made our ancestors succeed; (4) they prepared the way for English colonies in America; and (5) they actually began to colonize.

William Shakespeare. — Shakespeare, like Columbus (p. 264), came from the middle class. Shakespeare's father was a craftsman (p. 237) who made out of leather such useful things as coats, trousers, gloves, and purses.

William Shakespeare was born (1564) in Stratford-on-Avon, a town in central England. Every year thousands of Americans visit the house in which he was born and his grave in the beautiful parish church. We feel that Shakespeare belongs to us as much as to the English because he had done most of his great work before a permanent English colony was planted in America.

Shakespeare was one of the most wide-awake men that ever lived. He mingled with all classes of people, and he was quick to learn the thoughts and feelings of almost every kind of human being. His chief work was writing plays to be acted in London theaters. For many years he lived in London and helped to manage theaters.

The characters in his plays come from all classes — servants, craftsmen, merchants, lords and ladies. We have seen (p. 144) that the people who changed the map of western Europe had a high opinion of women. Shakespeare's plays have wonderful heroines as well as great heroes.

What we owe to Shakespeare. — (1) No one has surpassed Shakespeare in using the English language. Many sayings in his plays have become a part of our everyday speech. We often hear people use such phrases from Shakespeare as " bag and baggage," " true as steel," " elbow-room," " as merry as the day is long," " in my mind's eye," " What's in a name? " " a woman's reason," " there's the rub," " every inch a king." You may at some time have remarked : " I have not slept one wink," but you probably did not know that you were quoting Shakespeare. Some singers do not remember that Shakespeare wrote the song which begins :

> " Hark, hark ! the lark at heaven's gate sings."

Many people do not use more than 2000 words in their talk and writing. Shakespeare used about 15,000 different words, and the way in which he used them is even more remarkable than their number.

(2) Shakespeare's plays continue to affect the ways in which we think, feel, and act. If we despise human beings, Miranda, the heroine of his play *The Tempest*, makes us ashamed when we hear her say :

> " How many goodly creatures are there here !
> How beauteous mankind is ! O brave new world,
> That has such people in 't ! "

It is now more than three hundred years since Shakespeare died (1616), but some of his plays continue to be acted in our theaters. The printing presses of the United States use acres and acres of paper every year to supply schools with Shakespeare's plays.

The Elizabethan theater. — We have seen that the Greeks gave plays in open-air theaters (p. 81). The English miracle plays (p. 240) were shown in the open air, sometimes on stages that were drawn by horses to various parts of the town. Plays were later given in the courtyard of London inns. The Elizabethans built public theaters

A THEATER OF ELIZABETH'S TIME

From a drawing by Walter Godfrey showing reconstruction of the Fortune Theater in London. Built in 1599, this theater was destroyed by fire and rebuilt in 1623. Spectators sat in the galleries and even on the stage. The open space in front of the stage was known as the pit and was usually occupied by the common people.

which left only the " pit," the part in front of the stage, open to the sky.

In 1912 London built a theater after the model of Shakespeare's Globe Theater. An American who stood in the pit to see one of Shakespeare's plays given in this theater says that a sudden shower wet him nearly through before he could reach cover. He was so near the actors that he seemed almost to be taking part in the play.   There was no change of scenery.   A signboard told whether the scene was laid in a forest, in a palace, or by the seashore.

There were no women actors in Shakespeare's time. Boys played the parts of Shakespeare's great heroines, as well as of all other female characters.

The pit of the theaters that we attend to-day has been roofed over, as well as the stage and the balconies.   Specially painted scenery is used and changes of scene are shown. Women play the female parts.   Such changes have given us our twentieth-century theater.

Why Elizabethans could do so much. — (1) Elizabethans had great power of imagination.   By this we mean that they could dream dreams of doing great and unusual things.   They dreamed of founding a greater England in the New World and of sailing on every sea.

(2) Elizabethans had unusual will power, the power to act vigorously.   When Sir Walter Raleigh dreamed of founding a colony beyond the Atlantic, he started at once to found it.   Many dream of doing great things but never do them.   In regard to action, some people say : " To-morrow."   Elizabethans said : " To-day."

(3) Elizabethans had initiative.   When we do things at once because we tell ourselves to do them, we show initiative.   If we do things only when others tell us to do them, we lack initiative.   When boys and girls notice what the family needs and start to get it or to mend something *without being asked*, they show initiative.   Courage and daring went with Elizabethan initiative.   Drake and other Elizabethan sailors had initiative and daring which made them eager to humble Spain on every sea and able to overcome the Armada (p. 307).

These three powers, inherited from the Elizabethans,— imagination, will, and initiative, — enabled our forefathers to plant lasting colonies in America. Men had to have imagination to make an ax and a knife take the place of a dozen different tools. It took imagination to deal with unusual difficulties. Our ancestors needed will power to clear the land, build homes of logs, and stick to their hard work. The colonists needed initiative every day because there was no one to tell them what to do or to map out their changing work. The unsettled frontier was a school for initiative, which has always been one of the most prized qualities of Americans. There are some organizations, such as the Boy Scouts and the Camp Fire Girls, that are now trying to give boys and girls training in initiative.

Search for a Northwest Passage ; Newfoundland. — The first attempt at colonization was the result of trying to find a Northwest Passage from the Atlantic to the Pacific; that is, a passage by water from Europe to Asia, through or around the northern part of North America. Martin Frob'isher (1535–1594), an English sailor, dreamed of a Northwest Passage and sailed to Arctic waters three times, vainly trying to make his dream come true. The passage was really there, but was (and is) blocked by ice.

Sir Humphrey Gilbert, another English sailor, became interested in two things : (1) in finding a Northwest Passage, and (2) in founding a colony on the way to it. He took possession of New'foundland (1583) in the name of Queen Elizabeth "by right of the discovery of John Cabot" (p. 273). A turf of Newfoundland soil was delivered to Gilbert, "after the custom of England," as a sign that the first land in the New World had passed "forever" under the control of the English nation. He did not found a

WHAT MARTIN FROBISHER SAW IN THE ARCTIC REGION

From a book of 1580. Eskimos in the far north still use boats like those in the picture.

colony there because hunger, sickness, and cold forced him to sail for England with his two remaining little vessels after the loss of his largest ship with all her supplies. He intended to return early the next spring. He was in the *Squirrel*, a little ship of only ten tons. When a storm arose, the sister vessel sailed near, and some one heard Gilbert say : " We are as near to Heaven by sea as by land." He was then " sitting abaft with a book in his hand." At midnight the light of the *Squirrel* suddenly disappeared, and she was never seen again.

Sir Walter Raleigh. — The great Elizabethan writer and explorer Sir Walter Raleigh (rô′lĭ, 1552–1618), was really the father of the English colonies in America. He had helped send Gilbert (his half brother) to Newfoundland. Like Hawkins and Drake (p. 304), Raleigh was born near the coast of Devonshire in southwestern England. There he mingled with the sailors and heard their stories of Spanish cruelty. For the rest of his life he thought that Spain was the most evil spot in the world. His wish to found colonies that would make England stronger than Spain was due partly to his dislike of the Spanish religion (p. 301).

ROANOKE ISLAND AND VICINITY

Raleigh had the Elizabethan quickness of imagination and action. When he was a student at Oxford, a weak classmate who was a good archer asked in a helpless way what he could do about an insult. Raleigh replied instantly : " Challenge the bully to a duel with bow and arrows." When he saw Queen Elizabeth stop before a mud puddle, as quick as a flash he threw his velvet cloak in it for her to step on. This act won her favor, and she rewarded him so that he became rich and was able to plant colonies.

Raleigh's first colony. — Raleigh obtained from Queen Elizabeth a charter (document) giving him the right to discover and colonize " lands not actually possessed by any Christian prince nor inhabited by Christian people."

Raleigh wisely sent two ships in advance without colonists. He thought that he would thus be sure of finding the right place for a successful colony. The ships sailed into Pam'lico Sound on the coast of what is now North Carolina, and stopped at Ro'anoke Island. The captains reported that the soil was the most fertile in the world, that the Indians feasted them on rabbits, venison, and Indian corn, and that they saw one Indian in half an hour catch fish enough to fill his boat

Raleigh sent at his own expense the next year (1585) a hundred colonists to Roanoke Island. Within a year they were worried because supplies had not reached them from England. Just then Sir Francis Drake called at Roanoke Island to see and report to Raleigh how his colony was faring. The colonists insisted on his taking them back to England. A few days after they had left, three supply ships reached Roanoke Island. When those ships returned, they left fifteen men to hold the place. The little colony of fifteen men was never seen again.

Raleigh's lost colony. — In honor of Elizabeth, who was called the Virgin Queen because she was not married, Raleigh gave the name of Virginia to the country that he tried to settle. A year after the first colonists returned, he sent (1587) at his own expense a hundred and fifty men, women, and children to Virginia. The sailors disobeyed his orders to take them to Chesapeake Bay and left them on Roanoke Island as before. Soon after they arrived, a child was born, and was named Virginia Dare. She was the first English child born in America

John White, the leader of the colony and grandfather of Virginia Dare, sailed back to England, intending to return with supplies in a few months; but the war between England and Spain delayed him. It was four years before he again landed on Roanoke Island. The colonists had promised that if they moved they would carve on a tree the

name of the place to which they had gone. He found the word CROATOAN cut on a tree "in fair capital letters." Croatoan was an island at the southern end of Pamlico Sound, south of Cape Hatteras. A tribe of friendly Indians lived there.

A storm arose, and the captain, who cared nothing for the settlers, sailed away with White before he could

INDIANS SPEARING FISH
From a drawing by John White of the Roanoke colony.

hunt for the colonists. We do not know what became of Virginia Dare. No one ever heard from any member of the lost colony. Some thought that the savages killed all the settlers, but it may be that they went to live with the Croatoan Indians and became part of their tribe.

The result of Raleigh's efforts. — Raleigh failed to found a permanent colony, although he sent at his own expense five expeditions to Virginia. The value of the money he thus spent would more than equal a million dollars to-day. He believed that a new English nation would be founded in the New World, and his experiments were steps toward founding it.

Instead of rewarding Raleigh as he deserved, the weak

king who succeeded Elizabeth had him executed on a charge of treason. We should remember our indebtedness to Raleigh. The state of North Carolina, on whose soil he tried to plant his colonies, has honored him by giving his name to the state capital.

Unequal success of different classes. — We saw in Chapter XVI that the beginning of the rise of the middle class was one of the important facts of the Middle Ages. The middle class in England kept on improving their condition during the Elizabethan Age. Merchants, foreign traders, and manufacturers became so wealthy that many of them were raised to the rank of nobility. Elizabeth selected some of her best advisers and statesmen from the middle class. There was no longer the same sharp line drawn between the middle class and the nobility. In that age, even if a man successful in trade or manufacturing were not raised to the nobility, he might have more influence than a nobleman.

In the Elizabethan Age the clergy did not have so much influence in the government as the clergy had in the Middle Ages, but the bishops of the Church of England still sat in the House of Lords. The villeins (pp. 232–236) had become free, but as free laborers they were not prosperous.

The Elizabethan Age was a time of great prosperity for the upper and middle classes. Their initiative and energy gave them an advantage over the same classes in other parts of Europe. The upper and middle classes in England secured nearly all the benefits of the prosperity of the nation, while the laborers remained poor. Let us see what reasons there were for such lack of equality.

(1) In the reign of Henry VIII a large amount of land was taken from the monasteries and became the property

of the king and the upper classes. Some of the noble families in England to-day owe their wealth to these church lands.

(2) We saw in Chapter XVI that the villeins made their living by tilling land. When they became free, they paid rent for their holdings. In the sixteenth century, however, wool became very valuable, and land that had once been used for thousands of farms was turned into pastures for sheep. Pasture land did not need to be plowed and cultivated. Only one shepherd and his dog were needed to attend to the sheep on a tract of land that had once employed a hundred peasants to till it. Farm laborers were thrown out of work all over England. They had to beg or steal while the owners of the land were getting rich.

(3) Fifteen weeks' work would support a laborer and his family better when Columbus discovered America than fifty-two weeks' work a hundred years later. The large amount of gold and silver brought to the New World made prices rise. Wages did not rise so fast as prices, partly because laws had been passed to regulate the wages of laborers (p. 236).

We can now see why the laborers might be more willing than others to colonize the New World.

Laws for crime. — Many laws were passed to deal with unemployment and the crime that resulted from it. Under Elizabeth, Parliament passed a law that vagabonds or wanderers were to be whipped and have a hole burned through their ears unless they found some one who would give bond to keep them at work for a year. They were to be put to death if they were found wandering a second time.

Men flocked to London but often failed to find work. England tried to prevent stealing by hanging those who stole anything worth a shilling. She finally made three hundred crimes punishable by death, but conditions became still worse. When successful colonies were founded in America, men who might have been hanged for slight reasons were often sent there to work like slaves for a few years.

Why colonists came to America. — (1) The victory over the Spanish Armada made the English more patriotic than before. Nobleman, merchant, and laborer wanted their country to become greater, and one way to make it greater was by planting English colonies. Sir Walter Raleigh was patriotic enough to spend a fortune trying to found an England beyond the sea.

(2) Many wished to come to America because they thought that they could make a better living there. Some wanted free land on which to raise their food. Others hoped to find gold or to profit from trading with the Indians. At first some hoped that a passage would be found through America. A colony on such a Northwest Passage would be a good station on the way to the Indies (p. 274).

(3) In the seventeenth century religious differences sent thousands to New England, Maryland, and Pennsylvania. Many desired to go where they could worship God as they chose.

How colonizing companies were organized. — Raleigh's colonies had failed. Men realized that the expense of founding a colony was too great for one man, and so they did what the makers of steel or of electrical machinery often do to-day. Such people now get other men to join with them in buying shares of stock in a company. Each stockholder is part owner of the company. States to-day give what are called "charters" to companies. A charter means a written

paper which grants certain rights or privileges and states
what the company may do.

In England, the king granted charters. In 1606 he gave
a charter to two companies, called the London Company
and the Plymouth Company. Each company had the

SEAL OF THE VIRGINIA COUNCIL

The portrait is that of King James I. The arms are those of Great Britain (the lions), France
(the lilies), and Ireland (the harp). The Latin inscription reads: "Seal of the King of Great
Britain, France, and Ireland for his council of Virginia." The king of England was also king
of part of France from the time of the Hundred Years' War (p. 295) down to the reign of
Queen Mary (p. 299). The name France was kept in the title much longer (till 1801).

right to plant a colony on the Atlantic coast of North
America, in the great territory then called Virginia (p. 319).
The London Company planted the first successful American colony — later called Virginia — as we shall see in the
following chapter.

Colonists to have the rights of Englishmen. — One part
of the charter said that the colonists were to be governed
by a council in England and a council in the colony.
Another far more important part granted to the colonists
and their children the liberties enjoyed by those born and
living in England. We should also remember that Queen

Elizabeth first granted such rights to Raleigh's colonists. The English claimed two rights which the English colonists later demanded : (1) the right to have some voice about taxation, (2) the right to have representatives in the law-making body (p. 190).

Things to remember about the Elizabethans. — 1. The early English colonists were born in the Age of Elizabeth.

2. The United States still feels the influence of Shakespeare in its thought and speech.

3. The English theater began to develop rapidly in the Age of Elizabeth.

4. The Elizabethans were noted for their imagination, will power, and initiative.

5. They began English colonization in America. Sir Walter Raleigh sent at his own expense two colonies to Roanoke Island, North Carolina. Both were failures, but they aroused interest in colonizing the New World.

6. The middle class of merchants and manufacturers grew more wealthy and influential.

7. Many tillers of the soil became vagabonds when their lands were taken for sheep pastures. There was much crime, which severe laws did not stop.

8. The three chief reasons for colonization were (1) the patriotic desire to make England more powerful, (2) the desire to gain wealth or to make a better living, (3) the desire for freedom to worship God as the colonists chose.

9. Colonizing companies secured charters which gave the colonists the rights enjoyed by Englishmen.

Things to do. — Tell the class why the age of Elizabeth was great.

Mention any one quality that made Shakespeare unusual.

Describe an Elizabethan theater. How was it different from the theater of to-day?

Explain the quality of initiative to a person who has never heard the word.

Be able to make a three-minute talk on Sir Walter Raleigh and his colonies.

Explain why some classes wished to leave England when others were contented there.

What is meant by a colonial charter? What rights did it grant?

References for Teachers.— Channing, *A History of the United States*, Vol. I, pp. 122–130 (Gilbert and Raleigh), 143–163 (colonial charters); Greene, *Foundations of American Nationality*, 31–43; Tyler, *England in America* (American Nation Series); Wood, *Elizabethan Sea-Dogs* (Chronicles of America), 205–222; Hakluyt's *Voyages* (Everyman's Library, Vol. VII,— gives full matter about the Raleigh colonies); any good history of England, such as those by Mowat, Cross, or Green, on the reign of Elizabeth; Traill and Mann, *Social England*, Vol. III; Eggleston, *Beginners of a Nation;* Eggleston, *Transit of Civilization from England to America in the Seventeenth Century;* Brown, A., *Genesis of the United States;* Halleck, *New English Literature*, IV; Adams, J. Q., *Life of William Shakespeare;* Hart, *American History Told by Contemporaries*, Vol. I, pp. 89–101; *Encyclopædia Britannica*, articles on "Shakespeare," "Gilbert, Humphrey," " Raleigh, Walter," and " North Carolina."

For Pupils. — Haaren and Poland, *Famous Men of Modern Times*, 111–122 (Raleigh); Bacon, *Voyages of Adventure and Discovery*, XVII (Gilbert), XIX–XXI (Raleigh's colonies); Holland, *Historic Boyhoods*, 35–47 (Raleigh); MacDowell, *Book of Boyhoods*, 42–50 (Raleigh); Foote and Skinner, *Explorers and Founders of America*, 103–111 (Raleigh); Dutton, *Little Stories of England*, 153–160 (Elizabeth), 171–178 (Shakespeare); Bennett, *Master Skylark* (Shakespeare, fiction).

CHAPTER XXII

THE FIRST SUCCESSFUL ENGLISH COLONY

How Jamestown was settled. — The reasons already given (p. 323) caused one hundred and five colonists to sail on three small ships from London for America. There were on board many who were called gentlemen because they did not work with their hands. There were also four carpenters, a blacksmith, a barber, a mason, a tailor, a number of laborers, and four boys. The vessels came by way of the West Indies, and the voyage lasted four months.

The colonists were ordered to sail one hundred miles up a river, in a northwesterly direction if possible, and then plant a colony. Two reasons were given for this order: (1) They would be less likely to be attacked by Spaniards there. (2) It was thought that this river might be the Northwest Passage to the South Sea (Pacific Ocean).

The colonists sailed thirty-two miles up the James River and made a settlement at Jamestown; they named both the river and the town in honor of James I, the king of England. They chose this place because the water was thirty feet deep so close to the edge of the bank that they could tie their vessels to trees. Jamestown was the first successful English settlement in the New World.

Some great historians have called 1607, the date of the settlement of Jamestown, the third most important event in American history. They think that only two other dates are more important: 1776, the time of our Declaration of Independence, and 1492, the date of the discovery of America.

A Jamestown pageant. — The settlement at Jamestown is important because it was the beginning of what is now the United States. Would you not like to see a pageant of the chief events that happened there? As you read the rest of this chapter you may turn it into a pageant in your imagination, by trying to see the people as clearly as if they were acting before your eyes. Then you and your classmates may perhaps play parts of the chapter as a real pageant.

Only men and boys came on the first voyage to Jamestown. Women and girls followed later. The men needed

INDIAN ATTACK ON A PLANTATION

at once the muskets which they brought with them. When they first landed, " there came the savages creeping on all fours like bears, with their bows in their mouths," and wounded two Englishmen. The Indians were frightened away by the sound of the guns. The English ate some fine oysters which the Indians had been roasting.

It was early in May when the colonists landed at Jamestown. Their writings tell of the wild flowers, of beautiful strawberries, of singing birds, of deer, foxes, otters, beavers, and " wild beasts unknown."

We may next see the colonists building a fort at Jamestown and planting corn near it. They were trying to prepare for a long stay on this continent.

The red men in the pageant. — The colonists had no theater, but some friendly Indians showed them a dance which was more interesting than moving pictures. The faces of the Indians were painted with a mixture of colors — black, red, blue, yellow. Some had their eyes painted red, some white on a black background. The claws of birds were hanging from their ears. One red man stood in the middle and the rest danced around him, making frightful gestures and howling like a pack of wolves.

In the early days, after many colonists had died of starvation, a file of Indians might often have been seen on their way to Jamestown bringing corn, fish, and venison. " Otherwise we had all perished," said a colonist. Sometimes three or four colonists died during one night, and their bodies were silently carried out for burial. Forty-six had died, most of them of starvation, before the middle of the first September after their landing.

Two years later many starving colonists left Jamestown to live among the Indians. For eight weeks the Indians and their white guests could get nothing but oysters to eat.

The planting of gunpowder was one of the few amusing scenes in the early history of the colony. The Indians were curious about gunpowder and its strange power. When they were given some of it, they planted it as they would their seed corn to see how much it would increase.

What Captain John Smith did in Virginia. — No Jamestown pageant could be complete if it left out John Smith. Many of us have already heard of him. He was a young Englishman born (1579) in the reign of Queen Elizabeth.

Like other Elizabethans (p. 315), he loved to do things. His favorite text was: "Whatsoever thy hand findeth to do, do it with thy might." He was president of the Jamestown colony during its second year and saved the colonists from starving. We may picture him building a boat and trading with the Indians, sometimes bringing back to Jamestown as much as a hundred bushels of corn.

We may see him moving among the laborers and finding that they had for the most part waited

CAPTAIN JOHN SMITH
From his map of New England made in 1614.

on gentlemen "and never did know what a day's work was." So many expected to get rich quickly from finding gold, that they were not willing to do hard work. Smith forced both laborers and gentlemen to work. He knew that the colony could not exist unless every one worked. He would not allow any one to eat if he had not worked. He made some go to the oyster banks to dig oysters. Others had to plant

corn, go with him to trade with the Indians, cut wood, dig
a well, work on the fort.

After he had been president of the colony for a year, he
was so badly hurt by an explosion of gunpowder that he
had to go to England for treatment. After he left, there
followed what is known as the " starving time." At last
the colonists all went on board a vessel and set sail for England to escape their misery. But they were met by supply
ships near the mouth of the river, and returned with them
to Jamestown.

A statue of John Smith was erected at the site of
Jamestown (1907), three hundred years after it was
founded, to honor him for his service to the first successful English colony in America.

Pocahontas. — No pageant of early Jamestown could
leave out Pocahontas. She was a beautiful, brown-eyed
Indian girl. The English called her a princess, because
she was the daughter of Powhatan', the chief of the Powhatan tribe of Indians. John Smith has made her story
one of the best known in American history. In his
history he wrote that he was captured by Indians and taken
to Powhatan, who said that he must be killed. Smith's
head was fastened to a stone, and Indians got their clubs
to beat out his brains. Pocahontas begged for his life, but
her father would not listen. When she saw the clubs raised,
she " got his head in her arms, and laid her own upon his
to save him from death." The chief then spared Smith's
life, and adopted him as a member of the tribe, but later
let him go back to Jamestown.

From that time Pocahontas was the friend of the English.
She once came a long way through the forest at night to
warn Smith of an Indian attack. She often brought corn

to the colony.   Smith wrote the English queen that Pocahontas saved Jamestown from destruction.

While Pocahontas was staying at Jamestown after Smith had gone back to England, John Rolfe, an English gentleman, fell in love with her.   They were married in the Jamestown church.   Her two brothers, her uncle, and other friends, both Indian and white, were guests at the wedding.

In 1616, the year of Shakespeare's death, Rolfe took her to England, where she was given a royal reception as the daughter of a king. Powhatan sent with her one of his braves with orders to report the number of the English by notches on a stick. He got a long stick, but the poor Indian soon gave up the task and wondered how the English counted.

POCAHONTAS

Portrait painted in 1616.   The Latin means "In the twenty-first year of her age."

At the beginning of the return voyage to America, Pocahontas died (1617). She was buried in the church of St. George, at Gravesend on the Thames River.   Nearly three centuries after her death, Virginians placed in that church two stained-glass windows in her memory.   She left a son, from whom many proud Virginians have traced their descent.

Religious worship in Jamestown.—No picture of Jamestown should fail to show the interest of the colonists in religion.   One of their first acts was to prepare a place of

CHURCH AT JAMESTOWN

© *Galloway*

The tower is part of the church built in 1639–1647. The rest of the church was rebuilt at the time of the Jamestown Exposition of 1907.

worship. They used an old sail for a roof to keep off the sun and rain. The seats were logs. A bar of wood nailed to two trees fenced off the pulpit. The colonists soon built a church. Men were fined if they did not go to church. One governor of the colony sent an officer every Sunday morning to the homes of the colonists to force all who were well to go to church. One of the reasons given for removing a president of the council at Jamestown was that he came to Virginia without a Bible. He replied that he had put a Bible in his trunk before sailing and that some one must have stolen it.

One reason for establishing the colony was the desire of the English to convert the Indians to Christianity. Pocahontas was introduced to the English queen as the first Christian convert in Virginia.

The only church allowed in the colony was the Church of England, or Episcopal Church, as it is called in America.

Other scenes in a Virginia pageant. — Corn and tobacco, both found only in the New World, would have a prominent place in a pageant showing the settlement of Virginia. John Rolfe tried raising tobacco in his garden before he made his visit to London with Pocahontas. When he came back after a two years' absence, he found only five or six houses in Jamestown. Its streets were planted with

TOBACCO SHIPS IN THE JAMES RIVER

Redrawn from an old engraving. Many plantations bordered on the river, and tobacco was shipped directly from the bank of the river. Much tobacco was packed in great barrels which were rolled to the wharf.

tobacco. Its people had spread out in the country to raise tobacco. So it happened that Virginia became a colony of tobacco plantations and not of towns.

After tobacco became plentiful, the London Company that had settled Virginia sent over a shipload of young women (in 1619). A Virginia colonist could now have a wife if he could (1) get the girl's consent, and (2) give to the company 120 pounds of tobacco to pay for her passage to Jamestown. Virginia soon became a colony of homes.

A Dutch vessel brought in the same year twenty negroes to Virginia and sold them to work in the tobacco fields. Thus negro slavery began in English America.

The same year also saw the first step taken toward the kind of government that we have to-day in the United States. Each of the chief settlements in Virginia elected two representatives to sit in the first representative body chosen by English settlers in America. This body was called the " House of Burgesses " (bûr′jĕs-ĕz). It advised with the governor of the colony and his council, who were appointed by the London Company. It had its first meeting at Jamestown in 1619.

The king took away the London Company's charter (1624) and made Virginia a royal colony. This meant that the king appointed the governor and the council, and used the royal power in governing Virginia. The Virginians, however, kept on electing their own House of Burgesses, which was like the English House of Commons.

We thus see that Americans had practice in governing themselves almost from the beginning of the first colony.

What the Virginia colony brought from the Old World. — The English colonists in America did not begin everything anew. They brought with them a vast heritage from England. They brought over the English language, ready made for use in their daily life. They had English books, such as the translation of the Bible. They brought English home life to America. The parents taught their children as they had been taught in England. They worshiped God, and made the church an important part of colonial life. The colonists usually followed English law and customs.

They were heirs to a vast heritage from the Old World in general — knowledge which men had worked thousands of years to get. The colonists brought the arts of spinning and weaving wool and linen thread into clothing, of tanning leather, and making shoes. The Old World had taught them how to use fire, and how to smelt and use iron. It

COLONIAL FLINT-LOCK MUSKET AND POWDER HORN

There were no cartridges or percussion caps in those days. The musket was loaded by pouring powder into the muzzle and ramming the bullet down the barrel. The firing was done by a spark struck by the flint lock. The spark fell into a train of powder leading through a little hole to the charge in the gun.

had invented muskets and gunpowder which they brought for their protection. They knew the art of shipbuilding and they had the mariner's compass to help them in crossing the ocean. They had long used the Arabic numerals from 0 to 9, so that they did not need to use a notched stick as did the Indian (p. 332). They were in debt to men of long ago for patiently taming the common domestic animals, such as the cow, horse, hog, and sheep. These were brought to America. Many of their crops, also, were from seed brought to this country from the Old World.

Facts to be remembered about the Virginia colony. — 1. A successful English colony was founded at Jamestown in 1607.

2. The colony was helped in many ways by the Indians. Pocahontas is one of the heroines of American history.

3. John Smith, the savior of the colony in the early days, showed Elizabethan qualities (p. 315).

4. The Church of England was the only one allowed in the colony. All were compelled to attend its service.

5. The year 1619 saw (1) a shipload of young women, the

founders of homes, come to Jamestown, (2) negro slaves brought, (3) the election of burgesses, the first representative body to be chosen in America.

6. The cultivation of tobacco made the colony prosperous.

7. The Jamestown colonists brought the Bible, the home life, speech, law, and customs of the English; also domestic animals, seeds for crops, and knowledge which it had taken the world thousands of years to learn.

Things to do. — Draw up a plan for your Jamestown pageant. How would you divide it into scenes? What characters would you use? Which scene is the most interesting to you? Which character would you choose to represent in the pageant?

Tell the story of Pocahontas.

Tell the story of Captain John Smith.

Tell the story of corn and tobacco and their importance to the Jamestown colony.

Talk to the class about the heritage which the Jamestown colonists brought from England.

References for Teachers. — Johnston, *Pioneers of the Old South* (Chronicles of America), I–VIII; Tyler, *England in America*, III–VI; Brown, *Genesis of the United States;* Bruce, *Social Life of Virginia in the Seventeenth Century;* Channing, *History of the United States*, Vol. I, Ch. VII; Wertenbaker, *Virginia under the Stuarts*, 1–94; Greene, *Foundations of American Nationality*, III–IV; Fiske, *Old Virginia and Her Neighbors;* Goodwin, *Colonial Cavalier;* Johnston, *To Have and To Hold*, and *Prisoners of Hope* (fiction); *Encyclopædia Britannica*, article "Smith, John" (excellent estimate of him). Halleck's *History of Our Country for Higher Grades*, page xxiv, shows twenty important dates (see page 327).

For Pupils. — Holland, *Historic Girlhoods*, 93–106 (Pocahontas); Jenks, *Captain John Smith;* Hazard, *Indians and Pioneers*, 127–148; Rolt-Wheeler, *Coming of the Peoples*, 41–89; Griffis, *Romance of American Colonization*, 25–54 (Jamestown).

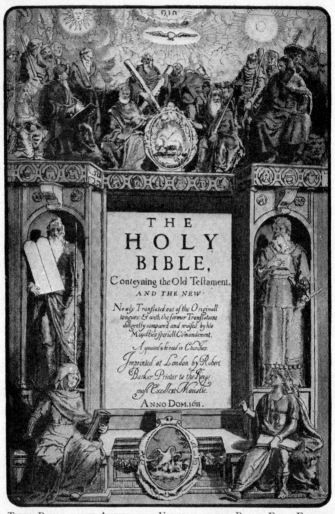

THE
HOLY
BIBLE,
Conteyning the Old Testament,
AND THE NEW:
Newly Translated out of the Originall
tongues: & with the former Translations
diligently compared and revised by his
Majesties speciall Comandement.

Appointed to be read in Churches.

Imprinted at London by Robert
Barker, Printer to the Kings
most Excellent Maiestie.

ANNO DOM. 1611.

TITLE PAGE OF THE AUTHORIZED VERSION OF THE BIBLE, FIRST EDITION

CHAPTER XXIII

HOW NEW ENGLAND WAS COLONIZED

A new line of kings in England. — Why were colonies
planted in New England? The answer is found in the history of England under Stuart kings. Queen Elizabeth was
the last of the rulers who belonged to the Tudor family (pp.
295, 298). The heir to the English throne was the king of
Scotland, the son of Elizabeth's cousin, Mary Stuart. He is
known as James I, the first of the Stuart line of English kings.
He and after him his son, Charles I, reigned from 1603 to
1649. Their acts left lasting marks on American history.

The Authorized Version of the Bible. — James I had
some of the most learned men in England make a simple
translation of the Bible (1611), a few years after the founding of the Jamestown colony. This translation was known
as the Authorized Version. It was soon brought to America
and read at morning and evening family prayers, at church
service, and at the burial of the dead. There are many
versions and translations of the Bible, but this has continued to be the one most used by English-speaking Protestants. It has greatly influenced the thought and the
speech of Americans as well as of Englishmen.

What the English people wanted. — Most of the English
people were at this time demanding more liberty. They
wanted it in two ways: (1) in religion, (2) in government.
They were determined to decide for themselves how they
should worship, and to have more of a voice in their govern-

ment.   The resistance of the Stuart kings to these two demands made many English people wish to come to America.
It was a direct cause of the settlement of New England.

Religious persecution. — When James I became king, the
Church of England (Episcopal Church) was the only church
allowed by the government.   There were two classes of
Protestants who wanted changes in worship :

(1) The Puritans wanted to " purify " the Church of
England without leaving it.   They did not like the surplice,

DRESS OF PURITANS ABOUT
1620–1630

or white linen robe, which the
clergy wore, and they did not
want the clergymen to be
called " priests."   Many would
have liked to change the
Prayer Book or to stop its
use.   The Puritans wished a
stricter Sunday, but James I
told the people that they
ought to give Sunday afternoon to sports and athletic
games.   Crowds went on Sunday to see bear-baiting, which
meant that a chained bear was
tortured by dogs.

(2) The Independents agreed with the Puritans but did
not think that the Church of England could be purified
enough.   The Independents left the Church of England
and founded a new church.

James I told both Puritans and Independents that he
would drive them out of the land if they did not worship
in the way taught by the Church of England.   He demanded that the clergy should accept the Prayer Book

without changes. Rather than do this, about three hundred clergymen gave up their places.

In the reign of Charles I, Archbishop Laud tried to make every clergyman, even if he was a Puritan or an Independent, accept the service of the Church of England. Laud ordered that the communion table should be placed in the east end of the church and that every worshiper should bow toward that table as he entered the church. Those who disobeyed him might be fined or have their ears cut off. Laud's persecution caused many to settle in New England.

Trouble over civil government. — By civil government we mean the everyday government of the people, apart from their control by the church in religious matters. The Stuart kings laid taxes without a vote of the lawmaking representatives of the English people sitting in Parliament. Charles I threw into jail without trial those who would not pay the tax. Just at the time when the English people were demanding more liberty, James I and Charles I were insisting more and more on the claim that, as kings, they ruled by divine right. That is, they believed that they received their kingdom from God and that their subjects had no right to object to what they did in matters of government. The English people, however, were fast coming to believe that the rights of the people were greater and more divine than those of the king.

The Petition of Right. — The House of Commons determined to make Charles I sign an agreement called the Petition of Right (1628), just as King John had been forced to sign Magna Charta (p. 187). The Petition of Right provided that the king should not imprison any one without a just reason. The king was forbidden to ask for loans or to lay taxes not voted by Parliament. He should not in time of peace set aside the regular laws as if the nation were at war. If he wanted to play king, he was told that he must obey the rules of the game given in the Petition of Right. Charles promised, but he did not keep his word. He ruled without a Parliament for eleven years. During that time he did not ask Parliament to vote taxes, but he raised money in one way or another to meet the expenses of government and of war. He also had men imprisoned without cause.

The civil war in England. — Charles finally had to summon a Parliament to get money to pay for war. He was fighting the Scotch because they refused to use the Prayer Book and to follow the service of the Church of England.

DRESS OF CAVALIERS ABOUT 1630

Parliament refused to vote taxes as the king wished. When five members criticized the king's action, he came with soldiers to arrest them. These members had been warned and fled. There could be no free government if the representatives of the people were not allowed to express their minds.

The king's attempt to stop free speech in Parliament led to civil war between his friends and those who wished a free Parliament. The king's followers were called "Cavaliers" because so many of them had horses to ride. Most of those who fought on the side of Parliament were Puritans or Independents. They were often nicknamed "Roundheads" because they clipped their hair short. Oliver Cromwell, one of England's great generals, finally became the head of the parliamentary army. He defeated the royal forces and captured the king.

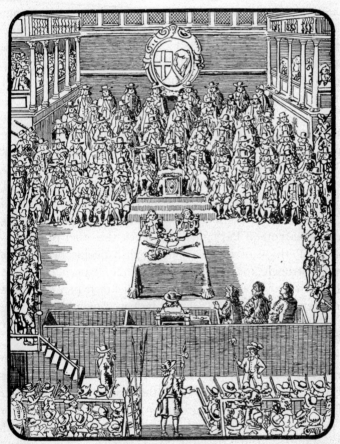

TRIAL OF CHARLES I

Redrawn from a book published in 1684. The king is the figure in the center with his back turned. He faces the large group of judges who are trying him. Notice the line of soldiers in front of the spectators.

While the people were trying to compel the captive king to agree to rule justly, he was plotting to bring foreign armies to England to defeat them so that he could again rule as he chose.   Cromwell's army then drove out of Parliament those members who gave any support to the king. The rest of Parliament decided that the people were the source of all power.   They had the king tried for treason because he had used arms against his subjects.   The court set up by Parliament found him guilty, and he was beheaded (1649).

England was then declared to be a Commonwealth or republic under the rule of Parliament, but Cromwell was in control until his death (1658).   During this time many Cavaliers went to the Virginia colony, which was friendly to the king.   In 1660 the monarchy was restored, and Charles II, the son of Charles I, became king of England.

After the Restoration, the king did not again lay taxes without a vote of Parliament, or break the other provisions of the Petition of Right.   The English people had won a great struggle for liberty.   Meanwhile, especially before the civil war, great numbers of Englishmen had left their country and had begun colonies in New England.

Why the first New England settlement was made. — In Nottinghamshire in northeastern England, there lived, early in the reign of King James I, a group of men who later made the first settlement in New England.   Most of them were plain farmers who read the Bible for themselves. They formed a little congregation and separated from the Church of England.   Some have for that reason called these Independents (p. 340) "Sep'aratists."   Their meetings were forbidden, and some of the members were imprisoned   The Separatists knew that people in Holland could worship as they chose, so they left their pleasant homes, with whatever they could carry, and tried to go there quietly. They were stopped, and much of what they had was taken from them. Some of them were thrown into jail. Most of them, however, finally reached Holland and settled in Leyden.

They called themselves " Pilgrims " because they said that they were on a journey or pilgrimage " to the heavens,

EMBARKATION OF THE PILGRIMS FROM HOLLAND ON THEIR WAY TO
AMERICA
Redrawn from a painting in the Houses of Parliament, London.

their dearest country." Their first pilgrimage was to Holland. The Pilgrims remained in Holland for nearly twelve years. During this time they had their own church and pastor and worshiped God as they pleased.

They found it hard to earn a living in Holland. The children had to go to work early to help support the family, and their bodies were bent with toil. They began to learn

the Dutch language and ways, and their parents feared
that they would cease to be English. Some of the boys
went to sea and fell in with bad companions. The Pilgrims thought that they might give their children a better
chance in America and at the same time serve God as they
chose. So these Pilgrims started on another pilgrimage, a
longer one than the Crusaders (p. 216) had ever attempted.

The settlement at Plymouth. — In 1620 part of these
Pilgrims sailed in the ship *Mayflower* for America. More
than a third of them were children. No other early English colony had so large a proportion of young people.

After some delay the colonists landed at Plymouth late
in December. The girls and women stayed on board the
Mayflower while the men and boys were building log houses.
The Pilgrims suffered so much from the cold winter that
half of the colony of one hundred and two died before spring.
Fewer children died than older people, and thus Plymouth
became more than ever a young people's colony.

How the Indians came to Plymouth. — In February
(1621) some Pilgrims left their axes in the woods when they
went home to dinner. Some Indians who had only stone
tools had been watching how quickly these wonderful axes
could cut down a tree. They ran away with the axes as
soon as the Pilgrims had gone. The Pilgrims might have
tried to compel the Indians to give the axes back, but they
found that making friends of the red men served better
than threats of war.

In March an Indian walked boldly among the Pilgrims and
surprised them by saying, " Welcome, Englishmen ! " His
name was Sam'oset. He had learned a little English from
fishermen who had visited the coast of New England. He
was the first Indian that the Pilgrims met, and they wanted

SAMOSET'S VISIT TO THE PILGRIM COLONY

to learn from him all that they could. He told them that the cleared fields which they found had belonged to a tribe of Indians who had died of the plague four years before. They noticed that he shivered when a cold wind rose, and they put a horseman's coat on him. The next day he came with other Indians, all dressed in deer skins. A Pilgrim wrote of this visit: " They brought us all our tools again, which were taken in the woods in our men's absence."

Samoset next brought Squanto, the only one who was left of the tribe that had lived at Plymouth before the plague. Squanto had survived because an English captain had taken him to Europe. Squanto had lived long enough in London to learn English. Another captain had brought him back on a fishing voyage, and he had found his way to the home of his tribe, but not one was alive to greet him. He stayed with the Pilgrims as long as he lived.

The Pilgrims might have starved the next winter if Squanto had not shown them how to raise corn in the fields where he had worked before he was taken to Europe. He told them to plant the corn in hills and to bury a fish or two under each hill for fertilizer. He showed them where enough fish could be caught. This was in April. He told them to plant the corn when the oak leaves were as big as the ears of a mouse. This was in May. They had found and paid for ten bushels of seed corn that had been buried by the Indians. The Pilgrims followed Squanto's advice in planting twenty acres, which yielded enough corn to feed them during the winter.

How peace was kept with the Indians. — The Pilgrims believed in peace. They treated the Indians fairly. April 1,

GOVERNOR CARVER'S CHAIR
In Pilgrim Hall, Plymouth. John Carver was the first governor of the Plymouth colony.

1621, is a noted day in Pilgrim history. On that day Squanto and Samoset acted as interpreters for the Pilgrims in making a treaty of peace with Mas'-sasoit, a great Indian chief. They agreed that the white men and the Indians should never harm each other; that they should aid each other if a third party declared unjust war upon either Massasoit or the Pilgrims; and that anything stolen by either race should be returned. This treaty was faithfully kept by both parties. Massasoit warned the Pilgrims when other tribes of Indians threatened them.

When Massasoit was so sick that he was expected to die, one of the Pilgrims, named Edward Winslow, visited him and helped to save his life by careful nursing and the right kind of food. When the Indian chief was well again, he said: "Now I see that the English are my friends. I will never forget this kindness."

Why we have a Thanksgiving Day. — The Pilgrims had the first Thanksgiving Day in 1621 after their corn was safely gathered and stored. They wished to thank God for his blessings in giving them homes in a new land, and large crops for food. Four young hunters were sent out to supply the Thanksgiving table, and they found the game plentiful. There were in the vicinity of Plymouth wild turkeys, quail, partridges, ducks, rabbits, and deer. Massasoit and many of his Indians were invited to the feast, and brought five deer. The Indians enjoyed themselves so much that they remained three days to feast and play games with the Pilgrims.

Thanksgiving Day is now observed every year in our whole country. It should always make us think of the Pilgrims, whose thankfulness and trust in God led them to establish this holiday.

How the people of Plymouth governed themselves. — The Pilgrims were not under the control of any company. Nobody had framed any laws for them. They governed themselves from the first day that they landed.

Before coming ashore, they drew up what is known as the Mayflower Compact, which began, " In the Name of God." This was an agreement " in the presence of God " that they would make for themselves " just and equal laws for the general good of the colony," and that all would obey these laws.

They elected their own governor. William Bradford was their governor for many years. Miles Standish, their captain, trained them as a little army for the defense of the colony. Sometimes all the male members of the Plymouth

MILES STANDISH'S SWORD, PLATTER, AND KETTLE
Now in Pilgrim Hall, Plymouth, Mass.

congregation decided questions of public interest. They once sat in judgment on two young men who had fought a duel, and sentenced them to remain for twenty-four hours with their feet tied to their necks. The young men, however, were released in an hour when they promised to offend no more. Duels were not again fought in the colony.

The Pilgrims had regular town meetings which all the voters attended. These town meetings did two things: (1) They elected town officers who attended to the roads, taxes, schools, and other matters which affected the welfare of the people. (2) They passed laws which the town needed. The Pilgrims had been used to such meetings in the parishes or districts around churches in England. These meetings suggested the New England town meeting, which taught self-government.

How the Pilgrims worshiped. — The Pilgrims left their homes in England and went to Holland because they put their religion above everything else. In America, they tried to obey the Ten Commandments and serve God. They kept the Sabbath day holy and went to church.

They worshiped God in their own way without any direction by bishop or king. Their church has become known as the Congregational Church because the entire congregation voted on all church matters, and each congregation was independent of any outside control. Their church, like their town meeting, was a school for self-government.

They had very few books, but they brought with them one of the most interesting books in the world. They read

GOING TO CHURCH AT PLYMOUTH IN 1622

The fort at Plymouth had a flat roof, with cannon on it. The building was used also as a meeting house.

in it the story of creation, of Ruth, of David and Goliath, of the lost sheep, and of the Good Samaritan. It was the fashion to read this book through several times. This book was the Authorized Version of the Bible (p. 339), which had been printed only a few years and was new to most of them.

How the Puritans settled in New England. — Charles I (p. 341), early in his reign, gave to some wealthy Puritans

NEW ENGLAND COLONIES

a charter for planting and governing the colony of Massachusetts in New England. The land which was granted to them was north of the Plymouth colony and extended westward "from sea to sea." These Puritans were beginning to fear that they might not succeed in having the Church of England "purified" as they wished (p. 340). They also were greatly displeased by the king's government (p. 341). They therefore decided to go, with many other Puritans, to found a new home in Massachusetts.

Their chief settlement was at Boston, which was founded in 1630. In the next ten years nearly twenty thousand Puritans came to New England, and made Massachusetts from the first a large and prosperous colony. The smaller colonies of New Hampshire, Rhode Island, and Connecticut were also founded by Puritans during those ten years. Some of the settlers in these later colonies came from Massachusetts, and some from England.

The Puritans in New England promptly left the Church of England and became Congregationalists (p. 351). They governed themselves, like the Pilgrims of Plymouth, not only in their form of worship but also in their civil affairs. In each town of Massachusetts, the same body of male voters controlled both the church and the local government. Every town also sent representatives to Boston to take part in a government for the whole colony.

The Pilgrims in Plymouth and the Puritans in Massachusetts were on very friendly terms. There was little

OLD TOWN HOUSE IN BOSTON

From an old print which follows the pencil drawing made by Thomas Joy, the designer. This building was the seat of the Boston town government from 1657 to 1711.

difference between them. The Plymouth colony grew slowly, and after seventy years (1691) it was made a part of Massachusetts.

H.-F. — 24

What the Pilgrims and Puritans brought from the Old World. — (1) The early settlers in New England had the same great heritage that the colonists brought to Virginia (pp. 335–336).

(2) They brought also a firm determination to worship God as they chose, to govern themselves as much as possible, and to vote their own taxes.

(3) They brought a deep respect for the Bible and for the Ten Commandments and made them the foundation of their government. They thus set a standard which has greatly influenced our whole country.

Facts to be remembered about the colonization of New England. — 1. The Authorized Version of the Bible (1611), printed during the reign of James I, influenced the thought and the language of American colonists.

2. Those who wished to " purify " the Church of England were called Puritans. Those who wished to found a new church were called Independents or Separatists.

3. Under James I and Charles I, both the Puritans and the Independents were persecuted, and many went to New England.

4. The English forced Charles I to sign the Petition of Right, which forbade the king (a) to imprison any one without cause, (b) to ask for loans or to lay taxes without the consent of Parliament, (c) to set aside the laws of the land in time of peace.

5. Civil war broke out when Charles I would neither keep his promises nor allow freedom of speech in Parliament. He was defeated, tried, and beheaded.

6. England became a Commonwealth with Oliver Cromwell at the head. Soon after his death the monarchy was restored, but the new king obeyed the Petition of Right.

7. The Pilgrims were Separatists who went first to Holland and then came to America; they settled at Plymouth, 1620.

8. The Pilgrims treated the Indians justly and kindly, and the Indians helped the Pilgrims.

9. The Pilgrims were the first to have a Thanksgiving holiday.

10. The Puritans founded the great colony of Massachusetts and other New England colonies.

11. The Pilgrims and Puritans had in America (1) nearly complete self-government, (2) an independent church where they could worship as they chose.

Things to do. — For what should we remember James I?

Compare Magna Charta with the Petition of Right. (See pages 187–188.)

Imagine yourself to be one of Cromwell's men. Tell why you are fighting against Charles I.

Do we to-day enjoy any of the rights for which men fought in the English civil war?

Show on the map the wanderings of the Pilgrims.

Build a log cabin, and in a pageant represent Pilgrims at their various tasks about the place.

Dramatize the first Thanksgiving.

Explain the statement: " The Pilgrims governed themselves from the first day that they landed."

What are some of the things the Pilgrims and Puritans brought from the Old World?

References for Teachers. — Consult any history of England for the reigns of James I and Charles I. Pollard, *History of England*, V; Gardiner, *Puritan Revolution;* Channing, *History of the United States*, X, XI; Harding, *New Medieval and Modern History*, XXI; Robinson, *History of Western Europe*, XXX; *Encyclopædia Britannica*, articles on " English History," " James I," " Charles I," " Cromwell, Oliver "; Bradford, *History of Plymouth Plantation;* Goodwin, *The Pilgrim Republic;* Usher, *The Pilgrims and Their History;* Arber, *The Story of the Pilgrim Fathers;* Greene, *Foundations of American Nationality*, V; Halleck, *History of Our Country for Higher Grades*, 64–77.

For Pupils. — Tappan, *England's Story*, VII (House of Stuart); Dickens, *Child's History of England*, XXXII–XXXIV (James I, Charles I, Cromwell); Dale, *Landmarks of British History*, IX (Stuart kings); Warren, *Stories from English History*, 255–289 (Stuart kings and Cromwell); Van Loon, *Story of Mankind*, 279–295 (Stuart kings and civil war); Ross, *Oliver Cromwell;* Haaren and Poland, *Famous Men of Modern Times*, 175–184 (Oliver Cromwell); Usher, *Story of the Pilgrims for Children;* Griffis, *Romance of American Colonization*, 94–128 (the Pilgrims); Holland, *Historic Girlhoods*, 107–123 (Priscilla Alden); Jenks, *Captain Miles Standish;* Hazard, *Indians and Pioneers*, 171–181 (Plymouth); Deming and Bemis, *Stories of Patriotism*, 1–18 (Indians, first Thanksgiving); Tappan, *Letters from Colonial Children* (John Billington of Plymouth); Rolt-Wheeler, *Coming of the Peoples*, 200–246 (Pilgrims).

CANOPY OVER PLYMOUTH ROCK

CHAPTER XXIV

HOW THE COLONISTS LIVED

The thirteen colonies. — We have seen how Virginia, the first English colony in the South, was settled (Chapter XXII). Four other colonies in that part of our country were founded by the English; namely, Maryland, North Carolina, South Carolina, and Georgia.

We have seen (Chapter XXIII) how the four New England colonies were founded by the English; namely, Massachusetts, Connecticut, Rhode Island, and New Hampshire.

In the region between the Southern Colonies and New England, the Dutch (p. 303) were the first to found colonies; but the land was taken from them by the English in 1664. Before long this middle region was divided among four colonies under English rule. The Middle Colonies were New York, New Jersey, Pennsylvania, and Delaware.

All of these thirteen English colonies, except Georgia (1733), were founded between 1600 and 1700, during the century following the defeat of the Spanish Armada (p. 306).

Colonizing meant a struggle to live. — Raleigh's colonies proved that it was not enough for settlers to be brought to these shores. The more important question was how to live after they had come. Those who have read the book called *Swiss Family Robinson* know how a father, mother, and four children lived after they were wrecked on one of the fertile South Sea Islands. Almost all that they had to do was to reach out their hands and pluck fruit. It took little effort to live. On the other hand, most of us have read *Robinson Crusoe*, and we know that it is the hero's struggle to get things that makes his story one of the most interesting ever written. Our own ancestors had some struggles like those of Robinson Crusoe.

BEAVER

The beaver has a rich chestnut-brown fur. Its head and body are about two feet long, and the broad, flat, hairless tail is about ten inches. The beaver lives most of the time in the water. It eats water plants and the bark of trees.

Let us imagine that we are colonists and set ourselves the problem of finding what we can do to live. Let us suppose at the outset that we own a tract of land partly or wholly covered with trees, on the eastern coast of what is now the United States.

We have land, trees, and water. The water may be the ocean, a harbor, or a river. It contains fish (pp. 319, 320) and perhaps oysters (p. 328), clams, and lobsters. The new country has valuable fur-bearing animals : beaver, foxes, otters, minks. The Indians tell us how to make clothing out of the skin of the deer and blankets out of that of the bear. The story of the first Thanksgiving shows that many wild animals and fowl could supply

MINK

The American mink ranges in color from a light yellow-brown to a dark brown. Its body is about fifteen inches long. It is a good fisher and feeds chiefly on fish and reptiles.

food at certain seasons of the year. Among these were wild turkeys, geese, ducks, quail, grouse, pigeons, rabbits, and deer.

The use of corn in solving the problem of food. — We cannot be sure of finding game and fish all the year, and so we must search for a food on which we can depend at all seasons. If we imagine ourselves meeting Indians and asking what they eat, we shall learn of a food new to Europe. The Indians will tell us that they live on corn when the snow is deep and game cannot be found, and that they take only a pouch of parched corn when they go on long journeys. If we meet Indians as friendly as Squanto (p. 347), they will tell us when and how to plant this new grain. They will also show us how to prepare the corn for cooking by making from it meal, hominy, and samp. They will teach us how to turn the meal into corn bread by baking it in the hot ashes and will tell us how long to boil the hominy and samp. The use of Indian corn helped to save the colonists from starvation in early colonial times.

© *Wide World*

WILD TURKEY

The turkeys on our farms are descended from turkeys domesticated by white men since the discovery of America.

There is a story that each Pilgrim once had only five kernels of corn a day for food. Each guest at a dinner in honor of the founders of New England sometimes finds five kernels of corn at his plate as a reminder of the famine which the founders endured and of the grain which saved them.

The building of homes. — The problem of something to eat comes first because we must eat while we work. Let us suppose that we have trees for material and axes for tools with which to begin building our home. We must notch the logs where they join at each corner of the house, so that they will lie close to each other and remain firmly in their place. We are told the story of a man who used such uneven logs that a wolf thrust his nose between them and bit the head of the sleeping man. In our house, we may drive wedges of wood in the crevices between the logs, and plaster them with mud.

If we see Indian wigwams made of bark, we may learn how to use bark for roofing our log cabin. On Manhattan Island, the site of New York, all but one of the houses in the first settlement made by the Dutch (1626) were built of bark.

COLONIAL FIREPLACE AND COOKING
UTENSILS

The "Dutch oven" (in front) was made of thin iron and had one side open to the fire. It had a shelf in the middle which made it possible to bake several things at one time. Notice the iron kettles for boiling, which are hung over the fire by chains.

The chimney of our log cabin will trouble us more than anything else. If we can find flat stones for the chimney, we may leave at one end of the house a hole eight feet long and four feet high. We can then build the fireplace and its stone chimney on the outside of the house. If we cannot find stones, we may have to make the chimney of small logs plastered on the inside with mud. All the family meals must be cooked in the fireplace. We can study our lessons by the blazing logs in the long winter evenings and watch the shadows play hide and seek around the room.

We may use oiled paper for windows.   If we are skillful
enough, we may make wooden hinges for the doors; but
most of us will probably hang our doors on hinges made of
the tough hide of some animal.

GUARDING THE CORNFIELD

Redrawn from a painting by General Seth Eastman, who spent much time on frontier duty
near the homes of western Indians.   This shows how Indian women protected the corn from
flocks of birds.

If we were colonial men or boys. — Nearly all the colonists at first lived by tilling the soil.   All the colonies from
Massachusetts to Georgia raised Indian corn, and the
people usually ate it every day in the year.   If we were
colonial men or boys, much of our work in the early days
would be in the cornfields.   We should find trees covering
our land in most places.   Before we did any planting, we
should girdle the trees by cutting through the bark.   This
girdling would kill them and keep them from putting forth
leaves which would shade the crops.   The next November
we should begin to cut down the trees, burning most of

them where they fell, but saving some for firewood. After oxen were brought from England, we should have to dig up many roots of trees before the ground could be plowed.

After the corn was planted, we should have to watch the fields to keep the crows and squirrels from pulling up the young shoots of corn. We should have to keep the weeds out of the corn until it was grown. As everything would have to be done by hand, raising a good crop of corn would take up much of our time until late in the summer.

BREAKING FLAX

This home-made machine was used for breaking the tough woody parts of the stalks of flax. The flax fibers remained unbroken and were afterwards cleaned. Notice that the upper slats in this machine fit between the lower slats so that the stalks were broken in several places at each blow.

As our colony grew older, we could plant fields of rye, barley, and wheat. Our gardens would grow peas and beans. We should plant pumpkins with our corn. We should also raise cows, sheep, pigs, and chickens, beginning with animals brought from the Old World or from other colonies.

We should not forget to raise a patch of flax. Flaxseed is sown in May. The plant grows rapidly and is ready to be pulled up in July. Then we should have a hard time separating the fibers from the rest of the stalk. What is the use of flax? That story is best told as part of the work of women and girls.

The work of colonial women and girls. — Let us again use our imagination and become colonial women or girls. Let us chat together and tell what we do.

In the first place, we do all the cooking for our families, which often number twelve or more, but cooking is the smallest part of our work. We make all the clothing for the family. The sheep furnish us with wool. The men shear it from the sheep and say : " Make out of this everything that we wear except our shoes." If we told you all that we do to that wool before you have a coat or stockings to wear, you would not have patience to listen to us.

Here is our spinning wheel, with which we spin yarn

SPINNING WOOL

The spinner holds a roll of soft carded wool in her left hand. The end of the roll is wound on the point of the spindle at the left. The large wheel is set in motion with the spinner's right hand, thus making the spindle rotate rapidly. The spinner steps back and stretches the roll to the right distance while it is being twisted into yarn. Then she allows the yarn to wind up on the spindle, and repeats the process with another length of the roll of wool.

from the fibers of wool. A girl of four can knit herself a pair of stockings from the yarn. We knit mittens and stockings for all the family. Sometimes we also knit a pair of mittens for the minister to wear when he preaches in cold weather. If he did not have them, his hands might freeze while he preaches a two-hour sermon in the cold meeting house.

The spinning wheel does not make cloth, but only thread or yarn that we weave into cloth. We use a loom to do the weaving.

A smaller spinning wheel makes linen thread from the fiber of flax. That thread is light brown even after it has been bleached thirty times. We use it in weaving handkerchiefs, towels, bed sheets, aprons, pillow cases, dresses, and shirts. To make the linen cloth white, we spread it on the grass and wet it several times a day for weeks. It is sometimes soaked in buttermilk at the last.

Besides cooking and spinning and weaving, we have other work. We do the mending and washing for all the family. This is the way we make soap: First we fill a barrel with wood ashes, pour water on them, and catch the brown liquid, called lye, in a tub under the barrel. Then we mix this lye with grease, and boil them together. The result is soft soap which looks like yellow jelly.

We catch the geese, put a stocking over their heads so they will not bite us, and pluck their feathers for our beds and pillows. If we sleep between two feather beds, we are never cold, even though the water in the room freezes solid.

We make candles of tallow or from the wax of bayberries. We prepare dyes from sumach berries and the bark of various trees. We make brooms of birch twigs or wheat straw. We make baskets. We help milk the cows, make butter and cheese, and take care that the hawks, foxes, and minks do not catch the chickens.

By the fireside. — In colonial times the family really sat by the fireside (see Frontispiece), as they seldom do to-day. Various kinds of work could be done in the evening before the blazing logs. The colonial boy often used his jackknife then to make some article, such as a red cherry butter paddle for his mother.

The members of the family often told stories by the evening fire. Let us listen to one, the tale of a fireside industry, as a boy tells the story:

Two boys wished to earn some money in the long winter evenings, and so they used their jackknives to make shoe pegs from hard maple. Their father carried the pegs in a bag to a market at some distance and stopped for the night at a town tavern. Some farmers on their way to market put up at the same tavern. One farmer, whose name was Meigs (mĕgz), stole out to the tavern stables at night and searched for grain to feed his hungry horse. He grabbed from a neighbor's sleigh what seemed to be a bag of oats and poured out a good mess for his horse. In the morning the boys' father went to his sleigh and missed part of the pegs. He found them under the nose of the sorrowful horse of Meigs. The boys nicknamed the man " Shoe-pegs Meigs," and that was the name by which he was known ever after.

What the home accomplished. — The colonial fireside was a school of service. It was this fireside service that made the members of the family quick to notice the wants of one another and happy to do what was needed to supply them. American patriotism began by the fireside when members of the home circle unselfishly helped each other.

It spread beyond the home to the colony, and then helped make us into a nation. The women and girls did the most to make the home, but the men and boys did their share in different ways. Colonial girls and boys were both, in their own way, like the Elizabethans (p. 315).

Life in the South. — The majority of the early colonists living north of Maryland made at home most of the articles which they needed. The southern colonists in the uplands also depended on home manufactures.

We have already seen (Chapter XXII) how the early Jamestown colonists lived. Settlers in Maryland, Virginia, the Carolinas, and Georgia, living near the sea or navigable rivers, made fewer things in their homes than the northern colonists. There were two reasons for this difference: (1) The soil and climate of these southern colonies were better fitted to produce things which the outside world wanted. Maryland and Virginia raised much tobacco. North Carolina had pine forests which produced tar and pitch for the British navy, as well as good lumber for building houses. The seacoast of South Carolina and Georgia grew rice. (2) Ships could easily carry to England the tobacco, tar, and rice and bring back articles which the colonists wanted.

A traveler wrote of the Virginians (about 1700) that they sheared their sheep more to cool them than to make clothes out of the wool. The reason was that a month's labor in growing tobacco might bring in exchange more clothing than two months' work at the spinning wheel and the loom. The clothing for the slaves, however, was often made on the plantation.

Virginians made enough from the sale of their tobacco in England to order from London for their wives such articles as silk shoes, flowered silk dresses, silk hose, ruffles, ribbons, kid gloves, and fans. Men ordered for themselves fine cloth suits lined with scarlet, summer suits, winter suits, shoes, wigs, and beaver hats. They also imported furniture

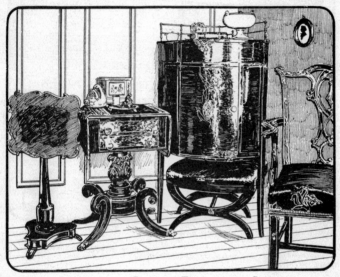

FURNITURE OF COLONIAL TIMES IN THE SOUTH
From left to right: tip-table, serving table, cabinet with a footstool underneath, chair.

and many common household articles which New England colonists made at home. Virginians sometimes complained to their London merchants that the fine goods shipped had been damaged by salt water and had filled their houses with cockroaches.

Those colonists who lived where it took less work to get needed things would have more leisure. Virginians and the other southern colonists came to have still more leisure because much of their work was done by negro slaves.

AN EARLY PICTURE OF THE CODFISH INDUSTRY AT NEWFOUNDLAND

After a copper-plate in Sir William Keith's *History of the British Plantation in America.*
A, The fisherman.   *B*, The hook.   *C*, Catching codfish.   *E*, Dressing codfish.   *G*, Carrying
the cod.   *H*, Cleaning it.   *M*, Drying it.   *I*, Press for extracting oil from the cod's liver.

The southern colonists, especially those in Virginia, had
more visitors in their homes and more amusements.   They
enjoyed dancing, music, and horse racing, which would have
been frowned on in New England.   A program of entertainment in Virginia (1737) announced that a pair of handsome
shoes would be given to the best dancer, that twenty
fiddlers would play, each a different tune at the same time,
and that twenty horses would race.

Class distinctions were carefully made.   Colonial Virginians loved a horse race.   After a tailor had raced his horse
with a doctor's in Virginia (1674), the county court fined the

tailor because " it was contrary to law for a laborer to make a race which was a sport only for gentlemen."

Growth of trade. — The northern colonists, as well as the southern, learned how to supply some things which other people wanted, and to get in return articles which could not be produced at home. Trade between New England and the West Indies began in this way: New England wanted molasses and sugar which she could not produce. The West Indies wished cheap food for the slaves that worked their sugar plantations. The sailors of New England caught, dried, and salted hundreds of thousands of codfish to sell as food for these slaves. The New Englanders also took to the West Indies barrel staves and lumber. The molasses received in exchange was made into rum in New England. Much of this rum was taken to the coast of Africa, where it was traded for slaves. The slaves were taken to the West Indies to be sold, or perhaps exchanged for molasses that would make more rum that would buy more slaves.

SHIPBUILDING IN NEW ENGLAND
Redrawn from old engravings.

New Englanders sometimes sold to England in one year as many as four hundred ships, built out of fine timber.

H.-F. — 25

The tall New England pines were sent to England to supply masts for her navy. New England was expected to buy manufactured articles from England in exchange. These were as various as clocks, furniture, fine cloth, and tools.

Life in towns. — The country was more important than the towns in the colonial age, because nine tenths of the colonial population made most of their living by tilling the soil. New England had many small towns in which the farmers lived near their church, but they worked their farms and managed their household industries in the way already described in this chapter.

Towns grew as trade increased. Boston, Philadelphia, New York, and Charleston were the largest colonial towns, but all were small as compared with cities to-day. Boston probably did not have more than 20,000 people (1750), and New York was then smaller. All were located where ships could reach them. Lack of good roads in the colonies made it necessary to carry things in ships or smaller boats that could ascend streams. Many colonists lived and died without taking a land journey farther than an automobile can now travel in half an hour.

The merchants who made their living by trade, that is, by buying and selling things, were an important class of citizens. At one time the greatest merchants in New York dealt in flour, crackers, and other articles made from flour. New York was also a center of the fur trade. John Hancock, the first signer of the Declaration of Independence, was a Boston merchant whose ships brought molasses, sugar, and other articles to the colonies. The houses of some of the wealthy colonial merchants were built of brick. They had the best furniture and ornaments that could be bought in Great Britain.

As cities grew larger, there were many men who could devote all their time to their trade. There were carpenters, blacksmiths, masons, bakers, butchers, candlemakers, shipbuilders, harnessmakers, tanners, weavers, tailors, and a few printers. Benjamin Franklin was a printer; his father was a candlemaker.

The decline in the use of homespun and of other homemade articles began with the growth of cities. Citizens made fun of homespun suits and old fashions. They wanted the best and the latest that could be made by skilled workmen who kept up with the fashions. John Hancock is pictured wearing in his Boston home a red velvet cap, a blue damask dressing gown lined with silk, a satin vest beautifully embroidered, black satin breeches, and red morocco slippers. A New York newspaper (1773) advertises " scarlet, buff, blue, green, crimson, white, sky blue, and other colored superfine cloths."

We should think to-day that there were few comforts even in the best colonial city homes. The houses had no running water, no hot water ready for bathing, no bath tubs, no furnaces or steam heat, no lamps or electric lights, — only candles, — no matches for kindling a fire. When fires went out, the citizens borrowed live coals from a neighbor or tried to strike sparks from flint to catch in tinder. Then they often had to blow themselves red in the face before they could get a blaze. In the morning, city dwellers as well as country people often had to break the ice in the water pail before they could wash their faces.

Colonial education. — Many Englishmen, as we have seen, wished to learn to read in order to understand the Bible (p. 300). Colonists who came from England brought this desire to read the Scriptures for themselves. An early law in Massachusetts began by saying that it was " one chief project of Satan to keep men from the knowledge of the Scripture," and ordered that children should be taught to read and write. Nearly all the towns in Massachusetts had schools before 1650. Harvard College, the first college in the colonies, was founded (1636) not long after the Puritans came to New England.

Boys might be taught in public or private schools or by private teachers in the home. Virginians often brought private teachers from England. Reading, writing, and arithmetic were the subjects commonly taught boys. A farmer insisted that he did not want his boys to know anything but the Bible and " figgers."

The following is a copy of a letter from a colonial boy in a private school. We must not judge him by his spelling for only a few could spell in those days.

To Mr. Cornelius Ten Broeck
        att Albany.
Stamford, the 13th Day of October, 1752.
Honored Fethar,

    These fiew lines comes to let you know that I am in a good State of Health and I hope this may find you also. I have found all the things in my trunk but I must have a pare of Schuse. And mama please to send me some Ches Nutts and some Wall Nutts; you please to send me a Slate, and som pensals, and please to send me some smoke befe, and for bringing my trunk 3/9, and for a pare of Schuse 9 shillings. You please to send me a pare of indin's Schuse. You please to send me some dride corn. My Duty to Father and Mother and Sister and to all frinds,

                I am your Dutyfull Son,
                    John Ten Broeck
Father forgot to send me my Schuse.

The colonists brought from England the idea that education was not so necessary for girls as for boys. The

work done in colonial homes showed how capable the
girls were, but it was long after colonial times before girls
were given the chance to get as good an education as boys.

The early colonial public schools
were usually for boys. An exami-
nation of the deeds in the county
in which Boston is situated shows
that nearly a hundred years after the
Pilgrims landed (p. 346), the majority of women could not sign their
names but had to make their mark
with a cross. When girls were
taught at all, they seldom learned
more than to read and write. Only
a few were taught arithmetic.

COLONIAL WRITING
MATERIALS

From right to left: goose quill pens
and inkstand, uncut goose quills,
and box containing sand to be used
on freshly written matter instead
of a blotter.

Religion. — We have seen (p.
333) that the Virginia colonists had
only the Episcopal Church, which
they were compelled to attend.
The Episcopal Church was the
regular church in all the Southern Colonies except Maryland (p. 375), and in that also after the early days. The
Middle Colonies had a variety of churches.

The chief church of New England was the Congregational
Church (p. 351). Each New England town had its meeting house, which was both the place of worship and the
social center of the town. It took the place of a newspaper. Notices of marriages, of farms and cattle for sale,
of auctions, of the election of town officers, of the price of
beaver skins, warnings against selling firearms to Indians,
the offer of a reward for the heads of wolves that killed
sheep — all were nailed to the meeting house.

The ministers were well educated and capable leaders in the colonies. At first many of the New England minis-

HOURGLASS

It takes an hour for the sand in the upper part to run through the small opening into the lower part.

ters were graduates of Cambridge University, England, and later of Harvard College. An hourglass was kept on the pulpit to show time. The upper half of the glass was filled with sand which ran to the lower half in an hour. The glass was then turned over. The sermons usually lasted two hours. Sometimes they were longer. The prayers were often an hour long. The early colonists did not complain of the length of the service. A shorter one would have seemed to them lacking in respect to God.

The meeting houses were not warmed in winter. Some people had fur bags made of wolfskins into which they could thrust their feet. Women and children sometimes had little foot stoves filled with coals. Dogs often came to church and lay on their masters' feet to keep them warm. Every one went to church. Religion was the most important interest in life for the colonists.

The Ten Commandments were law in early New England. The one beginning: "Remember the Sabbath day to keep it holy," was specially obeyed. If any one on Sunday was caught fishing, hunting, or taking a ride except to church, he was liable to be fined or imprisoned. One Sunday two young men on horseback were stopped on the highway by a town officer. "My grandmother is lying dead in the next town," said one of them. The officer allowed them to pass. As they galloped ahead, this young man shouted: "And she's been lying dead in the grave-yard there thirty years."

Freedom of worship. — The early New England colonies were founded by those who wished the right to worship

INTERIOR OF A MEETING HOUSE

Notice the foot stove on the floor, the hourglass on the pulpit, and the guns which the wor-shipers have brought to church with them.

as they chose, but they did not allow this right to others. Massachusetts drove out Quakers, while Virginia expelled Puritans.

Lord Baltimore has the honor of founding Maryland (1634), the first colony where all Christians could worship in their own way. He was a Roman Catholic, and he was interested in founding this colony because Catholics were not then allowed to have meetings in England. The Balti-mores sent over many settlers, including more Protestants than Catholics. For fifty years both worshiped side by side in peace. Rhode Island (1636) was the second

colony to grant freedom of religion. Pennsylvania was
founded by William Penn (1681) as a colony where Quakers
and people of other religions could worship as they chose.

WILLIAM PENN'S HOUSE, NOW IN FAIRMOUNT PARK, PHILADELPHIA
Penn lived several years in Philadelphia, in the colony he founded. His house has been
carefully preserved.

Freedom of worship for all came slowly, but it finally
came. Our Constitution, as we have seen, protects all in
the right to worship as they please.

Things to remember about colonial life. — 1. There were
thirteen colonies. All of these except Georgia were founded
in the century after the defeat of the Spanish Armada (1588).

2. Living in the colonies was a series of problems.

3. The first colonial houses were made of logs or bark.

4. Most of the early colonists were farmers.

5. The Indians taught the colonists how to raise corn.

6. The colonists produced the wool and flax which they
needed for making clothes.

7. Colonial women and girls cooked, spun, wove, made the clothing, pillows, sheets, towels, and soap, did the washing, mending, and nearly all of the other work needed in the home.

8. The fireside was the center of the social life of the family. The colonial home helped make the American nation.

9. Boys were taught how to read, write, and cipher. The education of girls was neglected.

10. Southern planters exchanged their tobacco and rice for things made abroad. New England sent dried codfish and lumber to the West Indies and supplied England with ships and masts.

11. Towns grew as trade increased.

12. The established church in the Southern Colonies was the Episcopal Church; in New England, the Congregational Church.

13. Maryland, Rhode Island, and Pennsylvania set the example of granting freedom of religion.

Things to do. — Explain the statement: " Our own ancestors had some struggles like those of Robinson Crusoe."

Imagine that you are colonists. Choose a place on the Atlantic coast or on a river flowing into it, and tell of all the ways in which you would try to get food.

Tell how you would build a log house.

Talk on the work of colonial men and boys.

Talk on the work of colonial women and girls.

Get some raw wool, and wash it in hot water and soap. Let each member of the class twist (spin) some into thread between the thumb and forefinger.

Suppose that you were a colonial girl and were asked in April to take steps to have the raw materials on hand for making your grandmother some handkerchiefs for Christmas. Tell each thing that you would do until the handkerchiefs were made.

Suppose that you were a colonial boy and were asked to make a fork, a broom, and traces for oxen to draw a plow. How would you do these things?

If you had been a colonial farmer, do you think you would have kept geese? Give the reason for your answer.

What animals would have been almost necessary for an early colonial farm?

What colonial work would you have enjoyed most?

Make candles by trying out beef or mutton tallow and dipping wicks into it again and again.

References for Teachers. — Andrews, *Colonial Self-Government* (American Nation Series); Andrews, *Colonial Period* (Home University Library), V–X; Channing, *History of the United States*, Vol. I, 485–495, Vol. II, Chaps. VI–VIII; Greene, *Foundations of American Nationality*, IX; Andrews, *Fathers of New England*, IV, V, VII, and *Colonial Folkways* (both in Chronicles of America); Earle, *Home Life in Colonial Days;* Fisher, *Men, Women, and Manners in Colonial Times;* Dunbar, *History of Travel in America;* Goodwin, *The Colonial Cavalier;* Eberlein and McClure, *The Practical Book of Early American Arts and Crafts;* Tryon, *Household Manufactures in the United States;* Clark, *History of Manufactures in the United States*, I–V; Weeden, *Economic and Social History of New England;* Halleck, *History of Our Country*, IV–X.

For Pupils. — Earle, *Home Life in Colonial Days*, I (homes of the colonists), III (the kitchen fireside), V (food from forest and sea), VI (Indian corn), VII (meat and drink), VIII (flax culture and spinning), IX (wool culture and spinning), X (hand weaving), XI (girls' occupations), XIII (jackknife industries), XIV (travel, transportation, and taverns), XV (Sunday in the colonies); Earle, *Child Life in Colonial Days;* Hart, *Colonial Children;* Tappan, *Letters from Colonial Children;* Prescott, *Day in a Colonial Home* (fiction); Wilkins, *In Colonial Time* (fiction).

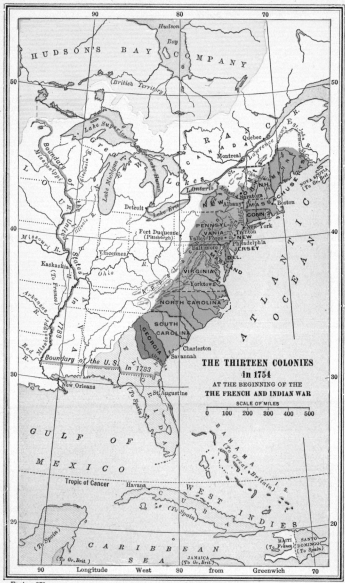

THE THIRTEEN COLONIES
in 1754
AT THE BEGINNING OF THE
THE FRENCH AND INDIAN WAR

SCALE OF MILES

0   100   200   300   400   500

CHAPTER XXV

HOW THE COLONIES BECAME A NATION

Restrictions on trade and manufactures. — European nations expected their colonies (1) to buy goods that the mother country made, (2) to produce raw materials that the mother country could use in her manufacturing, (3) to allow the mother country to do most of the manufacturing.

Holland, as we have seen (p. 303), was a liberal country, but her West India Company forbade the Dutch colonists in America to make any woolen, linen, or cotton cloth. The mother country wished to make these articles to sell to her colonists. France and Spain forbade their colonies to trade with foreign nations.

England was more liberal. She allowed home manufactures in her colonies, and permitted much foreign trade. She made the colonists angry, however, by forbidding them to manufacture articles of iron or steel or to make hats to sell outside the colony. She would not allow the colonists to sell to any foreign nation a number of special things, such as tobacco and masts. She forbade them to raise wool for sale.

Increasing trade (p. 369) made the colonists feel more independent and chafe under laws that hindered them in making or selling anything.

The French in North America. — The English colonists had several wars with the French in North America, and the outcome of the long struggle had a part in causing the Eng-

lish colonies to become a nation.   In 1754 the French held
more territory than the English.   The first permanent
French settlement in America was made in 1608 at Quebec,
the year after the English colony was founded at Jamestown.   More French people soon came and settled along the

THE BUILDING OF THE *GRIFFIN*

Redrawn from a picture in Hennepin's *Voyages*. This vessel was built in 1679, near the mouth
of Lake Erie, by Hennepin and other men under La Salle.   It was the first ship that ever
sailed on Lake Erie, Lake Huron, and Lake Michigan.

St. Lawrence River and in the region of the Great Lakes.
This territory was called New France, or Canada.

La Salle (là sàl'), a noted French explorer, was the
first white man to go from the Great Lakes to the mouth
of the Mississippi River (1682).   He claimed for France
all the region drained by the Mississippi and by the rivers

flowing into it. This territory extended west from the Appalachian Mountains to the Rocky Mountains. To make good her claim, France built a line of forts and fur-trading posts extending from Canada to the Gulf of Mexico.

England and France were often at war in Europe, and the war spread to the American colonies. The French made companions of the Indians and took part in their war dances. The Canadian Indians were ready at the bidding of the French to swoop down on the English colonists. From time to time, the French and Indians massacred men, women, and children in northern New York and New England.

France determined to confine the English colonists to a strip along the Atlantic coast, and she built a fort (1754) where Pittsburgh now is, because from that point she could control the Ohio Valley. The English colonists were also determined to have the furs and the rich lands in the interior.

What the struggle with the French meant. — War with France followed the erection of the fort which was built to close to the English the gateway to the West. England aided her colonies in this contest. This war, once begun, was fought to decide two things: (1) whether eastern North America should belong to the French or to the English, and (2) whether we should have the English or the French form of government.

The French and the English had very different ideas about government and religion. The French colonists were governed like children by their king. They did not vote for men to represent them in government. Every English colony elected a body of lawmakers, usually called an assembly. This body represented the people and voted the taxes.

The English colonists had come to prize liberty more than life. They knew that they would lose the right to govern themselves in everyday matters and also in religion if the French won. The French allowed only Roman Catholics in New France. The English Roman Catholics in Maryland were willing to have Protestants for neighbors.

The English colonists had more homes and children than the French colonists. Many of the French were merely fur traders without homes. The English, therefore, had more at stake in this struggle. If the French were the victors, the English would lose nearly everything for which they came to America.

The English colonists, aided by the mother country, won the war with the French. The government of the mother country (after 1707) was often called British instead of English; for England had united with her smaller neighbor, Scotland, and the name of the united kingdom was Great Britain. The treaty of peace (1763) was made between France and the British government. By it, France had to give to Great Britain nearly all her possessions in North America east of the Mississippi. Spain had aided France in the war, and so France gave to Spain the city of New Orleans and the territory between the Mississippi and the Rocky Mountains.

A step toward independence. — There were two reasons why the result of the war with France was a step toward American independence.

(1) The colonists needed the help of Great Britain as long as the French threatened them in the New World. If they had to be under the control of any nation, they preferred Great Britain. The colonists felt more independent as soon as the danger from France was past.

(2) The war with the French had been very costly and had plunged Great Britain in debt. In order to hold the newly won territory, it was necessary to place 10,000 British soldiers in forts extending from the Great Lakes to the Gulf of Mexico. It would be very expensive to maintain these forts, and Great Britain thought that her colonies should pay part of this cost, since the soldiers would protect them from the Indians. The taxes which she now tried to collect from the colonists were a direct cause of independence.

The habit of self-government. — England had so many troubles of her own at home (see Chapter XXIII) that she did not pay much attention to her colonies until they had formed the habit of self-government. Every town and every colony had practice in self-government.

After the French war, Great Britain found the habit of self-government in the colonies too firmly fixed to be overcome.

Great Britain's mistake. — The colonists of Spain and France paid taxes as directed by their home governments. Great Britain's colonists were unwilling to be governed in this way.

The early charters for colonization declared that English colonists should have all the rights of people living in England (p. 324). Magna Charta (p. 188) and the Petition of Right (p. 341) forbade taxation unless it was voted by representatives of the people. The colonists had no representatives of their own in the British Parliament. Great Britain did not ask the colonial assemblies to vote on the taxes she wished to impose on the colonies. " No taxation without representation " finally became the watchword of the colonists.

Great Britain's mistake was in not treating the colonists the same as the Englishmen in England. The restrictions on colonial trade and manufactures (p. 379) made many of the colonists angry, but the chief reason for separation from Great Britain was the way in which the colonists were taxed.

Increased taxation. — Long before the last colonial war with France, the British Parliament ordered the colonies to pay a tax on certain articles imported from other countries. Some of these things were molasses, spices, and silk. In one way or another, the colonists had escaped the payment of most of such duties. Ship captains often landed goods when the king's collector of customs was not present.

BURNING STAMPED PAPER IN THE STREETS

The Stamp Act required that stamped paper be used for newspapers and for all legal and official documents in the colonies. Many stamp agents were compelled to resign or else burn the stamps and stamped paper as they are doing in the above picture.

After the French war Great Britain began to collect the colonial duties. She used her men of war to keep track of vessels loaded with valuable cargoes. She also laid new taxes, such as the Stamp Tax, which the colonists refused to pay. Great Britain later placed a tax on tea, which the colonists would not allow to be landed.

The Revolutionary War begun. — Some men in Boston, disguised as Indians, threw overboard a shipload of tea so that no tax could be paid on it. Great Britain sent ships and soldiers to blockade the port of Boston until its people should pay for that tea.

The first Continental Congress, representing all the col-

BOSTON AND VICINITY IN THE REVOLUTION

onies except Georgia, met at Philadelphia (1774) to protest against Great Britain's acts and to ask for the rights of Englishmen. Great Britain did not heed this appeal.

Massachusetts chose a congress of her own in defiance of the order of the British general in command of the troops blockading Boston. This congress organized companies called " minutemen " because they were ready to fight at a minute's notice.

On the night of April 18, 1775, a body of British troops marched northwest from Boston to search for colonial military stores, such as muskets, powder, and ball. They also wished to capture Samuel Adams and John Hancock, two patriots who had been foremost in urging the colonists to resist. A minuteman by the name of Paul Revere galloped ahead and spread the warning so that the patriots escaped. (See Longfellow's poem, *Paul Revere's Ride*.)

At Lexington, Massachusetts, the next morning, the British soldiers fired on a company of sixty minutemen,

BATTLE OF LEXINGTON

From an old engraving. The minutemen are in the foreground and at the left; the British lines are advancing from the right. This battle occurred on the Common, or open space, in the center of the town. Many New England towns were built around such a common.

killing or wounding eighteen. The British then went to Concord to search for arms and ammunition. The patriots in one house plowed furrows in the garden, planted muskets in them like potatoes, and turned the next furrow over them. The British found some muskets and ammunition in another house and threw them into a pond. The minutemen at Concord then forced the British to retreat. More minutemen came from all sides and fired from behind trees and stone fences at the brilliant red coats of the British soldiers. The British lost 273 on the march back to Boston. This was the first battle of the Revolution, and the colonial patriots won it. Sixteen thousand of them then gathered to hold the British in Boston.

The Declaration of Independence.— The battle of Bunker Hill soon followed. Here the untrained patriots, as long as their powder lasted, successfully resisted the trained British troops.

The outbreak of war and Great Britain's refusal to grant the demands of the colonists caused the second Continental Congress at Philadelphia to issue our Declaration of Independence (July 4, 1776). A jury of historians (p. 327) has ranked this as the most important date in American history. It marks the beginning of the United States, which was formed out of the thirteen colonies (p. 357). The war continued for five years before independence was won.

THE RINGING OF THE LIBERTY BELL TO CELEBRATE THE DECLARATION
OF INDEPENDENCE

From an old engraving in the Library of Congress.   The bell in the Pennsylvania State House (now Independence Hall) had the inscription: "Proclaim Liberty Throughout all the Land Unto all the Inhabitants Thereof." This was the message rung out to the American people on July 8, 1776, when the Declaration adopted on July 4 was first read to the people.

This sentence from the Declaration of Independence shows why Americans wished to be free:

"We hold these truths to be self-evident, that all men are

created equal, that they are endowed by their Creator with certain unalienable rights, that among these are life, liberty, and the pursuit of happiness; — that, to secure these rights, governments are instituted among men, deriving their just powers from the consent of the governed."

Thomas Jefferson. — The Declaration of Independence was written by Thomas Jefferson of Virginia at the age of thirty-three. He was a graduate of William and Mary College in Virginia. He said that if he had to choose between education and a large fortune, he would take the education. He tells us that he sometimes studied fifteen hours a day. He could not have written the Declaration of Independence if he had not studied and known what the great writers on human liberty had said.

George Washington (1732–1799). — Washington was born on a Virginia plantation. He went to a little school, kept by the sexton of a church, where he learned how to

WASHINGTON, THE BOY SURVEYOR

Washington was engaged by Lord Fairfax as surveyor at the age of sixteen. Later he was appointed public surveyor of Virginia.

read, write, and cipher. Later, the forest, the wild animals, and the Indians became his teachers. At the age of sixteen he went into the forest as a surveyor. He camped out in the rain, shot wild turkeys and deer for his food, and met Indians.

His work as a surveyor shows one of the qualities for which he became famous. He never shirked any duty because it was hard or disagreeable. Surveyors often guessed at distances if the ground was hard to travel or if a stream needed to be crossed. Washington always carefully measured the necessary distances. Years later a lawyer who examined land titles said that Washington's surveys were the only ones on which he could depend.

We say of a man who can always be trusted that he has character. From boyhood to manhood Washington never failed in the hour of trial.

The hero of the Revolution. — The Revolution, after the first three months, centered around George Washington. He became commander in chief of all the colonial armies fighting against Great Britain. He had learned how to fight and to command soldiers in the war against France. Four bullet holes in his coat, received in one battle, showed that he was not afraid to expose himself when he needed quick action to rally his men.

Washington did not have enough powder and arms, but he skillfully held the British army in Boston until he could secure cannon. Then he seized Dorchester Heights, overlooking Boston from the south. The British saw that Washington had outgeneraled them. They sailed away in their fleet (March, 1776), but before the year ended they had taken the city of New York and a large part of New Jersey.

GEORGE WASHINGTON AND HIS GENERALS

On Christmas night, 1776, Washington crossed the Delaware River, marched to Trenton, New Jersey, and won the most daring victory of the war by capturing an army of 1000 Hessians. These were German soldiers hired by Great Britain to fight the colonists.

The next year Washington kept one British army busy near Philadelphia while a colonial army captured another British army under General Burgoyne at Saratoga (October, 1777). This victory made France feel that the Americans had a chance to win and led her to become their ally and furnish them money, soldiers, and ships.

Washington and his soldiers showed their patriotism in the following winter while in camp at Valley Forge, Pennsylvania. The soldiers were half-starved and poorly clad. Blood marked the footsteps of those without shoes as they walked over a crust of snow. The men knew that Washington himself was serving without pay, and they stood by him even under such hardships.

When the South was hard pressed, Washington sent there General Nathanael Greene, one of the ablest American leaders. Like Washington, Greene knew that there were times when a retreat might help win in the end. He fought successfully to weaken the forces of the enemy, to make them use up their supplies, and to drive them to the seacoast towns of the South.

Washington himself planned the campaign at Yorktown, Virginia, which ended the War of the Revolution. The British General Cornwallis had gone there to keep in touch with the British navy. Washington learned that a French fleet was coming north from the West Indies, and he asked its admiral to blockade Cornwallis by sea. Washington marched south rapidly with his own men and a large force of French soldiers.   Cornwallis and his army were trapped, and they surrendered (1781).   Washington, the guiding spirit of the Revolution, and his patriots, aided by the French, had won.   The United States became independent of Great Britain and was free to govern herself.

The Confederation of States. — Our first form of national government was known as the Confederation.   It had a central Congress, representing all the states.   It had the right to order taxes to be paid, but no power to collect them. It had to borrow from Holland and France to pay for the expenses of government.

Each state wanted to be independent enough to do as it pleased.   One state taxed articles coming from another state, just as we now tax goods coming from foreign lands. Such acts made the people of different states angry and might have led to war.   Washington and other thoughtful men saw that a stronger central government was needed.

The Constitutional Convention. — The Congress of the Confederation asked the thirteen states to send delegates to a Constitutional Convention at Philadelphia.   The object was to frame rules that would give the central government more power to make laws and to enforce them. Delegates came from every state except Rhode Island, and they chose George Washington as president of the Constitutional Convention (1787).   This body took nearly four months to write the Constitution under which we are now governed.   The Constitution was adopted by the states and went into effect in 1789.

The Constitution of the United States. — The Confederation had but one branch of government.   This was the lawmaking body called Congress.   The government under our Constitution has three branches :

(1) The Congress makes laws for our nation. It is divided into two bodies, — a Senate and a House of Representatives. The first power granted to Congress is the right to tax. It can put import taxes on sugar, cloth,

STAIRWAY IN INDEPENDENCE HALL, PHILADELPHIA

At the right is a portrait of George Washington. At the left is a memorial tablet which reads: "The State House of Pennsylvania, Consecrated by the Memories of the Events," etc. This building was the meeting place of the Continental Congress when the Declaration of Independence was adopted; also the meeting place of the Constitutional Convention.

and other articles brought from abroad. It has passed a law taxing incomes.

(2) The Constitution provides for a President and directs him to see that the laws are obeyed. It gives him the command of the army and the navy. If people in any state or city should refuse to pay the taxes laid by Congress, the President could use the army and navy of the United States if necessary to force payment.

(3) The Constitution provides for national courts, with the Supreme Court at the head, to decide (a) cases that affect the United States, (b) cases that affect foreign nations and their citizens, (c) disputes between states and between citizens of different states.

The Supreme Court of the United States decides what the Constitution means when people do not agree about it. It decides whether laws passed by Congress and by the states can be allowed or whether they are void because they conflict with the Constitution.

Part of our Constitution an Old World heritage. — Our Constitution is based only in part on the experience of our forefathers in this country. They made use of the Old World's experience. The English Magna Charta (pp. 187–189) calls for many rights like those in our Constitution. The Constitution says that every person accused of crime shall be tried by a jury. People had trial by jury before America was discovered. The Constitution is a body of rules for a representative government. Our ancestors brought from England their knowledge of representative government, which means choosing a few men to represent the rest in some place where laws are made. The colonists' idea of "no taxation without representation" came from Great Britain; for the representative British House of Commons had the right to vote all the taxes.

How the new government was started. — Our government under the Constitution began in 1789 with the election of George Washington of Virginia for President and John Adams of Massachusetts for Vice President. No other man but Washington was thought of for the presidency. The beginning of our government under the Constitution has been called the fourth most important event in American history. The three dates that rank as more important than 1789 are 1776, 1492, and 1607 (p. 327).

PRESIDENT-ELECT WASHINGTON AT TRENTON ON HIS WAY TO NEW YORK
A memorial arch was put up for the occasion, and Washington was formally welcomed. Thirteen girls, representing the states, strewed flowers in his path.

Our country did not really become a nation until George Washington sat in the presidential chair. Under him our Constitution became the supreme law of the land. This was proved, for example, when Congress passed a law to tax whisky. The makers of whisky in western Pennsylvania rebelled and drove away the United States collectors. Washington made use of his constitutional power and sent an army there to compel obedience to the nation's law.

Things to remember. — 1. European nations believed in restricting the trade and manufactures of their colonies.

2. The colonies and Great Britain were successful in a war with France and forced her to give up her lands east of the Mississippi.

3. The war with France plunged Great Britain in debt and led her to put increased taxes on the colonies.

4. The colonists refused to pay the taxes because they had the rights of Englishmen, who were not taxed except by their own representatives.

5. The colonists threw overboard a shipload of tea so that taxes could not be paid on it. Great Britain sent ships and soldiers to blockade Boston until it paid for the tea.

6. War began April 19, 1775, when British soldiers tried to arrest some patriots and seize colonial military stores. Independence was declared July 4, 1776.

7. George Washington was the commander in chief of the American forces.

8. French aid helped Washington win the battle of Yorktown, which ended the war.

9. The Congress of the Confederation represented the thirteen states from 1776 to 1789. It was not given enough power.

10. The Constitutional Convention drew up our present Constitution, which became the supreme law of the land. It gave the new Congress greater powers and ordered the President to see that the nation's laws are obeyed.

11. George Washington was elected the first President of the United States (1789), and he started our present government under the Constitution.

Things to do. — Explain what is meant by representative government. What does "No taxation without representation" mean?

Tell the story of George Washington before 1775.

Tell about some of George Washington's work during the Revolution.

Give reasons for calling Washington one of the world's great men.

Memorize the part of the Declaration of Independence given on pages 387–388.

Look up an account of the battle of Yorktown and tell how France helped us win it.

Give three points of difference between government under the Confederation and that under the Constitution.

What are some of the ideas that our Constitution borrowed from the former experience of the Old World?

How did the government under the Constitution begin?

References for Teachers. — Clark, *History of Manufactures in the United States*, I–IX; Channing, *History of the United States*, Vol. II, Chs. VIII–XIX, Vol. III; Greene, *Foundations of American Nationality*, XVI–XXVIII; Van Tyne, *Causes of the War of Independence;* Egerton, *Origin and Growth of English Colonies*, VI; Schlesinger, *Colonial Merchants and the American Revolution;* Wilson, Ford, or Lodge, *George Washington;* Wrong, *Washington and His Comrades in Arms* (Chronicles of America); Fiske, *American Revolution;* Trevelyan, *American Revolution;* Fiske, *Critical Period of American History;* McLaughlin, *The Confederation and the Constitution* (American Nation Series); Farrand, *Fathers of the Constitution* (Chronicles of America); Hart, *American History Told by Contemporaries*, Vol. II; Halleck, *History of Our Country for Higher Grades*, IX, XI–XIV.

For Pupils. — Sparks, *Men Who Made the Nation* (Washington, Franklin, Samuel Adams, Alexander Hamilton, and Thomas Jefferson); Hawthorne, *Grandfather's Chair* (Liberty Tree); Hart, *Camps and Firesides of the Revolution;* Scudder, *George Washington;* Mace, *Washington, a Virginia Cavalier;* Tappan, *American Hero Stories* (Washington, The Young Soldier, A Winter at Valley Forge); Holland, *Historic Boyhoods*, 73–86 (Washington); Foote and Skinner, *Makers and Defenders of America*, 9–103 (American Revolution), 117–129 (Jefferson and Hamilton); Haaren and Poland, *Famous Men of Modern Times*, XXV (Washington); Van Loon, *Story of Mankind*, 323–333 (American Revolution).

CHAPTER XXVI

HOW WE HAVE BEEN OF SERVICE TO THE OLD WORLD

Repaying our debt. — While studying this history, we have been watching the Old World. We have learned what our country inherited from the Old World, and how our country freed itself and became a nation.

We have learned how much we are in debt to the Old World. We know that we are the heirs to all the comforts, the inventions, and the knowledge which the world has painfully struggled to get during thousands of years. We are glad that our nation has been able to give something back to the Old World, — that our people have succeeded in repaying a part of their indebtedness.

Men that have influenced the Old World. — Let us remember three men whose work and example have specially helped the Old World. First, there is George Washington. His love of country, his honesty, courage, and patience are a heritage for the entire world. His example has caused many to try to be more like him. Great Britain is almost as proud of him as America and has statues of him in public places. Englishmen have said that Washington taught the British Empire how it must treat its colonies in order to succeed. His life has shown the world what patriotism and character can accomplish. His definition of character was " acting right every time."

Daniel Webster, one of America's greatest orators, standing by the completed Bunker Hill monument, said: "America has furnished to the world the character of Washington. And if our American institutions had done nothing else, that would have entitled them to the respect of mankind."

Another American useful to his own country and to the world is Benjamin Franklin, a poor boy born in Boston, who moved to Philadelphia and became a printer. He retired from active business at the age of forty-two. He defined leisure as "time for doing something useful." For the rest of his life he worked mostly to benefit others. He invented bifocal glasses, a stove for heating rooms, and other things for which he refused to take a patent.

FRANKLIN'S EXPERIMENT WITH LIGHTNING

His famous experiment with a kite sent up into a thunder cloud proved to the world that lightning is a form of electrical energy.

His writings have had perhaps a greater influence on the Old World than those of any other American. His sayings of Poor Richard, first published in *Poor Richard's*

Almanac, have been translated into all the chief languages of Europe, as well as into Chinese. They are to-day as much liked as ever. Their influence for saving and industry is so great that banks here and abroad continue to reprint them. These are some of Poor Richard's sayings that have been often reprinted :

" Early to bed and early to rise makes a man healthy, wealthy, and wise."

"One to-day is worth two to-morrows. Have you somewhat to do to-morrow? Do it to-day."

" None preaches better than the ant, and she says nothing."

The life of Abraham Lincoln has had strong influence on the Old World. The poor people who have lived where only the great could hope to rise to places of honor, have liked the story of Lincoln, who was born in a log cabin. They read about his learning to write on shingles by the light of the fireplace, and about his poking the fire to get enough light to read *Æsop's Fables*, *Robinson Crusoe*, and the few other books that he had. They have been interested to hear that he split fourteen hundred rails to get the homespun cloth for one pair of trousers. They have been thrilled by the story of how he became President and freed the slaves. Pictures of Abraham Lincoln have been found in the huts of far-off Siberia. Perhaps no other man has made so many wish to come to a land where it is possible for any one, rich or poor, to accomplish great things. An heroic statue of him stands opposite Westminster Abbey in London.

How our nation has helped to feed and clothe the world. — By clearing the land and working hard to raise bread and meat, American farmers have helped to feed the world. The hides of American cattle have supplied millions of people with shoes. American cotton plantations have

© *Galloway*

STATUE OF LINCOLN IN LONDON

This is a replica of the statue by St. Gaudens in Chicago. The tower seen at the right is
on the Houses of Parliament.

given the world most of its cotton clothing. American inventions have made it possible for the common man to
be as well dressed as were many of the wealthy before
America was settled.

An American, Cyrus H. McCormick, invented a mower
and reaper that enabled one man to do the work of twenty.
Americans invented a machine that threshed grain as fast
as seventy-five men could do the work with flails. The
reaper, thresher, and other improved farm machinery are
used in South America, Europe, and Asia.

The United States gave to the world cheaper clothing
as well as cheaper bread. A little more than a century ago
cotton was too high priced for clothing because it took so

long for men to separate the seeds from the cotton. Eli Whitney, a Yale graduate, invented (1793) the cotton gin which rapidly removed the seeds from the fiber. As a result, the world soon had cheap cotton clothing.

Elias Howe invented a sewing machine (1846) which made clothing more cheaply. Machines that would make shoes soon followed.

Charles Goodyear (1800–1860) made the whole civilized world his debtor by showing how to harden rubber so that

RUBBER TIRES FOR AUTOMOBILES   *Brown Bros.*

it would make overshoes, waterproof clothing, and thousands of other needed things. Those who use automobiles with rubber tires and the other rubber articles that his invention made possible ought to realize their debt to Goodyear. He received no pay for his invention, and he died a poor man, saying: "The advantages of a career in life should not be estimated exclusively by the standard of dollars and cents.   Man has just cause for regret when he sows and no one reaps."

Improved means of communication given to the world. — American inventors led the way in giving to the world new ways of communication.   Samuel F. B. Morse, a New Englander, invented the electric telegraph (1844).   The use of this telegraph began in America and then was extended to Europe and to other parts of the world.   Before the invention of the telegraph and the laying of the Atlantic cable, it had taken a month or more to send a message to England and receive a reply.   It took a rider thirty-two hours to carry a message from New York to Boston.   A man on horseback succeeded in taking an important message from the President in Washington to Nashville in nine days (1812).   Before the coming of the telegraph, newspapers could not get recent news from the outside world.

While Alexander Graham Bell was teaching deaf and dumb pupils in Boston, he invented the telephone (1876), which still seems a marvel to us.   Wise men had declared it impossible to talk with any one a mile away.   Some of them lived long enough to be able to talk by telephone from New York to San Francisco.

It took Thomas A. Edison a long time to give the world a working phonograph (1888).   Because of this invention, the world may continue to hear the beautiful songs of the great singers who have died.   Pupils in any part of the world may learn from the phonograph how to pronounce the words of foreign languages when the teacher is absent.

Americans succeed in flying. — Two young Americans, Orville and Wilbur Wright, watched birds as they flew and hawks as they soared.   Then they made gliders which could sail in the air and carry a man.   They worked on a light

THE FIRST SUCCESSFUL FLIGHT OF AN AIRPLANE

This flying machine was made by Orville and Wilbur Wright of Dayton, Ohio.   The test flight shown here occurred in 1903 at Kitty Hawk, North Carolina.   In this first form of airplane the propeller was behind the pilot.   Notice that the machine has skids on which to alight, instead of wheels.   Notice also the little car and the track used for giving the airplane a start before it could rise in the air.

gasoline engine to propel the glider.   Their first flight (1903) with this engine lasted twelve seconds.   This was the first machine heavier than air that had raised itself by its own power, flown for some distance, and alighted without being wrecked.   They gradually extended the distance that they could fly.

Americans made the first successful airplanes.   The World War was the first to use an air navy.   France has a statue of Wilbur Wright as a conqueror of the air.

One of the world's great discoveries. — Surgical operations are now common.   Before the middle of the nineteenth century, they were rare.   The agony in serious operations was too great for most human beings to endure.

It would shock us to know the number of deaths that modern surgery might have prevented.

Who would find the magical power of putting the patient to sleep during an operation? The dream of such a power seemed too wonderful to come true. George Rogers Clark, the hero who won the Northwest for us during the Revolution, injured his leg so that it had to be cut off. The best that could be done for him was to place drummers outside his window and have them beat the stirring march that had urged his soldiers on to victory. Thus he stood the operation.

A little after 1840 four Americans were trying to solve the problem of finding something that would cause insensibility to pain. The first was Dr. Crawford W. Long of Georgia, who gave ether to make a patient unconscious while a tumor was removed (1842). Dr. Long did not publish his discovery, and the other three Americans did not know what he had done. Horace Wells, a dentist of Hartford, Connecticut, used nitrous oxide gas for the painless extraction of teeth (1844). He told another dentist, William Thomas Green Morton, of Massachusetts, of his discovery. Morton studied the subject with Dr. Charles T. Jackson, a Boston chemist, who told Morton that sulphuric ether would produce insensibility to pain. In October, 1846, Morton administered ether while a surgeon removed a tumor from a patient in Boston. This operation was reported to the world, and it resulted in the use of ether as an anæsthetic throughout the civilized world.

Immigration. — We have seen that American inventions made great changes in the world. Let us next think of what Americans have done as a nation for the Old World.

Our nation performed a great service for humankind

by inviting immigrants to come to our shores as long as there was plenty of good land. No other country ever gave so many newcomers such an opportunity for improving their condition.

Generous treatment of other nations. — There are ways of helping foreign peoples other than by bringing them to America. Sometimes they can be served better at home than here. It has sometimes been said that America has too great a love of money. In reality it would be hard to find a nation that has been less swayed than the United States by love of the " almighty dollar " in its treatment of other nations.

Brown Bros.

SUGAR MILL, CUBA

The production of sugar from sugar cane is the leading industry of Cuba.

Our nation went to war to free the Cubans from the tyranny of Spain. We did not keep Cuba as Europe thought we would after the war which freed her. Instead, we showed her how to educate her children better, how to clean up her cities and to be more healthy, and how to govern herself. We freed her more than a quarter of a century ago and have not sought to annex her.

At the end of the Spanish War we could have taken the Philippines for nothing, but we paid Spain $20,000,000. The Filipinos were not a nation ready for self-government, and we did not wish to turn them back to Spain. We have sent our teachers, doctors, and nurses to the Philippines to try to show the people there how to live so that they will be able to govern themselves. This nation does not regret that the Philippines have cost more in dollars and cents than they will ever repay.

A FILIPINO STRIPPING HEMP

The production of Manila hemp is one of the chief industries of the Philippines.

When other nations tried to get as much Chinese territory as they could, a secret society known as the "Boxers" started to drive out foreigners (1900). They killed the German minister and some other foreigners. The United States, European nations, and Japan sent troops to China and put down the uprising. China was made to pay $330,000,000 for the expense of sending soldiers and for the lives of foreigners whom the Boxers had killed. The share given to the United States was $24,000,000, which was three times our losses and expenses. Our government returned two thirds of this sum to China. The money has been used to pay for educating Chinese students in the United States. We asked for the "Open Door" for our trade in China, on the same terms as for the trade of other nations; but we used our influence to keep China free and independent. As a result of our fairness, China trusts us to-day.

When we spent billions of dollars in helping win the World War, we set a good example in " seeking nothing for ourselves but what we shall wish to share with all free peoples," — as President Wilson said when we entered the war.

The spirit of individual service to other nations. — We have seen how our government has helped other peoples. What have Americans done as individuals?

The names of those who have tried to be Good Samaritans to the rest of the world would make a very long list. Many American teachers, missionaries, doctors, and Red Cross workers have given their service to other peoples. Every time there is some unusual distress abroad, we send help as individuals. People from every state in the Union sent money for years after the World War to the Near East Relief Committee. Individuals gave freely to help feed the starving children of our former enemies in the World War. Millions of our dollars went promptly to Japan after her terrible earthquake (1923). The American Red Cross watches the entire world to see where it can relieve suffering. An agency founded with private money (Rockefeller Foundation) is working to improve the health of people all over the world.

How Americans saved the world from a scourge. — Dr. Walter Reed, a surgeon of the United States army, headed a commission that went to Cuba (1900) to try to find at the risk of their lives what caused yellow fever. They had the clothes of yellow fever patients put in their sleeping rooms, but no one caught the disease in that way. Dr. Reed thought that yellow fever as well as malaria might be carried by mosquitoes. Dr. Jesse W. Lazear allowed a suspected mosquito to settle on his hand and draw blood. He caught yellow fever and died from it. This hero gave up his life to discover the secret for the benefit of mankind.

RED CROSS NURSES IN A PARADE ON FIFTH AVENUE, NEW YORK, DURING THE WORLD WAR

Yellow fever had been a scourge in cities as far apart as Lisbon and New Orleans. Each of those two cities sometimes had as many as 7000 die of yellow fever in one summer.

After Dr. Lazear's discovery, the American sanitary officer in Havana had every pool of water and every marsh in the vicinity either drained or covered with oil (1901). Before this Cuba had been a breeding ground for yellow fever. In a few years (1910) there was not a case of yellow fever on the island. By saving Cuba, our nation also saved itself from this disease. The world is in debt to Americans for showing how to prevent yellow fever.

A FRONTIER FORT

In times of war with the Indians a fort such as this served as the refuge of settlers on all the near-by farms. Notice the surrounding stockade, with a narrow platform inside, near the top, for the use of the defenders.

Our contribution to free government. — Our Declaration of Independence showed our belief in equality. We are sharing with the Old World the ideals of the largest successful republic in the history of the world. Our republic inspired the French people to throw off the yoke of king and nobles at the time of the French Revolution (1789). The Spanish colonies in South America followed our example in declaring themselves free from Spain and in forming republics. China, which has a larger population than the United States, is trying to form a successful republic.

Our first colonial settlements were on a frontier. " Frontier " in American history means the edge of an unsettled tract of country where the settlers are few and where the things that civilized people enjoy are hard to get. The frontiersmen, for example, having no nails, were ingenious enough to make and use wooden pins instead. For one hundred and eighty years our country had a frontier, and it developed these five qualities, which it is our duty to preserve and to pass on to the rest of the world: (1) ingenuity, (2) self-reliance, (3) independence, or the desire of people to govern themselves, (4) the belief in equality, that all should be given an equal chance and not be denied the right to rise because they happen to be born poor or are not the sons of the great, (5) democracy, which means (a) that all should have an equal voice in government, and (b) that all should share in the duties as well as the rights of good citizens.

The experiment of American democracy has led many countries in other parts of the world to make improvements in their government.

The common school. — In the Old World the children of nobles and of the wealthy went to one school; those of the poor went to another school if there was any for them. The American frontier had so few inhabitants that it was lucky if it could have one school for all. For this reason the fashion gradually spread in America to have common schools everywhere, in country and in city.

There could be no equality if education cost so much that the children of the poor could not afford it. The people of the United States gradually learned that education should be made free for all children, from the first grade through the high school and later through the state universities. We thus set an example for the Old World.

The public school is now a common meeting place for children of all people. All classes mingle here and learn

FOOTBALL ON THE PLAYGROUND OF A PUBLIC SCHOOL

The school-teachers of to-day, like Vittorino da Feltre (p. 256), encourage games and other kinds of exercise to promote health and to train the body as well as the mind.

to know each other. Our public schools have taught the rest of the world a wonderful lesson in democracy.

A problem: Comparative rank of our inventions. — Before 1776, the date of our Declaration of Independence, there were only seven inventions or discoveries of the first rank : the use of fire, alphabetical writing, Arabic numerals, the printing press, the mariner's compass, the telescope (invented in the seventeenth century), and the steam engine (patented by a Scotchman in 1769).

See if you can find seven inventions or discoveries of any other single nation that have influenced the world more than the seven inventions or discoveries of those Americans whose names are given below : —

Eli Whitney, Samuel F. B. Morse, Cyrus H. McCormick, Alexander Graham Bell, Thomas A. Edison, Orville and Wilbur Wright, Dr. Crawford W. Long and the other Americans who aided in the discovery of anæsthesia.

If you cannot find any other single nation that has produced since 1776 seven inventions that have changed the world as much as these, you must not be boastful, but only thankful that our country has been of so much service to the world. Our country is thus only partly repaying the world for the heritage which she has received.

Things to be remembered about our service to the Old World. — 1. Washington, Franklin, and Lincoln are great Americans who still influence the whole world.

2. American inventions — the mower and reaper, thresher, cotton gin, vulcanization of rubber, telegraph, telephone, phonograph, and successful airplane — have made great changes in the world.

3. Americans discovered how to make surgery painless, and how to escape the scourge of yellow fever.

4. America gave millions of immigrants a chance to rise. Our country freed the Cubans and the Filipinos from Spanish misrule, and helped win the World War.

5. Our Declaration of Independence emphasized our belief in equality and influenced others to throw off the yoke of king and nobles.

6. America set an example by having public schools for the children of all.

Things to do. — Explain how Washington influenced the Old World.

Specify in what ways Franklin's influence is felt to-day.

Why is Lincoln admired abroad?

If all the sewing had to be done by hand, what would be the result?

Tell what a different world this might be if some one had not found how to vulcanize rubber.

What proportion of the news in your paper comes by telegraph?

Give examples of time saved by use of the telephone.

Give a talk on the work of Orville and Wilbur Wright.

Why is the discovery of anæsthesia of vast importance to the world?

Specify some ways in which Americans have helped the people of other countries.

Tell the story of the victory over yellow fever.

Mention two things that the American frontier accomplished.

References for Teachers. — Thompson, *The Age of Invention* (Chronicles of America); Schurz or Charnwood, *Abraham Lincoln;* Franklin, *Autobiography;* Ford, *The Many-sided Franklin;* Hendrick, *Age of Big Business* (Chronicles of America), III (William Kelly, first maker of Bessemer steel), IV (Alexander Graham Bell and the telephone); Iles, *Leading American Inventors;* Bates, *Story of the Cotton Gin;* Goddard, *Eminent Engineers* (Elias Howe); Casson, *Cyrus Hall McCor-*

mick; Casson, *Romance of the Reaper;* Casson, *History of the Telephone;* Turner, *The Frontier in American History.* For Washington, see reference on page 397.

For Pupils : Thayer, *Life of Benjamin Franklin from Boyhood to Manhood;* Parton, *Life and Times of Benjamin Franklin;* Watson, *Poor Richard's Story: Life of Franklin;* Whipple, *Story of Young Benjamin Franklin;* Franklin, *Poor Richard's Almanac;* Nicolay, *Boys' Life of Abraham Lincoln;* Baldwin, *Abraham Lincoln;* Haaren and Poland, *Famous Men of Modern Times* (Washington and Lincoln); Foote and Skinner, *Makers and Defenders of America,* 230–257; Bachman, *Great Inventors and their Inventions,* 105 (Eli Whitney), 121–141 (Elias Howe), 142–160 (Cyrus H. McCormick), 208–227 (Samuel F. B. Morse), 228–246 (Alexander Graham Bell), 247–253 (Thomas A. Edison), 253–261 (Orville and Wilbur Wright); Rolt-Wheeler, *Thomas Alva Edison;* Thompson, *Age of Invention,* VII (Charles Goodyear); Parkman, *Conquests of Invention,* 8–26 (Cyrus H. McCormick), 63–80 (Eli Whitney), 87–103 (Elias Howe), 107–131 (Charles Goodyear), 158–185 (Thomas A. Edison), 298–309 (William Kelly), 325–343 (Orville and Wilbur Wright), 350–378 (Samuel F. B. Morse), 379–395 (Alexander Graham Bell); Holland, *Historic Inventions,* VI (Whitney), X (Morse), XI (McCormick), XII (Howe), XIII (Bell), XIV (Edison), XVI (Orville and Wilbur Wright); Darrow, *Boys' Own Book of Great Inventions,* II (telegraph), III (telephone), VIII (aviation); McFee, *Stories of American Inventions,* II (Fulton), III (McCormick), IV (Morse), V (Howe), VI (Bell), VII (Edison), VIII (phonograph), XI (airplane); Tappan, *Heroes of Progress* (McCormick, Goodyear, Morton, Howe, Field, Bell, Edison, Goethals); Kaempffert, *Popular History of American Invention.*

INDEX

Abbeys, in England, 210
Acropolis, of Athens, 75, 81
Actors, in Elizabethan theater, 315
  in Greek theater, 82
Adams, John, Vice President, 394
Adams, Samuel, 385
Adrianople, battle, 149
Ægean Sea, early civilization, 52
Æneid, 122, 254
Æschylus, dramatist, 81
Æsop, writer of fables, 85–86
Africa, explored by Portuguese, 261
  Roman province, 103, 108
Agora, Greek market place, 55
Airplane, American invention, 404, 416
Aladdin, story, 161
Alaric, Gothic leader, 160
Alexander the Great, 67–70
  conquests, 70
  death, 69
  Hunting the Lion (picture), 68
Alexandria, 69, 70, 59
Alfred the Great, boyhood, 172
  promotes English learning, 175
  reign, 173–176
  statue and monument, 176
Alphabet, Egyptian, 29
  Greek, 60, 47
  history of, 46–47
  Roman, 98, 47
America, discovered, 271
  Northmen in, 171
  where history begins, 3
American colonies, companies for founding, 323–324
  government, 335, 349, 353, 381, 383
  heritage, 335, 336; *see* Heritage
  life, 357–376
  restrictions on trade, 379
  Revolution, 382–395
  rights granted by charters, 324
  thirteen, 357
  war with France, 381–383
  why colonists came to America, 323
American Red Cross, 408
Americans, democracy, 410–411
  heritage ; *see* Heritage
  service to Old World, 398–413
Amphitheaters, Roman, 117

Anæsthesia, discovery of, 405
Ancient times, ended, 156
Andronicus, author, 122
Angles, 143, 153, 168; *see* Anglo-Saxons *and* Teutons
Anglo-Saxon Chronicle, 175, 213
  quoted, 171, 175–176, 181
Anglo-Saxon language, 193
  words in English, 193–198, 203
Anglo-Saxons, Angles and Saxons, 143, 153, 168
  found the English nation, 168
  life, 170, 177–178, 195–197; at table (picture), 178
  unite with Normans, 180–181
Animals, domestic, 13, 42
  in colonies, 336, 358, 362
Anno Domini, 132
Antigone, Greek play, 81
Aphrodite, goddess, 72
Apollo, god, 73, 132
Apprentices, in medieval crafts, 239, 240
Aqueducts, 116–117
Arabia, herdsmen in, 34
  Mohammedan conquest, 159
Arabian Nights, stories, 161
Arabic numerals and words, 203
Arabs, 35
  civilization and science, 202–203, 248
  in Holy Land, 216
Arachne, myth of, 73–74
Arch, history, 39, 116, 117, 210
Architecture, Babylonian, 39
  Egyptian, 20, 25
  Gothic, in England, 208–212
  Greek, 75–76
  Roman, 104–105, 116–117
Argos, Greek city, 53, 55
Aristophanes, dramatist, 80
Arithmetic, beginnings of, 41
Armada, Spanish, 306–308, 323
Armor of a feudal warrior, 223, 230
Art, cave men's, 12
  Egyptian, 26–28
  Greek, 77–79
  Italian, 255
  of Near East, 40, 42, 44, 46
  revival of, 255
  Roman, 103, 105